Employee Engagement
&
The Failure of Leadership

DAVID WEST

Engagement ↔ Loyalty pg 6.
disengaged = - sickness, Absentism
                - staff retention
                - underperforming
                - presenteeism - demotivated - uninterest.

Excesive pressure + workload too High. pg 6
- uncertainy
- unfair managers
- lack of development.
- No feedback or given opportunity to participate in business decisions.
* lost of trust in senior management.
* Pay does not create Loyalty (p. 12)
- Problems that stop EE = Pay does not create loyalty
  CEO gets CEO+Cup+Employees However Pay discrepancy between
  • Special reward for good work. affect Engagment
  • Trust; fair pay   (How it is distributed)
  • Paid for failure too much (pay for not performing).

Pg 30: How can senior Mangmt expect loyalty, going the extra mile from employees, when they can not lead by example.

Pg30: lack of leadership from the top.
- How to generate a CULTURE of INNOVATION + CREATIVITY.

Pg 40 Loyalty is a 2 way street: loyalty is "earned"
     So it is engagement

Copyright © 2012 David West B.A. Ph.D.
All rights reserved.

ISBN: 1468004158
ISBN 13: 9781468004151

About the Author

Dr David West gained his first degree in Philosophy and Logic from the University of Exeter and his Doctorate in Philosophy from the University of Leicester. He taught at University for several years including a happy time at Acadia University in Canada. His business career included Ford Motor Company and Xerox, primarily in line management roles. He was a partner in an accounting firm before branching out on his own, first with Behavioural Science Systems and latterly creating and founding The Working Manager. During his consulting career, he worked with companies in Europe, Asia and North America. David West is married with two grown up children and lives in London, England.

Dedication and Thanks

This book is dedicated to Henri Debuisser, the best manager I ever worked with, who taught that people respond to being supported and trusted, and to the memory of Herb Lewis, Professor of Philosophy at Acadia University, who taught that the patient collection and collation of ideas leads to understanding.

I first thank my wife, Jenny, for her amazing help in bringing this book to fruition and for her love during 43 years of marriage. May there be many more. I also thank the erstwhile members of *The Working Manager* International Editorial Board, and in particular Luis Eduardo Bastias, Jharna Sengupta Biswas, Helen Kelly, Burke Pease and Alan Hamblin. I have spent many happy hours discussing leadership with Robin Stuart-Kotze and Rick Roskin. Without those discussions, this book would never have been written.

This book was prepared using as a basis the material that I wrote for *The Working Manager Ltd* (www.theworkingmanager.com) and I thank that company for its permission to use the material. Needless to say, the opinions expressed in this book are those of the author alone and in no way represent the opinion of *The Working Manager Ltd* or its directors.

A note on spelling

I write in 'English' English and thus spell *'colour'* with a *'u'*. However, in quoting an author I retain the spelling that he or she uses, for example using *'defense'* instead of *'defence'* in quotations from American authors. I prefer *'s'* to *'z'*, thus *'organisation'*, but in the quotations *'organization'* is more common.

What this Book is About

Employee engagement is the single most serious issue in management today. Its apparently inexorable decline will soon spell the end of Western economies. If you cannot compete on price (and the West cannot) you must compete on creativity and quality. Without employee engagement, neither of these is possible.

Employee engagement is not the result of some initiative quite detached from leadership. It is not something that someone (HR?) can take care of while line management get on with the job (which would be what exactly?) Employee engagement, when it appears, is the result of really effective leadership. The lack of employee engagement that we experience today is nothing less than a failure of leadership.

The commercial organisation is the primary way that we bring together people, investment and raw materials to create economic growth, products, jobs and, equally importantly, human well-being and satisfaction. Profitability enables this social purpose. Such organisations are not for short term gains or making CEOs rich, attitudes which have brought capitalism to a crisis point.

Most employees in most organisations seek to do their best, often in spite of management and its processes, many of which disengage people, add useless cost and serve only as grist to the cynics' mill. This applies equally to not-for-profit and public sector organisations.

The only way is ethics. If employees are to feel engaged with a company, they need to feel proud of it. Only a company that takes a positive view of ethics can expect employees to find compelling purpose in their work.

This book is about the meaning of employee engagement, the context in which employee engagement can be understood and the organisational culture required for its existence. I feel very deeply about all this. William Wordsworth said that poetry was emotion recollected in tranquillity. That is not a bad guide for prose either. However, I cannot pretend that I have always been tranquil in my writing.

I start with an introduction to the nature of employee engagement and its rarity to establish what it is we are talking about and to set out the size of the problem. I proceed to describe the major causes of the lack of engagement and then seek to communicate an understanding of engagement and its context. Finally, I summarise in bullet form the message of employee engagement and what has to be done.

> *What is needed in business is a return to kindness and a rejection of obscenities like huge compensation packages for CEOs. I think that it is a sin to sack thousands of people and then accept a million-dollar bonus, a sin of the human spirit.*
>
> Anita Roddick

Contents

Preamble:
Hawthorne & Lordstown ... xi

1 The meaning:
engagement and its rarity ... 1

2 The problem I:
the boss is an alien ... 11

3 The problem II:
loyalty is a two way street ... 39

4 Towards understanding I:
the context – not a pill you can take ... 59

5 Towards understanding II:
the culture and the paradigm shift ... 95

6 Towards understanding III:
control and creativity ... 121

7 Towards a solution I:
being ready to think differently ... 159

8 Towards a solution II:
at least don't disengage ... 185

9 Towards a solution III:
the only way is ethics ... 221

10 Summary:
the main points in bullet form ... 247

I'm a man who believes that right is right and wrong is wrong. Treat me right, and I will give you my all. Treat me wrong, and I will give you nothing.

Johnny PayCheck

Hawthorne and Lordstown

The Hawthorne experiments, which took place as long ago as 1927, are famously important in showing that scientific management, a concentration solely on the physical aspects of routines and procedures, is inadequate. Forty five years later, in 1972, General Motors demonstrated that they had not been paying attention.

At their Lordstown plant in Ohio, they designed the most efficient, sophisticated and fastest production lines ever. Equipped with the latest power tools, the line was designed by the very best cost-cutting teams from General Motors' Assembly Division to build a car known as the Vega - and it was a disaster.

Before the introduction of the Vega line, grievances and disputes in the plant stood at about 100; afterwards, they rose to 5,000. Production, worth $45 million at 1972 prices, was lost due to staggering levels of absenteeism. As Peter Herman of MIT wrote at the time:[1]

> *Most workers are locked into their jobs at Lordstown because they can't get better work or money elsewhere. It is this money which makes them bear the deadening monotony of the same operation performed over and over and the inexorable rate of the line which does not permit any variation in pacing. People at Lordstown often work a compulsory 50-hour week; 10 hours a day doing the same job. A rate of 100 cars an hour means that the worker has to repeat his or her operation every 36 seconds. The Vega itself becomes a hated object.*

One worker described his feelings about working at Lordstown thus:

> *You do it automatically, like a monkey or dog would do something by conditioning. You feel stagnant; everything is over and over and over. It seems like you're just going to work and your whole purpose in life is to do this operation, and you come home and you're so tired from working the hours, trying to keep up with the line, you feel you're not making any advancement whatsoever. This makes the average individual feel sort of like a vegetable.*

Peter Herman reports how the scene at the change of shifts was eloquent testimony to the workers' hatred of their working conditions. The shift going into work hung around their cars in the parking lot or idled slowly towards the plant. In contrast, the workers coming off the shift dashed out of the plant, leapt into their cars and went racing away with horns blaring and tyres squealing.

After a while, GM raised the speed of the assembly line further. As another worker said:

> *We were already working hard, but it got ridiculous after they raised the speed of the line. The first day they brought out a sign, 'First time in GM history, 100 cars/hour,' and some of the old-timers cheered, but I just thought we were fools to take it. Then they started getting competitive, and told us that the first shift ran 110 cars an hour. Pretty soon even the old-timers got sick of that sh*t and said, 'If first shift wants to put out 110 cars, f*ck it, let 'em. We're not going to do it.*

During 1971 absenteeism, already high, increased further and many workers began letting cars go by on the line without doing their job. There were also cases of active sabotage. Joseph A. Arena tells us[2] that:

> *... problems with the Vega's quality had begun almost immediately after the car's introduction. In November 1970, the Washington Post reported that the height of the Vega's undercarriage trapped the vehicle in automated car washes ... On April 8, 1971, GM sent a letter to Vega owners asking them to return their cars for 'product improvements' that included fixing a loose carburettor choke lever, insufficient clearance, a windshield wiper nut which could become loose and a fuel tank filler neck subject to gasoline spillages. By July 1972, there had been three major recalls affecting 500,000 cars, nearly the entire production runs in the 1971 and 1972 model years. One of these recalls, in*

> May 1972, targeted 350,000 cars with carburettor defects that could 'cause the throttle to stick in a partially open position.'

and that

> ... consumer reports consistently placed the vehicle at the bottom of overall quality rankings for a wide range of problems, going so far as to list the car as 'not recommended' in 1975, the only subcompact that received this distinction.

Car Survey.org carried a review which tells this from experience.

> What things have gone wrong with the car? Almost anything that could go wrong, did. Brakes serviced and largely replaced at under 10,000. At 17,000, post major service, after 70+ miles of expressway, rough running began just before toll plaza. Clouds of smoke etc. while stopped. Tow required. Chevrolet dealer replaced head gasket and did assorted other major repairs. Astronomical cost. Brake linings/pads replaced a second time by Chevrolet. Corroded exhaust system replaced before 28,000. Engine begins to backfire. Dealer services. Muffler blown off a few weeks later. Gear shift knob falls off. Assorted corrosion problems although not driven in snow/salt. At 31,000 miles, head gasket blew again, giving off sufficient smoke to acquire ticket for excessive smoke (three weeks after service and inspection.) Dealer estimate, for engine and other repairs said to be essential, exceeds value of car. Says no special warranty, but after pressure, contacts Chevrolet Region which pays for most of engine repair. Transmission begins to be troublesome in the 30s. Locks up completely and estimate for replacement exceeds value of car. Car scrapped under 40,000miles/8 years as not worth repairs.

Someone who worked on the line commented:

> I worked on the Vega line at Lordstown when it first started in 1970. While there definitely were labor problems, there also were design problems. My job was to fasten the transmission to a frame rail under the car. Most of the time the holes in the frame didn't match with the transmission. As a result, I often had to use 'cheaters' - metal screws - instead of bolts. As I recall there also was a problem with the aluminum heads in the field.

Joe Kelly writes[3]:

> The union proposed that team assembly be used. This was rejected by the management. Unfortunately, management's effort to increase productivity through

classical means mobilized the young assembly line workers to full scale confrontation with management.

The Lordstown strike is now as much part of industrial relations legend as the Tolpuddle Martyrs in the UK and the Ludlow Massacre in the USA. Of course, this is history and the introduction of robots has materially altered the face of the production line. Nevertheless, management will insist on repeating similar mistakes: creating jobs which kill the spirit rather than enhance involvement, commitment and engagement.

> Take this job and shove it,
> I ain't workin' here no more.
> My woman done left,
> And took all the reason,
> I was working for.
> Y' better not try to stand in my way,
> Cause I'm a walkin' out the door.
> Take this job and shove it,
> I ain't working here no more.

Lyrics by David Allan Coe, sung by Johnny Paycheck

1

THE MEANING: ENGAGEMENT AND ITS RARITY

I knew that if I could get the people in the company to want the company to succeed as badly as I did, there would be no problem we could not solve together.

James Lincoln – Lincoln Electric

There is a world of difference between doing a job and wanting to do a good job. There is a world of difference between wanting to do a good job and really putting your back into it. There is another world of difference between hard work and dedicated hearts and minds.

Do you want people to go the extra mile in your company? Do you want them engaged in their work, putting their heart and soul into what they are doing, dedicating themselves to the success of the operation, and making a strong commitment to achieving the best results possible? If your answer to those questions is 'yes', then let's ask what are you, and what is your organisation, doing to make people want to do that bit more. What does your leadership do to capture their hearts and minds?

An employee of **Southwest airlines**[4] writes:

> *I am convinced that there is NO better job on earth than the job I currently have as a ramp agent for Southwest Airlines. Not to be confused with a ramp agent for any other airline. As Southwest ramp agents we enjoy one of the absolute best compensation packages on earth, bullet proof job security (Southwest being the most healthy airline in the country as well as a union shop), and the greatest company culture and work atmosphere there is.*

People feel good there, they say, because:

> *It's an absolutely great place to work.*
> *Leaders ... go out of their way to offer praise and encouragement.*
> *...people can start out at the bottom and go on to become Directors, VPs, Sr. VPs and into the Executive Office.*
> *There is a positive vibe in the offices where we are encouraged to and expected to treat each other well.*
> *My interaction with upper management has been nothing but positive.*
> *If you go in and do an outstanding job, upper management will take notice.*

Does this mean the work in Southwest is easy? No.

> *It's definitely not for everyone. It takes a certain type of individual who is able to handle the type of work that you'll be expected to do. You'll face adversity in the form of weather, high volume, time constraints, long hours, and responsibility. In other words you'll have essentially 20 minutes to connect ground services, position ground equipment to the plane, load over 100 bags and thousands of pounds of freight, do so in a weight and balance friendly manner, act as the last line of defense as far as making sure the plane is sealed and ready for flight, then take command of a 40 million dollar aircraft and move it from the gate out onto the taxi way via a push back tug vehicle. That's the job in a nutshell. If you're up for it, or if you're like me and actually LUV the work, you're going to be a very happy person.*

95% of Southwest employees approve of the leadership of Gary C. Kelly, Vice Chairman and CEO.

This book is about achieving that extra mile but nothing of worth is achieved without effort. So unless you are prepared to change the way you lead and manage, change the way your systems deal with people, you had better not read any further. Just put this book back on the shelf. Loyalty is a two way street and so is engagement.

Radical change

Some of the factors that hinder or prevent employee engagement are easier to deal with than others. Some require a fairly radical change in thinking and some require a change in behaviour of senior management itself. You have to give to get and some of the changes you are not going to like.

Indeed, much of what goes on in the typical organisation is inimical to employee engagement. It disengages people, is seen as useless cost and serves only as grist to the cynics' mill. In fact, many if not most employees in the average organisation seek to do their best and do what is right, *in spite of* the organisation and its management. Early retirement is very often a matter of good people getting tired of trying; tired of fighting useless procedures; tired of struggling against those who poison the organisation.

Can an organisation be turned around? Can employees become fully engaged? Yes, but understand that the idea of employee engagement does not live in a vacuum. If you want to treat the subject seriously then you must understand its context. If you don't then you have no right to be monkeying around with things like employee engagement. That would be as dangerous as driving a car before you've had a lesson or passed a test.

If you really, really mean it, you can get it but employee engagement will demand a change in organisational culture. It will probably cause a fair amount of upheaval and require you to manage with a firm eye on the soft skills as well as the hard. It will require that the top team gets involved with people and things like emotional intelligence, active listening, delegation, development, consultation and participation as well as getting to grips with the difference between intrinsic and extrinsic motivation.

In particular, employee engagement is not something you delegate to HR and then forget about. Actually, it is not something you delegate to HR at all, whether you forget about it or not. It is not a process or a project. You have to understand its meaning.

Do I have to?

A lot of managers really can't be doing with all this. They prefer to maintain a distance between themselves and employees, seeing people management as largely unnecessary and even undesirable. (A common enough view is that if people are paid well enough, they should be happy to do what they are told.) If we add that employee engagement may well require that the top team reins in its own freedom to act and even limits the way and the amount it pays itself then, let's be frank, many senior managers are going to think this is beyond the pale.

If this is your view, recognise that you cannot expect employee engagement. If you 'do' employee engagement badly or halfheartedly, you will make things a lot worse. You will just increase the credibility gap between management and staff. The last thing that is needed is 'just another programme' that no one believes in. Just remember that you have admitted defeat. A company whose employees are engaged will outperform an ordinary company. Look at Nucor, John Lewis, the Royal National Lifeboat Institution, Lincoln Electric and Southwest Airlines.

If you don't want anything to do with employee engagement, please do one thing for us. Don't pretend. Don't tell lies about your employees being your most valuable asset, about how you put employee development first and how you constantly seek your employees' views. You don't; so don't make things worse by saying you do.

So what do we mean by employee engagement?

Still with us? Right. So let's get going by describing employee engagement and its rarity. What is meant by employee engagement? The UK's Chartered Institute of Personnel and Development (CIPD) says[5] that it:

> ... *can be seen as a combination of commitment to the organisation and its values plus a willingness to help out colleagues (organisational citizenship). It goes beyond job satisfaction and is not simply motivation. Engagement is something the employee has to offer: it cannot be required as part of the employment contract.*

The CIPD goes on to say:

> *Employers want employees who will do their best work, or go the extra mile. Employees want good work: jobs that are worthwhile and turn them on. More and more organisations are looking for a win-win solution that meets their needs and those of their employees. What they increasingly say they are looking for is an engaged workforce.*

In a later report, the CIPD expanded[6] its definition to read:

> *We define employee engagement as being positively present during the performance of work by willingly contributing intellectual effort, experiencing positive emotions and meaningful connections to others. We see engagement as having three core facets:*

- *intellectual engagement or thinking hard about the job and how to do it better*
- *affective engagement or feeling positively about doing a good job*
- *social engagement or actively taking opportunities to discuss work-related improvements with others at work.*

The Work Foundation says[7] that:

> *Employee engagement describes employees' emotional and intellectual commitment to their organisation and its success. Engaged employees experience a compelling purpose and meaning in their work and give of their discrete effort to advance the organisation's objectives.*

Sounds good doesn't it? A touch of *motherhood, apple pie and the flag* perhaps, but highly desirable nonetheless.

IT'S RARE

> *Collins Dictionary experts compiled (2011) a list of words no longer used. Among these words are 'cyclogiro', a cross between a plane and a helicopter, and 'charabanc', meaning a motor coach. Another of the words that has gone out of use is 'supererogate' - to do or perform more than is required.*

THE MEANING

The problem is that anything resembling employee engagement is rare. In a 2008/9 study of 600 UK organisations[8], the Work Foundation found that:

- 49% found sickness and absenteeism an issue
- 33% had problems with staff retention
- 33% felt staff underperformed
- 25% experienced 'presenteeism' - de-motivated uninterested staff

A 2008 Gallup study found[9] that only 29% of US employees could be said to be engaged while 17% are actively disengaged. The 2009 Ipsos Loyalty Study found[10] less than 30% of US employees to be loyal to their company while even fewer thought their employer deserved any loyalty.

(Loyalty and engagement are not the same but one would argue that in management they are intimately related. While it is no doubt just possible for an employee to be loyal but not engaged, it would be difficult to see this as anything more than an exceptional and passing case. Again, it is possible for an employee to be engaged but not loyal but it would at least be psychologically unusual. In practice loyalty is required for engagement and engagement requires loyalty. One builds upon the other.)

And in case you think that the loyalty problem is primarily about employees, check this out. In 2006, Peter Cappelli, George W. Taylor Professor of Management at The Wharton School, found[11] that 52% of all executives would say 'yes' to an invitation from a search firm to interview for another job – and that the willingness to say 'yes' actually increased the higher an individual was in the hierarchy.

In 2010, the CIPD reported[12] that employee satisfaction was at an all time low. Only 25% of employees found much excitement in their work while the number of employees saying that they were under excessive pressure at work had increased. A third of employees felt their workload was too high. The most dissatisfied were younger (18–24) employees, which hardly bodes well for the future. Twenty percent of employees expected to lose their jobs during the recession; 32% of employees believed their managers were unfair and not committed to their organisation; 47% received no coaching;

39% no discussion of training needs and 28% no feedback. Only half felt informed about what was happening within their organisations.

The survey also showed trust in senior leaders to have reached an all time low. Only 33% of employees trusted their senior management. Very few employees had confidence in them and almost none said senior managers consulted them about important issues.

Glassdoor.com[13] runs a continuous opinion poll of employee satisfaction in US companies using a 0-5 scale where 5 indicates very satisfied. The number of respondents per company is rarely enough to be statistically significant. However, it is noticeable that only nine companies score more than 4.0 (or 80%.)[14]

THE LIVING DEAD

Professor Rick Roskin writes (for *The Working Manager*[15]):

> *If you've ever worked for a big company, you've probably seen it yourself: the sad sight of dead wood. People who come to work but don't have clearly-defined jobs; people who have titles and may appear on organization charts but don't feature much in contribution to ideas, progress, or making life better for others in the workplace.*

Can this be widespread? In his book, *The Living Dead, Switched Off, Zoned Out: The Shocking Truth about Office Life*, David Bolchover[16] answers with a resounding yes and provides some astonishing statistics:

- 40% of all casual drugs users in the US (people who use drugs just once a month) choose to do it at work.

- 20% of people who take drugs at work do so at their workstation.

- One in five US workers has had full on sex with a co-worker during working hours.

- One third of UK young professionals are hung over at least twice a week on working days. Two thirds admitted to having called in sick due to alcohol at least once in the previous month.

- 75% of internet porn site visits occur during the 9-to-5 working day.

- More than half of the UK's 14.5 million pet owners say they would need between two and five days off from work to grieve for a dead pet, while 10% said they would need up to two weeks.

- UK employees most often take Monday (23%) and Friday (25%) as sick days. Wednesday has the lowest off-sick rate with 8%.

Twenty percent of UK employees say they are actively disengaged at work. Roskin, in his review[17] of this book, says:

> *In my own practice I've named one leadership style 'Defector'. I'm not alone in searching for the 'Defector gene' and failing to find it; it seems not to exist. Rather the mind-numbing, Dilbert-like environment of many jobs shapes the behaviour of those who display a zombie-like existence from 9 to 5 - even if away from work they are the most energized of people, working long hours with friends, charities or on personal pursuits.*

Roskin sees the popular television series *The Office* as painting a more and more realistic picture of the daily tribulations of life at work; a make-believe world with a make-believe language and make-believe jobs. He argues that business leaders must recognise and acknowledge the serious challenges concerning the 'living dead'. Sadly, it seems to be his view that few will make an effort.

> *After all, they have a vested interest in perpetuating the idea that their company has a dynamic, creative and motivated workforce.*

Even when they don't.

TRUST

Edelman Loyalty[18], the leading independent global PR firm, publishes an annual *Trust Barometer* and argues that trust and loyalty, with customers and employees, go hand in hand.

> *It's long past time to abandon the old adage that 'love makes the world go round.' Today, if anything keeps the world turning, it's trust. Without trust,*

> *there's no benefit of the doubt given, everyone becomes a hapless fact-checker, and nothing gets done, no governmental decisions made, and little gets bought or sold in the marketplace.*

Richard Northedge, writing *Why Nobody Trusts Business Anymore* for BNET, took data from the 10th edition of the Edelman Trust Barometer reporting on a year (2008) unlike any other.

> *Government bailed out banks in New York and London. Melamine-laced baby formula rolled off assembly lines into the homes of Chinese parents. American auto executives descended on Washington hungry for handouts. An Illinois governor was led away in handcuffs. And as a $50 billion Ponzi scheme collapsed, an Indian tech mogul's fraudulent enterprise started to crumble.*

The Edelman Trust Barometer said:

> *In no country is trust in a more dismal state than in the United States, where government, business, and media are all distrusted by respondents (ages 25 to 64) to do what is right, even with a new administration elected to power. Trust in U.S. business — at 38% down from 58% last year — is the lowest in the Barometer's tracking history ... even lower than in the wake of Enron and the dot-com bust.*

It seems that few people trust business leaders or believe what they are saying. The Edelman report for 2008 said:

> *Only 29% view information as credible when coming from a CEO declining from 36%. In the United States, which has seen a revolving door of high profile CEOs, trust in information from a company's top leader now sits at a six-year low, at 17%.*

In her 2009 book, *Top Talent: Keeping Performance up when Business is Down*, Sylvia Ann Hewlett shows[19] that compared with 2008 the percentage of talented employees with feelings of loyalty to their companies has dropped from 95% to 53%. She says:

> *If you measure loyalty to employer, trust in your current company, engagement with your present job, everything is plummeting. One rather amazing figure is that top talent is spending 56% of its time looking for the next job. That's a terrible thing to be doing all day everyday, week in, week out. Because you are being relied upon to fuel renewal and growth for the company you are in.*

It is not surprising that companies yearn for employee engagement:

- *a combination of commitment to the organisation and its values plus a willingness to help out colleagues (organisational citizenship).*
- *employees who will do their best work, or go the extra mile.*
- *employees (who) experience a compelling purpose and meaning in their work and give of their discrete effort to advance the organisation's objectives.*

* * *

2

THE PROBLEM I:
THE BOSS IS AN ALIEN

The rich run a global system that allows them to accumulate capital and pay the lowest price for labour. The freedom that results applies only to them. The many simply have to work harder, in conditions that grow ever more insecure, to enrich the few.

Charles Moore (one time editor of the *Daily Telegraph*)

It is not that people don't want to get involved. A few employees no doubt have no interest in whatever they do but the great majority are anxious to believe in what they spend a rather large slice of their lives doing. The issue is that management just makes it so difficult. Senior management, in particular, has become one of the major factors hindering employee engagement. Senior managers appear to inhabit a different world.

A 2008 Bain Consulting study revealed that 81% of senior leaders believed their organization delivered superior customer service yet only 8% of their customers agreed. The study refers to the problem as a 'Customer Service Gap.' Whatever the customer service trouble is called, the root cause is leaders, many of whom have never worked the front lines servicing customers.[20]

Reuters Friday October 28, 2011

Research from Income Data Services - a unit of Thomson Reuters - showed that directors of companies on Britain's FTSE 100 index enjoyed a 49% rise in total salaries the last year. The FTSE index itself has not increased at all over the last 20 months.

'With the FTSE 100 down on last year and most staff getting pay rises of less than 2 per cent, these bumper settlements prove that chief executive officers' pay bears no resemblance to performance or economic reality,' said TUC general secretary Brendan Barber.

'This is a concerning report, particularly at a time when household budgets are very tight,' the UK Prime Minister David Cameron, said.

'This damning report shows just how much these pampered directors are removed from the lives of working people struggling to hold onto their jobs and paying soaring energy, food and transport costs,' Unite General Secretary Len McCluskey said.

Let's take pay. Richard Lambert, the head of the employers' lobby group the Confederation of British Industry (CBI), said, April 2010, that chief executives risked being seen as aliens because their pay is so out of step with that of the population at large. [21]

> *If leaders of big companies seem to occupy a different galaxy from the rest of the community, they risk being treated as aliens. It is difficult to persuade the public that profits are no more than the necessary lifeblood of a successful business if they see a small cohort at the top reaping such large rewards.*

Pay does not create loyalty. Go all the way back to the Roman statesman and philosopher, Seneca (the younger, if you want to be picky) who said, *'Fidelity purchased with money, money can destroy.'* Indeed, the lack of pay does not preclude loyalty. After all, many people invest loyalty in a club, a social movement or a charity for which they give rather than receive. What matters is what WG Runciman described in his book *Relative Deprivation and Social Justice*.[22]

> *People are roused to political action as a result not of absolute changes in their material conditions but of changes relative to the circumstances of those with whom they compare themselves.*

You are much more likely to be upset by finding out that someone who does the same work as you is paid a lot more, than you are to be upset by how much you are paid in absolute terms. You expect some people to be paid more (or less) than you but you also expect a rationale to this and for the discrepancy to be within bounds.

While a CEO does not do the same work as an accounts clerk or a marketing assistant, we do expect that there is some consistency, some rationale, to pay scales. Is there any? The Hutton report of December 2010[23] said:

> *Pay dispersion has widened over the last decade. This trend has been most pronounced among public listed companies: in 2009 median pay for FTSE 100 chief executives has risen to 88 times UK median earning and 202 times the national minimum wage, up from 47 times and 124 times respectively in 2000.*

In May 2011, the High Pay Commission[24] published a report entitled *More for Less: what has happened to pay at the top and does it matter?* It showed that in 2010 CEO total pay of the Footsie was 145 times the average salary. On current trends, the report indicated that this would rise to 214 times by 2020. The report said:

> *High pay in the financial sector generates the strongest feelings among the British public and trust in the banking sector has plummeted. In 1983, 90% of us thought banks were well run – better run even than the BBC or police. Now just 19% think this is true. But public anger over bank bonuses has not stopped staff in 11 European banks increasing their pay by 7% in the year from 2009. Nor has it stopped Barclays giving bankers three times as much in bonuses as it paid investors in dividends, HSBC revealing that its highest paid banker got £8.4 million and the financial services regulator the Financial Services Authority (FSA), showing that 2,800 staff in 27 banks received more than £1 million in 2009.*

Senior executive pay has become almost totally removed from the experience of workers. Take the example reported by the *Independent newspaper in 2010.*

> *Staff at six UK airports owned by BAA have voted three to one in favour of striking in a dispute over pay, their union says. Heathrow, Stansted, Southampton, Glasgow, Edinburgh and Aberdeen airports would have to close if strikes went ahead, BAA said, as key staff such as firefighters were due to take part.*
>
> *Staff accepted a pay freeze in 2009 and their union, Unite, described the offer for this year - a 1% increase, with the possibility of an extra 0.5% if the union agrees to changes to the company's sickness agreement - as 'measly' and 'nothing short of confrontational'.*
>
> *The company has also said there will be no additional summer bonus this year, which is usually paid if BAA makes a profit, and is worth about £700.*

Contrast this with the report in the newspaper, *The Daily Mail*, who became very hot under the collar when in May 2010, it reported that Frank Chapman, chief executive of the gas production firm BG, in 2009 during the middle of the recession, *'scooped a pay and pension package worth an astonishing £28 million.'* The paper went on:

> *(This) comes as families are being crippled by average gas bills of £750 and around four million households are in fuel poverty, spending more than 10 per cent of their income on heating their homes.*

While BAA employees were striking over 1.5% pay increase and a £700 bonus, Mr Chapman apparently received a basic salary of £1.14million, a bonus of £1.6million, £5.26million from a long-term incentive scheme and £15.5million from share options. This package was worth over 1,000 times the average UK full time salary of just under £28,000. Just to make sure he did not feel hard up and had enough to pay his gas bill in the future, he:

> *... also enjoyed a £4.6million boost to his pension pot, which means his gold-plated retirement package has a transfer value of £14million.*

Sean O'Grady, Economics Editor of the Independent, reported[25]:

> *Recession or not, the UK's top executives are still earning a typical £3.1m a year each – with a 'poor correlation' between their pay and shareholder value, according to two of the country's leading authorities in the field. MM&K, a business consultancy, and Manifest, which advises institutional investors on how to vote at corporate AGMs, say that the typical pay of a FTSE-100 boss rose by 5 per cent since the slump began in 2008. Looking over a ten-year horizon, the researchers found that despite widespread share-price declines, CEO remuneration has quadrupled.*

The most highly paid CEO in the US in 2009 received $141 million (excluding any share options, of course.) Try and put this into perspective. The average 25 year old American male with a University degree would need to work for 2,350 years (yes, that is two thousand, three hundred and fifty years) to make what the most highly paid US CEO made in just one year – and that year being 2009, the middle of the recession.

Bob Diamond, CEO of Barclays will receive £27 million in 2011 (1,042 times the median wage). He is now most famous for saying that the time for remorse is over and that bankers should stop apologising! (So for just how long should one be remorseful for ruining the world economy?)

SPECIAL REWARD FOR SPECIAL WORK?

Of course, you might expect that CEOs were being rewarded for exceptional performance. If you found out that they were not, your relative deprivation might show even more. If you get paid only if you produce results, you are likely to be very annoyed to find that someone else gets the money (and indeed a lot more) whether they produce or not.

Well, prepare to be really annoyed. Writing *An Insider's Look at CEO Pay* for BNET, Jeffrey Pfeffer says[26]:

> *... the relationship between CEO pay and performance is astonishingly small. One meta-analysis found that firm (company) performance accounted for less than 5% of the variation in CEO pay.*[27]

Forbes produces a list of the CEOs in the USA and their pay. They also analyse the CEOs' performance and evaluate that against their earnings.

They then rank order the efficiency of the CEOs. You'd hope that the highest paid would also be the most efficient, would you not? Here is the 2009 rank order of the highest paid CEOs and next to them the Forbes efficiency ranking[28].

ranking in pay	ranking in efficiency
1	90th
2	82nd
3	163rd
4	89th
5	78th
6	38th
7	no data available
8	no data available
9	no data available
10	31st
11	184th
12	no data available
13	82nd
14	no data available
15	no data available
16	20th
17	98th
18	no data available
19	20th
20	181st

Exhibit 1

Thus the highest paid CEO in 2009 ranked 90th in efficiency - which may be to say he wasn't worth the money. Here are the most efficient CEOs and where they ranked in the pay list for that year. The most efficient CEO - the one most worth what he or she was paid - ranked 135th in actual pay.

ranking in efficiency	ranking in pay
1	135th
2	463rd
3	286th
4	427th
5	295th
6	341st
7	133rd
8	182nd
9	312nd
10	412th
11	373rd
12	431st
13	157th
14	23rd
15	130th
16	40th
17	236th
18	241st
19	349th
20	16th

Exhibit 2

So who decides how the CEO gets paid? At a conference on corporate governance[29], sponsored by the Rock Center for Corporate Governance at Stanford University, Professor David Larcker said that the senior executive *'pay explosion that's generated so much outrage before and after the financial crisis'* should be blamed entirely on corporate boards, especially those that are comprised entirely of CEO appointees. He said:

Compensation consultants will justify any level a board wants to pay.

CEOs themselves decide what they get paid! While a small brake has been put upon executive compensation by shareholders in recent times – a trend that we can all applaud - it is still true that their compensation is set by the executives themselves.

> ### AIG
>
> AIG is an American insurance company, once the 18th largest public quoted company in the world. Trading in credit derivatives, it collapsed in September 2008. The US government was forced to nationalise the company and support it with $180bn in loans. Its share price fell from a high of $70.13 to a mere $1.25. In March 2009, AIG announced that they were paying out $165 million in executive bonuses and that total bonuses for the entire company could reach $1.2 billion.
>
> President Obama found it,
>> ... hard to understand how derivative traders at AIG warranted any bonuses, much less $165 million in extra pay. How do they justify this outrage to the taxpayers who are keeping the company afloat?
>
> Senator Chuck Grassley said,
>> I would suggest they follow the Japanese example and come before the American people and take that deep bow and say, I'm sorry, and then either do one of two things: resign or go commit suicide.
>
> Senator Richard Shelby said,
>> Now you're rewarding failure. A lot of these people should be fired, not awarded bonuses. This is horrible. It's outrageous.
>
> The Independent newspaper reported that five senior executives at AIG threatened to quit if their compensation was cut.

Listen to Anita Campbell, writing for *Small Business Trends*, and think about relative deprivation:

> Let's be very clear on what the public's outrage is about — and not about. The American public is not outraged with the majority of hard-working employees at AIG. No, this outrage is directed toward a relative handful of people. The outrage stems from the take-your-breath-away size of the bonuses — and because so much money is being divvied up in the hands of a few.

With stories like these around – and the truth is that they are around and will be more and more common as the High Pay Commission points out – is it very surprising that employees, bargaining for perhaps a tiny increase in pay, find it difficult to express their loyalty to an organisation paying a CEO in the tens or even hundreds of millions a year whether that CEO is any good or not? If senior executives can pay themselves these vast sums (in many cases without justification), how much loyalty will the average employee feel towards them? Indeed, how much loyalty do they deserve? The disconnect is almost total, and so is the disengagement. The CEO inhabits a different world: an alien indeed.

> The total pay in the financial year 2010/11 of Mick Davis, chief executive, Xstrata, the mining company, was £18,426,105. In a statement, the company said, *'it does not consider a ratio comparison between executive and non-Board employees to be a useful way of assessing the fairness and balance of Xstrata's remuneration practices.'*[30]

TRUST

The Work Foundation carried out extensive research in the UK with private and public sector employers. They listed the major factors in organisational effectiveness. Eighty one percent mentioned fair pay and 75% a culture of trust.[31]

Will Hutton wrote[32]:

> *Principles of fair pay are urgently needed, both to guide those who determine pay and to reassure the wider public that such principles exist and are being followed, certainly in the public sector over which the government has direct control. But such principles are impossible without a more robust definition of fairness than just a disposition towards reasonableness. In the report, I define fairness in pay as the due desert for discretionary effort which delivers desired results; reward should match the employee's actions and contribution.*
>
> *Embedded in this notion is proportionality: due desert should rise proportionally as individuals make more of a contribution. It should not rise limitlessly; there are boundaries not least because no one individual in any organisation*

can argue that every improvement is due to his or her actions alone – thus the case for some multiple of top to bottom pay. But fair pay also involves an attitude towards luck and process. Individuals should be paid for their effort and contribution, not for the luck of being in the right place at the right time. And pay should be determined by an impartially fair process.

The High Pay Commission[33] says:

The inability of boards to exert influence and the concerning trend of having current executives on remuneration committees has meant that a key mechanism for controlling pay has failed and may even have contributed to its growth. The alternative mechanism, namely shareholders, has also proved ineffective in reining in executive pay.

THE EXPERIENCE OF FAILURE

Edelman 2010 Trust Barometer[34] says:

In the US, Western Europe and BRIC countries, more than 70% say that actions such as firing non-performing managers, repaying bailout money or reducing the pay gap between senior executives and rank and file workers would restore their trust in the company. In the US, the numbers skew even higher – with almost 90% of respondents citing non-performing managers and repaying bailout money as pathways to trust.

By any yardstick AIG's management was a failure, so what happens when people fail? In a tragically ironical coincidence, the *Independent* newspaper reported[35] that in the UK:

The Government is to reduce a welfare budget that is 'completely out of control' by a further £4bn, George Osborne said last night. The Chancellor, who announced £11bn of savings on welfare in June, said he would no longer provide the money for the unemployed to make a 'lifestyle choice to just sit on out-of-work benefits.'

On the same day, it informed its readers that there was no danger in Martin Sullivan - whose last job was as CEO of AIG and who had been described by the financial channel CNBC as one of the worst CEOs of all time - swelling the ranks of the unemployed. He has been appointed deputy chairman of Willis, the insurance broker. He also received a severance package of around $48 million.

How do employees and senior managers fare when they fail? Let's go to Ontario and take a look at the rules for termination of employment in Canada. They are reasonably simple as *settlement.org* says:

> *In most cases, if you are fired or laid off for more than 13 weeks, your employer must tell you ahead of time. This is called notice. Your employer must give you notice in writing. And in most jobs, if you are fired without proper notice, your employer must pay your normal wages for the weeks you should have been given notice. This is called 'termination pay'. If you are laid off permanently, the same rules apply.*
>
> *Severance pay is not the same as termination pay. Severance pay is another payment that some people get when they lose their jobs. You only get severance pay if you have worked at least 5 years for your employer and your employer pays out wages of at least $2.5 million a year in Ontario, or at least 50 people will be losing their jobs within a 6-month period because the business is being cut back. Severance pay is one week's pay for each year of employment, up to a maximum of 26 weeks.*

So what do you get if you are made redundant (fairly) from the job as a manager in Canada by, say, a retail company closing down in the recession? Not a lot. Let us suppose that you are on a one month contract and have been with that employer for 10 years. You are now on $50,000 a year - which according to the Government of Canada Labour Market Information is above average for the retail sector. By my calculations, you get $13,782. Oh, and 5 cents.

The UK employment law provides five potentially fair reasons for dismissing an employee:

- Conduct (the employee's behaviour is seriously unacceptable)
- Capability (the employee can no longer do their job)
- Legality (for example where the loss of a driving licence means the taxi driver cannot drive legally)
- Redundancy (where there is insufficient work)
- Some other substantial reason (!)

THE PROBLEM I

The compensation limits for unfair dismissal in the UK at the time of writing stand at £8,700 basic award and £58,400 compensatory award. So in the UK, even if you are dismissed *totally unfairly*, then the maximum you get is a bit less than £68,000 (and perilously few get that.)

> The television channel STV reported[36] the case of Mr Alexander Shand, '*a man with an unblemished 11-year record,*' who was fired for failing to clock out for a hospital appointment. It seems that he had clocked in for work as normal around 7.45 in the morning and told his manager he had a hospital appointment at 9 o'clock. Having been told there was no problem, Mr Shand left the plant at 10 minutes to 9 and was away for half an hour. In his hurry to get there and back, he forgot to clock off and so the company terminated his contract, arguing that Mr Shand's behaviour amounted to gross misconduct because by not clocking out he was effectively stealing money from the firm.
>
> You will be glad to hear that Mr Shand won an action for unfair dismissal and the company was ordered to pay him £8,009. He still lost his job, of course.

By contrast, Kate Kelly, writing for the *Wall Street Journal* in November 2007, described the behaviour of the Bear Stearns CEO.

> A crisis at Bear Stearns this summer came to a head in July. Two Bear hedge funds were haemorrhaging value. Investors were clamoring to get their money back. Lenders to the funds were demanding more collateral. Eventually, both funds collapsed.
>
> During 10 critical days of this crisis - one of the worst in the securities firm's 84-year history - Bear's chief executive wasn't near his Wall Street office. James Cayne was playing in a bridge tournament in Nashville, Tenn., without a cellphone or an email device. In one closely watched competition, his team placed in the top third.

> As Bear's fund meltdown was helping spark this year's mortgage-market and credit convulsions, Mr. Cayne at times missed key events. At a tense August conference call with investors, he left after a few opening words. In summer weeks, he typically left the office on Thursday afternoon and spent Friday at his New Jersey golf club, out of touch for stretches, according to associates and golf records. In the critical month of July, he spent 10 of the 21 workdays out of the office, either at the bridge event or golfing, according to golf, bridge and hotel records.

Bear Stearns collapsed in 2008 and was sold at a fire sale price to JP Morgan Chase.

FAILURE AND REWARD

The working man or woman does not get rich from being fired and you may argue that this is as it should be. Failure should not be rewarded. Otherwise people would seek failure. As Professor Stuart-Kotze writes for *The Working Manager*:

> *Delegating responsibility is a contract. If the recipient agrees to take on a job, then he or she must fulfil their side of the bargain – they are accountable for the results. That implies that they will give their very best effort. On the leader's side of the contract, the commitment is to provide necessary support when required – but not to take back the responsibility for the task. Failure is acceptable, given best effort, but people who don't give full and honest effort need to be dealt with summarily.*

Now take a look at Michael Brush's article[37] on *MSN Money*, written in 2003 well before the 2008 banking crisis but at the end of the 2002 recession. Here we learn that:

> *The shares of Gemstar-TV Guide International fell to $3.40 from almost $50. Former CEO Henry Yuen received a severance payment of $22 million and was made chairman.*

> *At Clear Channel Communications many executives had a seven-year rolling contract that renewed every day. If fired, they were guaranteed salary and bonus for the rest of the contract - 7 years pay.*

Had things changed come the 2008-11 recession? No. AOL dismissed CEO Randy Falco but continued paying his $1 million salary and $7.5 million in bonuses through 2010.[38] Former Merrill Lynch chief Stanley O'Neal, in charge when the firm did the subprime thing, received a $161.5 million retirement package. Angelo Mozilo, *'who as co-founder and chief of mortgage lender Countrywide bears a good bit of the blame for the subprime mess,'* collected more than $73 million.[39]

We learn that NYSE chief executive Duncan Niederauer was awarded total compensation of $7.1 million for 2008 - his first full year in the job - including $4 million 'performance' bonus. The exchange's performance was a $738 million net loss. The stock price fell 68%. And so it goes on. As Michael Brush writes:

> *The sweetest sound on Wall Street these days? 'You're fired.' Regular folks may get a modest pension or maybe just a box for their personal items. But for Wall Street CEOs, the exit sign needs at least eight digits.*

IS IT ALL TO DO WITH THE RECESSION?

On June 7 2010, Daniel Gross wrote[40]:

> *Of all the mysteries of the BP oil spill, perhaps the most baffling is: Why does BP CEO Tony Hayward still have a job? Hayward was in charge when the disastrous blowout at the Macondo well in the Gulf of Mexico took place, and he's been in charge as BP has failed - and failed, and failed again - to stop the flow of crude oil into the Gulf. What's more, his (unbacked-up) reassurances and poor turns of phrase ('I want my life back') have aggravated the damage to BP's public image.*

A month later Reuters reported:

> *BP Chief Executive Tony Hayward will collect a pay and pension package worth at least 11.8 million pounds ($18.03 million) when he steps down from his role at the company.*

Gloriously, a BP spokesman immediately:

> *... dismissed the report as 'rumours,' adding that Hayward remained chief executive and had full support of the board.*

Very soon after that full support being given, Hayward was replaced. As Richard Ferlauto, director of pension investment policy at the American Federation of State, County and Municipal Employees, asked,

> *What does 'pay for performance' mean if you ignore performance?*

Mark Hurd, CEO of Hewlett-Packard, allegedly fiddled his expenses to the tune of about $20,000. Why on earth he did it, when he earned $30.3 million in 2009 and $42.4 million in 2008, is beyond most people. The answer seems to lie in the old adage, *'Cherchez la femme.'* According to the writer Lance Ulanoff[41]

> *Hurd left HP in disgrace. He mis-represented travel and expense reports and reportedly had a relationship with a contractor that, according to HP's board, violated its 'Standards of Business Conduct.' In the end, Hurd resigned and saved HP's board the trouble of firing him. Hurd later settled a sexual harassment suit.*

The received opinion in the US, as the law firm Charles Russell[42] says, is that

> *... while some employees regard exaggerating their expenses as a perk of the job, such behavior almost always results in summary dismissal for gross misconduct. Further, employees dismissed in these circumstances are likely to find it difficult to obtain new work as a reference that reveals gross misconduct for a dishonesty offence is not an attractive prospect for a future employer.*

In the UK also, such fiddling often and even usually ends in summary dismissal; that is dismissal on the spot and without notice. However, for Mr Hurd, things were different. In exchange for releasing HP from future litigation, Hurd received $12.2 million in severance plus vested options and restricted stock yielding a total of $34.6 million.[43]

Aliens? Yes.

All in this together?

The UK Prime Minister, David Cameron, appealed to ordinary people to help in the crisis that the banking fiasco has caused, using the rallying call: *'We are all in this together.'* Really? The Institute for Policy Studies[44]:

Corporate executives, in reality, are not suffering at all. Their pay, to be sure, dipped on average in 2009 from 2008 levels, just as their pay in 2008, the first Great Recession year, dipped somewhat from 2007. But executive pay overall remains far above inflation adjusted levels of years past. In fact, after adjusting for inflation, CEO pay in 2009 more than doubled the CEO pay average for the decade of the 1990s, more than quadrupled the CEO pay average for the 1980s, and ran approximately eight times the CEO average for all the decades of the mid-20th century. American workers, by contrast, are taking home less in real weekly wages than they took home in the 1970s.

The *Independent* again:

The TUC will today (10 September 2010) attack bosses for enriching themselves with pension pots averaging £3.5m at a time when staff retirement benefits are being slashed. Its research – analysing the pensions of 329 directors from 102 of Britain's top companies – will also show that the highest-paid directors in each company have pension pots worth an average £5.26m, providing an average annual pension of £298,503 a year.

Joanne Segars, chief executive of the National Association of Pension Funds, the UK's biggest workplace pension body had:

.. concerns that directors pension arrangements are not linked to performance ... This raises the spectre of directors reaping substantial rewards for failure. Their generous pension entitlements appear to allow them to run a company into the ground before retiring in luxury.[45]

Leo Mullin was granted 22 years of pension credit when he became CEO of Delta Air Lines. Leo Mullin 'retired' in January 2004 at the age of 61. When his retirement was announced the company's shares rose 5%. *USA Today* wrote[46]:

Mullin spent much of this year fighting to clear up an executive compensation flap. Last spring, as airlines were seeking federal aid and Delta was seeking pay concessions from employees after furloughing thousands, the airline revealed it had paid Mullin and his team tens of millions of dollars in bonuses and bankruptcy-protected pension payments. Mullin later gave up millions in compensation and the pension payments were stopped, but many employees remained resentful.

Resentful? Not surprising. It doesn't sound as if we are all in this together, does it? Mr Mullin now serves as Senior Advisor at Goldman Sachs, Merchant Banking Division. Perhaps Mr Mullin doesn't 'do' irony.

Loews lost $182 million from continuing operations in 2008, and its stock price sank 44%. Its board paid the CEO $7 million; 8% more than in 2007. Loews directors decided it *'wasn't fitting'* to consider the insurance division's $750 million loss or the $750 million of write-downs in the oil exploration unit. Course not!

Oh, and please don't ask why the bank bosses were paid so much. Either they knew what they were doing (and therefore were crooks) or they didn't (and therefore were idiots.) What indeed does 'pay for performance' mean if you ignore performance? [47]

In 2009, Ben Willmott, Senior Public Policy Adviser at the CIPD[48], reported that:

> *Our research highlights the dissatisfaction people feel with the rewarding of failing senior executives. Failing chief executives and directors should not be financially rewarded when they leave organisations when their leadership has contributed to poor business performance. 'Rewards for failure' are contributing to a deep-seated sense of unfairness amongst employees who feel they've been less well treated. This needs to be addressed if trust in senior leadership teams is to be rebuilt.*

Holding back?

The Hay Group study of executive pay in 2010 showed that executive cash remuneration increased in 8 of the 11 European countries surveyed, mainly as a result of a recovery in cash bonuses. So the executives led their companies to a recovery did they? Well actually, no. Simon Garrett of the Hay Group said[49],

> *Annual bonuses this year have jumped back up quite a lot but they are not necessarily related to companies' profits.*

The Hay Group says,

> *Bonus payouts were helped by companies revising the bar for performance-based bonuses because of the weak economy.*

THE PROBLEM I

Great! So they lowered the performance bar in order to make sure they got their bonuses. (Do you think they did that for their salespeople? That is, reduced their targets so they could get their commission?) [50]

% change cash income 2010 over 2009

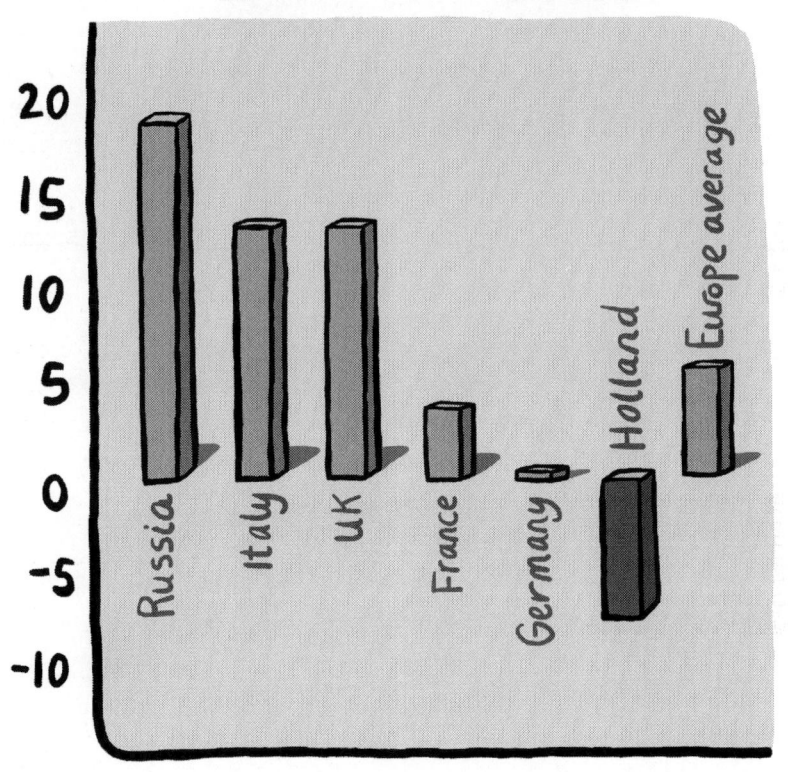

Exhibit 3. Source Hay Group

From the diagram, you may note that in the Netherlands, executive earnings fell by 7%. Why? Because performance targets remained unchanged. Dutch companies supported corporate pay restraint especially where companies were bailed out with public funds. At least a shred of decency exists, if only in the Netherlands.

Research released August 2010 by BDO[51], examining the link between executive pay, was surprised (!) to find that:

... the CEOs of companies with the best performance did not necessarily receive the highest pay increases. While overall, CEOs of companies with positive shareholder returns received pay increases and those with negative shareholder returns saw pay decreases, there were notable exceptions to this trend, especially in the margins for each group.

Why engagement then?

The outlandish compensation and the failure experience (or lack of it) of CEOs, alienates employees when we ought to be clear that leadership of a company is an honour, a recognition of skill, knowledge and performance, which also brings duties towards the long term survival and success of the organisation.

Senior executive behaviour and compensation has been a major factor hindering employee engagement. It is improbable that any employee will feel loyal to people whose only loyalty seems to be to themselves. Given how they have managed pay, senior executives can no longer appeal for employees to go the extra mile. No one will listen. In fact, they have probably cut off all communication between themselves and employees. They are truly aliens living in an alien world. Listen to Blogger Scot Herrick:

> *When was the last time the Senior Management of a corporation took a pay cut to help keep people employed? When was the last time the Senior Management of a corporation gave up their golden parachutes to keep people employed? Employee loyalty was on life support for decades, beginning in the early 1980s. With this current downturn, it has officially died.*
>
> *Employees don't owe the company anything except an honest day's work. That's what they get paid for and that's what they should deliver. Loyalty is a myth that has gone the way of the unicorn and the fire breathing dragon. Loyalty is an anachronism. Business is a cutthroat enterprise.*
>
> *The tragedy is that the only people who didn't realize it until it was way too late were the ones outside the executive board room. There are 10 million people out of work. Most of them were loyal. Virtually none of them are CEOs. Do the math.*

Herrick's facts can be disputed. That he states what very many employees feel, cannot be. Charles Moore, the official biographer of Baroness

(Margaret) Thatcher and one time editor of the *Daily Telegraph*, the high Tory right wing UK newspaper, shared with the readership of that newspaper (August 2011) his anxiety that the left may have been right all along about business and people. It was he who wrote the passage quoted at the beginning of this chapter:

> *The rich run a global system that allows them to accumulate capital and pay the lowest price for labour. The freedom that results applies only to them. The many simply have to work harder, in conditions that grow ever more insecure, to enrich the few.*

This litany of greed, reward for failure, hypocrisy and downright dishonesty has come to be regarded as almost normal. This is not an account of a few bad apples in the barrel but an account of how senior management conducts itself almost as a matter of course. How on earth can such people make any appeal to the ordinary employee to go that extra mile? Why is employee engagement so rare? Because there are so few leaders who deserve it.

LEADERSHIP

I have subtitled this book, *'The failure of leadership.'* There are many descriptions of leadership. One that is popular stems from James McGregor Burns and has a moral dimension.

> *Transformational leadership is about hearts and minds, about empowering people not controlling them. The word 'transformation' means change and transformational leadership is about empowering everyone in the organisation to learn, seek change and improvement, never to be satisfied with what is done today. It is based upon trusting skilled, dedicated, intelligent people to do what they have learned is best, to take responsibility immediately (indeed to seize it) and to share leadership throughout the organisation. The leader's job is to facilitate increased learning, trust and understanding.*[52]

We are experiencing a dreadful lack of leadership from the top. In his book, *The Future of Management*, Gary Hamel[53] gives a list of questions management must ask itself in an attempt to generate a culture of innovation and creativity; to *facilitate increased learning, trust and understanding*. These include:

- How can you create a company where the spirit of community rather than the machinery of bureaucracy, binds people together?

- How can you enlarge the sense of mission that people feel throughout your organization in a way that justifies extraordinary contribution?

- What are the biggest gaps between the rhetoric and reality in your company? What are the values it has the hardest time living up to? What's the espoused ideal you'd like to turn into an embedded capability?

Greed and insulation from the effects of failure breed no spirit of community to bind people together, no sense of a common mission, no extraordinary contribution, no ideals and no values. Leadership implies not demanding extravagantly better terms and conditions than anyone else, and indeed can demand the acceptance of worse. It certainly implies making sure that everything that is done is in the interests of the organisation – and its shareholders, employees and other stakeholders.

If this implies a form of sainthood, then so be it. Organisational leadership in today's organisations is not easy. If people slip from the highest standards that such leadership demands, then they are not worthy as leaders. In such cases, society has to take the most severe action, to protect its very way of being.

Are all CEOs guilty?

Dan DiMicco, CEO of Nucor, took a 43% reduction in pay in 2009. DiMicco's earnings were not small at $1.99 million but were far smaller than the average for the top 500 company CEOs at $8 million apiece. DiMicco's earnings are calculated on the same basis as the employees of Nucor. While he earns a lot more than the average steel worker, at least the way that he is paid is the same and is transparently so.

As the High Pay Commission said[54]:

> *The 18% bonus awarded to the CEO of John Lewis in 2011 was welcomed universally, because it was accompanied by an 18% bonus for the rest of the*

staff. While 18% of the CEOs wage may be a significantly larger amount in real terms than 18% of the cashier's wage, it is clear, transparent and linked to the success of the business.

Lincoln Electric CEO John Stropki Jr picked up $4.6 million in 2009, down 4% from the previous year. In particular, his non-equity incentive plan bonus fell to $858,144, a 55% decline from 2008.

At Southwest Airlines in 2008, CEO Gary Kelly received $900K in salary – $440K in base pay, plus a $460K bonus – with his total package valued at $1.7 million. Kelly took a 10% pay cut in April 2009 *'and until such time as the company's quarterly results improve.'*

None of these people are badly paid. None, however, are among the high earners. All are CEOs of very successful companies where employee engagement is high. It is also noticeable that in the case of Nucor and John Lewis, the CEO is paid on the same basis as the employees. If the amount of money is somewhat alien, at least the method of calculation is familiar.

John Lewis employees (known as 'Partners' because in fact they own the business) every year complete a survey. Despite the recession, the 2009 results showed an increase in the average satisfaction score (from an already good base.) Of its principles, John Lewis says:

The Partnership's ultimate purpose is the happiness of all its members, through their worthwhile and satisfying employment in a successful business. Because the Partnership is owned in trust for its members, they share the responsibilities of ownership as well as its rewards, profit, knowledge and power.

The John Lewis Partnership aims:

> *to make sufficient profit from its trading operations to sustain its commercial vitality, to finance its continued development and to distribute a share of those profits each year to its members, and to enable it to undertake other activities consistent with its ultimate purpose.*
>
> *to employ people of ability and integrity who are committed to working together and to supporting its Principles. Relationships are based on mutual respect and courtesy, with as much equality between its members as differences of responsibility permit. The Partnership aims to recognise their individual contributions and reward them fairly.*
>
> *to deal honestly with its customers and secure their loyalty and trust by providing outstanding choice, value and service.*
>
> *to conduct all its business relationships with integrity and courtesy and to honour scrupulously every business agreement.*
>
> *to obey the <u>spirit</u> as well as the letter of the law and to contribute to the wellbeing of the communities where it operates.*

John Lewis Partnership plc results for the year ended 29 January 2011:

- *Gross sales up £784.8m, 10.6%, to £8.21bn*
- *Group operating profit up £41.3m, 10.6%, to £431.0m*
- *Profit before Partnership bonus and tax up £61.3m, 20.0%, to £367.9m*
- *Partnership Bonus of £194.5m; 18% of salary (equal to more than 9 weeks' pay)*

The Chairman, Charlie Mayfield, said:

> *We're a long-term business, held in trust for the benefit of our Partners. Where we have made significant changes to the structure of our business, we have done so by engaging Partners. And, most important of all, our Partners have shown their commitment to continually improving what we do every day. The profits we make go to Partners and to improving the business for the future.*

> *I'm delighted that today we've announced that Partners will receive a bonus of 18%, an average of more than 9 weeks' pay. In addition we have paid £267m into our pension fund in the last year. We continue to offer a non-contributory final salary pension to Partners with more than three years service and our main pension fund has moved into surplus on a funding basis. Looking to the future, while we expect more difficult conditions for much of the year, we are confident of our plans. We will invest £0.6bn this year and expect to create 4,300 new jobs.* [55]

I doubt that you have forgotten that 2010 was in the depths of the bank inspired recession.

Until such time as senior executive pay is reduced, is tied properly to performance and is calculated using methods which are both transparent and similar to those used to calculate employee pay, the CEO and his immediate staff will still be seen as aliens. To that extent, nothing that they say about going extra miles, or being all in this together, will connect in any way with those who are being asked to put in extra effort. Otherwise, there is no such thing as employee engagement. This is a failure of leadership

To repeat what the Hutton report said:

> *Principles of fair pay are urgently needed, both to guide those who determine pay and to reassure the wider public that such principles exist and are being followed ... I define fairness in pay as the due desert for discretionary effort which delivers desired results; reward should match the employee's actions and contribution ... due desert should rise proportionally as individuals make more of a contribution. It should not rise limitlessly ... And pay should be determined by an impartially fair process.* [56]

Outside of a small number of companies, the way that CEOs are paid, whether or not they succeed, cannot but make any engagement with them impossible. Any appeal to loyalty such a person might make would fall on stoney ground and with great justification. CEOs are bad news.

> Richard Hall, writing in the *Independent*[57], said that the top executives of FTSE 100 companies in Britain received a median pay increase of 32% in 2010 compared with the increase in average employee wages of 2%.
>
> > *A report by the consultancy firm MM&K and the corporate governance specialists Manifest found the pay of executives in Britain had little relation to performance or shareholder value. The increase was more than treble the 9 per cent rise in the FTSE 100 share index over the same period.*
>
> Brendan Barber, general secretary of the Trades Union Congress said:
>
> > *These figures prove that directors' pay arrangements bear little resemblance to economic reality. Despite mediocre performance, corporate Britain continues to enjoy lavish and risk-free awards. As senior executives grab an ever-greater slice of Britain's dwindling earnings pool, ordinary workers face having their wages held back – with alarming consequences for consumer spending, household debt and the strength of our economic recovery.*[58]

WHAT IS SENIOR MANAGEMENT FOR?

If you are now asking yourself what on earth most senior management is for, then so are many other people. The author Jim Collins compared[59] high-performing companies to otherwise similar but low-performing companies. His research team sought a correlation between executive compensation and performance. They found none. CEOs just do not do very well. As McKeown and Whiteley say[60]:

> *Some 70 per cent of mergers fail; 70 per cent of outsourcing projects fail; 70 per cent of business processing re-engineering projects fail. They fail at this rate by their designers' own measures - profitability and return to shareholders.*

Senior management incompetence? Here is a list, in the UK only, of some of the fines levied on the financial sector alone in the year from June 2010 to May 2011:

- *£33.3million on JP Morgan for failing to ensure proper segregation of clients' money.*

- £17.5 million on Goldman Sachs for failing to keep the Financial Services Authority informed of an SEC investigation into its activities.
- £7.7 million on Barclays Bank for investment advice to customers to whom it sold savings plans.
- £3.5 million on Bank of Scotland for complaints handling failures.
- £2.8 million on Royal Bank of Scotland and Natwest Bank for failing to investigate customers' complaints.
- £2.275 million on Zurich Insurance for losing personal details of 46,000 customers.
- £1.575 million on Société Générale for transaction reporting failures.

Actually, it appears that there is one thing that CEOs achieve. The Institute for Policy Studies reported, in August 2011:

> We have no evidence that CEOS are fashioning, with their executive leadership, more effective or efficient enterprises. On the other hand, ample evidence suggests CEOs and their corporations are expending considerably more energy in avoiding taxes than perhaps ever before – at a time when the federal government needs more revenue to maintain basic services for the American people.

The report says that 25 of the top 100 US companies paid more to their CEO than they did in taxes.

Revolution?

There may have been some signs that the requirement for transparency of directors' salaries is having an effect. Some companies have indeed held back a little. However, transparency is not required for pensions. The *Independent* reported (9 August 2011) that the average FTSE 100 director is now in line for a pension 29 times that of the rest of the workforce. While final salary schemes have been closed to 97% of rank and file employees, 350 companies have kept such schemes open for directors.

Sean Farrell wrote (*Independent* newspaper October 24, 2011):

> *Shareholder revolts over pay have hit record levels this year as investors, stung by criticism of their inertia before the financial crisis, seek to rein in excessive rewards at Britain's top companies. With more than two months left of 2011, 15 companies in the FTSE 100 have suffered investor votes of 20 per cent or more opposing remuneration reports or deliberately abstaining.*
>
> *The biggest revolt so far this year was at WPP, the marketing giant, whose 42 per cent rebellion was entirely made up of votes against with no abstentions. XStrata was the next biggest with 39 per cent of votes withholding support. The mining company's remuneration report has attracted protest votes in each of the last three years. George Dallas, director of corporate governance at F&C Asset Management, says increased activism on pay is a response to the Stewardship Code[61], which was introduced last year. The code requires institutional investors to monitor the companies they hold shares in and tells them to act together when necessary to hold boards to account.*

In 2011, an anti-capitalist movement which started in the USA has taken hold in cities around the world. As their website says:

> *Occupy Wall Street is a people-powered movement that began on September 17, 2011 in Liberty Square in Manhattan's Financial District, and has spread to over 100 cities in the United States and actions in over 1,500 cities globally.*

In Melbourne, police caused violence in evicting demonstrators who had been camping in the city square, scenes emulated in other Australian cities. In London protesters set up a second campsite in Finsbury Square within the financial City of London following the encampment at St Paul's Cathedral. Chicago police arrested protesters while in Germany thousands of people took to the streets in Frankfurt, Berlin, Cologne, Munich, Dusseldorf and Hanover to voice outrage over corporate greed.

The writer, Howard Jacobson, put it this way[62]:

> *We've been hearing the business community telling us for years that no amount of money is too much to pay to get the best. And we've been watching their eyes glaze over when we ask why the same principle doesn't apply, say, to teachers, who are of more importance to society than CEOs. But this time even the defenders of the indefensible appear to know their time is over. Allow your greed to turn the world in which you exercise it into a hell hole, and where's*

the advantage (never mind the fairness) of your £18m? It might even be that through the clouds of defeated self-interest a glimmer of understanding is beginning to dawn about the practical meaning of inequity. So the tent people are winning this one hands down. They don't even have to say much. Just let the unimaginatively selfish panic before their steady scrutiny and ultimately condemn themselves.

Is it capitalism itself which is the problem? Well, it was for Karl Marx but then he was talking about real capitalists, people who put up their own money to create companies for their own profit. (Don't forget that Friedrich Engels was from a family of business owners.)

However, we do not have capitalism in this form today. It might be better to describe the current situation as 'managerialism'. The managers, whose earnings are the subject of such outrage, do not own their companies. The early capitalists at least risked their own money. The managers today risk very little.

We have no alternative to capitalism in one form or another and so what we must do is to set controls on the behaviour of the managers. We need regulation for clearly we cannot depend upon decency and morality - and self-regulation has become a very poor joke. The cause of the banking crisis was the greed and incompetence of the managers. However, what allowed that greed and incompetence to flourish was the removal of banking controls.

* * *

3

THE PROBLEM II: LOYALTY IS A TWO WAY STREET

There was one woman I worked with who'd been with the company all her life – and remember most people there were only earning an average of £18,000. Every year she put money into the share save scheme and almost overnight she saw the value of all her savings just wiped out.

That was to help her in her retirement. She was doing the right thing. People at the top played fast and loose not just with customers, not just with taxpayers but also people who worked there. That was one of the saddest things from a personal perspective. People lost all faith in the organisation they worked for, as well as losing their savings and their jobs as well.

Rachel Reeves, Member of Parliament and shadow cabinet, speaking of her experience working for HBOS, the bank that went bust in the 2008 crash.[63]

THE PROBLEM II

Loyalty is earned. Loyalty is a two way street and so is engagement. If loyalty has been damaged by the gulf between senior executive pay and the normal employee's experience, it has been further sundered by redundancy and by the weasel words that surround it.

The more that employees are willing to go the extra mile, the less senior management has to pay for work done, the fewer people it needs to employ and the more it can pay itself. Fair enough if the reward for harder work is a better salary and job security but neither of these are on offer. So is employee engagement a con-trick? Can you be loyal to someone who shows no loyalty to you?

The Institute of Leadership and Management runs an annual Index of Leadership Trust. In its 2010 report[64], The ILM argued that:

> *Trust is integral to effective leadership – leaders must motivate and inspire people to follow them. Trust creates more efficient organisations, reducing staff turnover, absenteeism, stress and the costs of doing business. And it is leaders who build trust. At times of great uncertainty and threat, only the most trusted leaders will inspire the confidence and commitment needed to ensure success.*

During the recession, ILM research in particular revealed

> *… that where the organisation had managed to avoid job losses, CEOs and line managers enjoyed increased levels of trust. However, where redundancies and site closures occurred, trust levels fell sharply.*

The ILM goes on to say that this is even more marked for CEOs.

> *Employees see CEOs as bearing far more responsibility than line managers for the scale of the impact of the recession on their organisations, depressing trust levels accordingly.*

A long time ago (and it does indeed feel like another galaxy) people stayed with a company for life. In that galaxy, loyalty to one's company was a bit like loyalty to a football team. In *What makes a true football fan?* Simon Kuper and Stefan Szymanski discuss[65] the true fan as portrayed in Nick Hornby's book, *Fever Pitch*.

> *As far as life allows, the Hornbyesque fan sees all his club's home games. (It's accepted even in the rhetoric of fandom that travelling to away games is best left to unmarried men under the age of 25.) No matter how bad his team*

> gets, the fan cannot abandon them. When Hornby watches the Arsenal of the late 1960s with his dad, their incompetence shames him but he cannot leave: 'I was chained to Arsenal and my dad was chained to me, and there was no way out for any of us.'

Gideon Rachman[66] quotes an archetypal declaration of faith from a Carlisle United fan, Charles Burgess:

> There never was any choice. My Dad ... took me down to Brunton Park to watch the derby match against Workington Town just after Christmas 41 years ago – I was hooked and have been ever since ... My support has been about who we are and where we are from.

A long while ago, loyalty to one's company was a bit like this. Perhaps it also had to do with the company pension. Jumping between jobs had a damaging effect on one's pension at retirement age and so this was another reason to stay loyal. That reason has disappeared obviously. With very few exceptions, and a declining number of those, the good old company pension scheme has disappeared (except for senior management of course.)

Psychological contract

Pension reasons or not, job security and job tenure have been seen as major parts of the psychological contract, a concept introduced by Chris Argyris in his 1960 book *Understanding organizational behavior*[67]. Jacqueline A-M. Coyle-Shapiro, Lynn M. Shore, and M. Susan Taylor summarise the current concept of a psychological contract as follows:

> ... the psychological contract is composed of an employee's beliefs about reciprocal, promissory obligations between himself or herself and the organization. These beliefs relate to what each party is entitled to receive and bound to provide in exchange for the other's contributions.
>
> The notion of exchange is an important part of this contract. The employee expects to make contributions to the relationship, but these are contingent, in part, on expected contributions by the employer. Thus, it involves not what one would like from the relationship, or what he or she expects from the relationship, but rather, what one believes should or must be exchanged because of promises that have been made or obligations that have been established between the two parties.[68]

Just as a job description can never capture what a job is about, so a contract of employment can never capture what it means to be a proper member of an organisational community. In any job, there are many things that need to be done - implied, assumed, just a matter of common sense or part and parcel of doing such a job professionally - none of which are referred to in a job description. In a similar way, the psychological contract goes beyond any contract of employment.

The psychological contract covers informal, imprecise mutual expectations of all sorts of behaviours; from working late when something needs to be completed, covering for several colleagues off sick, digging the boss out of trouble when he or she has made a mistake, to making allowances when a loyal employee has a bad day, ante-ing up some expenses when overtime cannot be paid or doing one's damndest to avoid a redundancy.

Professor Jackie McCoy of the University of Ulster and Alan Elwood[69] connect the psychological contract with what they call 'organisational citizenship' whereby employees *make voluntary contributions that go beyond the specific task performance.* They argue that this type of behaviour is crucial to the resilience of an organisation. A vital part of the contract is a sense of fairness. The deal may be informal and unwritten but it must be honoured by both sides. As the CIPD says[70]:

> *In order to display commitment, employees have to feel that they are being treated with fairness and respect.*

Despite the changes in employment conditions over the last twenty or thirty years, the feeling that job security is very much part of the psychological contract is still strong. As the CIPD also says[71]:

> *The traditional psychological contract is generally described as an offer of commitment by the employee in return for job security provided by the employer - or in some cases the legendary 'job for life'. The recessions of the early 1990s and the continuing impact of globalisation are alleged to have destroyed the basis of this traditional deal since job security is no longer on offer. Research suggests that in many ways the 'old' psychological contract is in fact still alive. Employees still want security.*

Violation of the contract leads to feelings of injustice, deception or betrayal among employees. Again, it's like football.

> *Many times I have found myself sitting in an 80 per cent empty stadium, trying to generate heat from a barely edible burger and wondering if I was going to get home before midnight. Half of me wants to congratulate myself for being a 'loyal fan' and for turning out on a frozen November evening, while the more sensible half is saying, 'I must be a fool to be here.'*[72]

It's football's greatest crime to talk of switching allegiance and just as the genuine fan will not give up on his team, the engaged employee will stick by his or her company through thick and thin.

Broken

There is little doubt that in most companies today, the contract between managers and employees has broken down and with it has gone employee loyalty. In 1996, the New York Times survey found that since 1980, a family member in one-third of all U.S. households had been laid off[73]. That was in the period 1980-1996. What would you estimate today? That a half of all households have a member who has been made redundant at some time? Two-thirds? The Chartered Management Institute 2010 survey reports that *'78% of managers say that they have previous experience of redundancy.'* [74]

The Ipsos Loyalty Study found that only about 25% of US employees think their employer *deserves* their loyalty[75]. In his book, *Charging Back Up the Hill*[76], on the subject of how to bring about recovery after mergers, acquisitions, and downsizings, Mitchell Lee Marks quotes the survivor of a downsizing:

> *There is no loyalty here; no one is going the extra mile after this. Two years ago, we worked sixty-five-hour weeks. People were willing to do it, because it was a great place to work and we were doing something that mattered . . . From here on in, it's just a job for me. I'll put in my forty hours and that's it.*

In December 2008, Towers Perrin carried out research into the effects of the recession. It revealed[77] that many employees were worried about how they'll be affected by the recession. Nearly half (45%) said they believed they faced greater risk that their job will change or be eliminated, and even more (55%) believed the risk that their future earnings would plateau or decline had increased.

They were right to worry. Towers Watson showed[78] that 74% of US companies instituted redundancies or lay offs during the recession.

Senior management is the enemy

Research in America by the Institute for Policy Studies has shown[79] that there is a direct correlation between what CEOs get paid and how many staff they lay off or make redundant.

> *In 2009, the CEOs who slashed their payrolls the deepest took home 42% more compensation than the year's chief executive pay average for S&P 500 companies.*

Keiningham and Aksoy[80] write:

> *Wall Street often rewards layoffs by treating them as a sign that management is serious about getting a company's financial house in order.*

Senior managers expect and indeed receive praise and reward for downsizing. Their reward is of course the employees' pain. So is it not somewhat irrational to expect employees to give loyalty, to go that extra mile and become emotionally engaged in an organisation that not only has no qualms in throwing them out when it suits them, but actually sees getting rid of them as something to be proud of?

Henry Hornstein, in *Downsizing isn't what it's cracked up to be*[81], says that:

> *Most analysts perpetuate these traditional and unoriginal attempts at turnaround by praising organizations 'for doing the right things' such as downsizing. Research has shown that the decision to downsize is a political one rather than one based on any valid financial rationale. That is, downsizing decisions undertaken by organizations are taken because that is what managers have decided to do rather than because they expect to realize any real financial benefits.*

The interests of the employee and the interests of the senior executives are diametrically opposed. If senior management is successful in reducing headcount, resisting pay increases and minimising costs of employment, they are seen to be successful, and can pay themselves more; 42% more as it turns out. Senior managers are not just aliens but enemy aliens.

So isn't employee engagement indeed a con trick? It certainly isn't a case of us all being in this together. Any loyalty is not reciprocated. Take the example of continuous improvement. CK Prahalad says[82]:

> *Continuous improvement is desirable - but think about its implications. We are telling employees: 'If you do not become more efficient, you will lose your job to your competitor.' The employees can understand that. But we are also saying, 'If you become very efficient, you will lose your job to productivity improvement' - and that they do not understand.'*

In a key phrase, he goes on:

> *How long do you expect employees to continuously improve without them recognising that the implication of such improvement is loss of jobs?*

Prahalad argues that continuous improvement must go hand in hand with continuous growth and is possible only when growth enables retraining and redeployment. If continuous improvement leads only to redundancies and lay-offs, then sooner or later the three card trick is laid bare and no one wants to play the engagement game again.

Downsizing and morale

Thomas A. Hickok shows[83] that downsizing changes the relationship between the boss and the employees. It reinforces top down management and actually reduces involvement. Both, of course, have a negative impact on engagement. He goes on to say:

> *Accompanying this change is a shift in emphasis away from the well-being of individuals in the direction of the pre-eminence and predominance of the organization as a whole.*

His study finds that

> *... the employer-employee relationship has moved away from long-term and stable in the direction of short-term and contingent.*

Senior management seeks short term gains, well aware that they will not be in the company long. Employees are not seen as the most important asset whatever the company's PR department says. The well-being of employees is no longer seen as important and

> *... it appears working relationships have changed away from being 'familial' in the direction of being more competitive.*

Why is this so? Well, have you ever seen a collaborative game of musical chairs? You might think that only those downsized, feel the pain. However, as Rick Roskin says, writing for *The Working Manager*:

> *The effects of downsizing on workers are well documented. Although survivors maintain their jobs and their pay, their sense of security about jobs and pay decreases, which may lead to lower productivity, resistance to change, and reduced commitment to the organization.*
>
> *Moreover, the job restructuring that occurs because of downsizing often increases role conflict, role ambiguity, and role overload which may result in greater interpersonal difficulties at work as well as decreased organizational commitment. Finally, they are often left with a deep sense of survival guilt.*
>
> *One of the most important effects of downsizing may be the challenge to workers' expectation that good performance will result in long-term employment. In fact, it is argued that downsizing causes a fundamental shift in the psychological contract between worker and employer.*

Downsizing brings decreased loyalty and morale, lower trust levels, breakup of high performing groups, cultural damage, self-protection strategies among employees, decreased risk-taking, lower levels of employee involvement, increased top-down management, increased management and employee stress.

Why would an employee give loyalty to an organisation that takes only a short term (and selfish) view, changing direction and employment at the drop of a hat?

Downsizing doesn't work

CK Prahalad wrote that downsizing is:

> *... like corporate anorexia; it can make you leaner and thinner, but it won't make you healthier.*

He invited management to:

> ... think what might have happened if companies had used all the 'redundant' brainpower they got rid of to imagine new markets for tomorrow, or to build new core competencies that would give them an advantage in those markets.

You may argue that downsizing is a necessary part of management. After all, management has to reduce costs in the face of competition and recession. Well, it might be a good argument if downsizing worked but there is a chorus of research that says it doesn't. As Jeffrey Pfeffer of Stanford University, has said:[84]

> There are two things to say about downsizing: It seldom works and is often done incorrectly.

In his book, *Management Myth: Why The Experts Keep Getting It Wrong*[85], Matthew Stewart recounts a story of how the consultancy he once worked for was sent into a chain of menswear shops. The advice was to cut the staff by 30% and to replace full-time staff with part-time staff. What they actually replaced was a set of employees with a long term commitment to a career in the company and to its customers, with a set of people with no long term prospects and thus with only a short term commitment to the money they earned. Motivation levels in the company collapsed as did the standards of customer service and the company fell into bankruptcy a short while later.

In a similar vein, Keiningham and Aksoy[86] report research using the American Customer Satisfaction Index indicating that:

> ... firms that engaged in substantial downsizing experienced large declines in customer satisfaction. Unfortunately for those firms, the index has proven to be a good predictor of future earnings. The current trend toward downsizing in US firms may increase productivity in the short term, but the downsized firms' future financial performance will suffer if repeat business is dependent on labor-intensive customized service.

Hickok[87] writes:

> ... downsizing has failed abjectly as a tool to achieve the main raison d'etre, reduced costs. According to a Wyatt Company survey covering the period between 1985 and 1990, 89% of organizations which engaged in downsizing

reported expense reduction as their primary goal, while only 42% actually reduced expenses.

One of the reasons why cost reduction is not achieved is that voluntary redundancy attracts only the most confident (and best) employees. All too often, the good people leave and are then employed back again as consultants and contractors.

Henry Hornstein writes[88]:

> *Downsizing has a negative effect on corporate memory and employee morale, disrupts social networks, causes a loss of knowledge, and disrupts learning networks. As a result, downsizing risks handicapping and damaging the learning capacity of organizations. Further, given that downsizing is often associated with cutting costs, downsizing firms may provide less training for their employees, recruit less externally, and reduce the research and development budget. Consequently, downsizing 'hollows out' the firm's skills capacity.*

Downsizing, a somewhat dim-witted, knee jerk response, usually fails to have any benefit for the company and acts in the opposite direction to employee engagement. The redundancies it causes severely damage the contract between management and staff. Instead of the hard work of growing a company and engaging their people in the search for growth, managers take the apparently easier and certainly lazier and failed opposite route.

CAN IT BE DONE?

Can it be done? Can it really be true that organisations can prosper while giving and receiving loyalty and engagement? Well, take Nucor. Helen Kelly, writing for *The Working Manager*, invites us to picture:

> *A firm with operations in forty-nine locations across seventeen US states - employing 12,000 people of whom seventy work at corporate headquarters – that:*
> - *has never had a layoff in over forty years in business*
> - *seeks to hire people who are first and foremost curious, creative, straightforward, thorough and highly articulate*
> - *operates without committees, task forces, lengthy handbooks, performance appraisals or paper trails*

> - *delegates all operating decisions and most of its budget to front-line teams of friendly, smart, decisive people*
> - *expects of employees only that they: know the job, ask questions and experiment, share what they learn: what's new that works and why, what doesn't go right and why, do what it takes to prevent the wrong things happening again, let management know how they can help*
> - *and whose CEOs job description and his operating philosophy is: 'Hire the right people, give them the resources and tools to do the job, and then get the hell out of their way.'*

Did they suffer during the recession? Of course they did.

> *CHARLOTTE, N.C., Jan 26, 2010 /PRNewswire via COMTEX/ – Nucor Corporation (NYSE: NUE) announced today consolidated net earnings of $58.9 million (down from) $105.9 million for the fourth quarter of 2008. For the full year of 2009, Nucor reported a consolidated net loss of $293.6 million or $0.94 per diluted share, compared with net earnings of $1.83 billion or $5.98 per diluted share for 2008.*

Did they lay off anyone? No, they did not.

> *Nucor Q4 2009 Earnings Call Transcript, January 26 2010*
>
> *Dan DiMicco: The benefit that Nucor and companies like Nucor have had ... is they haven't laid off their employees. We've been able to get in there immediately to meet customers' needs. Some of our competition took time to gear backup again and we've benefited from that and we will continue to benefit from that.*
>
> *John Ferriola: I would like to add one thing, building upon Dan's comments of no layoff practice. As a result of that we used the difficult times last year to develop new products. We expanded our product range in virtually every one of our product groups and that has helped us weather this storm and will help us weather the storm going into 2010.*

Nucor is, of course, an exception. It is an amazingly well run company deeply loyal to its staff and receiving deep loyalty in return.

RBS – LOYALTY AND FAILURE

The psychologists call it 'cognitive dissonance' - psychological conflict resulting from simultaneously held incongruous beliefs and attitudes. Listening to what management says about *'firmly believing that our employees are our most valuable assets'* while watching the disparity between employee and senior executive salaries grow and lay-offs increase makes any belief in what management says just that bit tricky.

Most companies just talk a good game. What they actually do is made worse by the contrast with the weasel words that they use. The Royal Bank of Scotland **had a** head of human capital strategy, Greig Aitken. According to Aitken:

> *We had a good starting point when the HR director and I came up with our employee engagement proposition in 2001. We already had a global employee survey, for which we got a response rate of 87%. Employee engagement is not just about employee satisfaction. It is about the discretionary effort that differentiates high-performing staff.*

The CEO of RBS (Sir) Fred Goodwin enjoyed his nickname of 'Fred the Shred' gained for cutting costs and jobs. He built up the bank with acquisition after acquisition: NatWest, Coutts, Adam & Co, Direct Line, Ulster Bank, Churchill, Citizens Bank in the US and the one that finally broke the bank: ABN Amro. He then ruthlessly cut costs making staff reductions to generate bigger short term profits.

Fred was fired after RBS had to be bailed out by the government. (Failure of risk management at RBS was *'obvious'* said the new chief executive Stephen Hester.) In April 2009, RBS, by then virtually owned by the UK Government after its monumental failure, started to announce a series of rounds of job losses which have gone on ever since.

As the government's share in RBS rose to 84 per cent and as job losses exceeded 25% of RBS employees, one cannot avoid the conclusion that RBS words about employee engagement were just that: words. The *response rate* of 87% and the *discretionary effort that differentiates high-performing staff* must feel really great today.

As Rob MacGregor, national officer at the union, Unite, said[89]:

> *Just three weeks ago, staff were boosted to hear of the £1.1bn half-year profit, yet today thousands of them are told that they have no future at the bank. The scale of the cuts announced today beggars belief and staff across the country today will be left reeling from this news. We continue to see a financial services sector which thinks the skills and expertise of its staff are a disposable asset with scant regard for the high level of service these very same staff provide to their customers.*

COMPLAINTS

In February 2011, the Financial Ombudsman reported, in the second half of 2010 compared to the first half, that at Santander, total complaints fell by 20%. At Barclays, they fell by 4%. At HSBC, they fell just a little at 1%.

At Lloyds they *rose by 14%* while at RBS total complaints *rose by 41%*. Natwest, part of the RBS group, ran an advertising campaign on their 'improving' customer service. Complaints at Natwest also *increased by 41%*.

What you say matters. If you want to talk about *'the discretionary effort that differentiates high-performing staff'* then make sure that the company deserves that discretionary effort.

A GUARANTEED EMPLOYMENT POLICY?

I received this letter from Hermann Schwin of St Mary's University in Canada, asking how realistic a guaranteed employment policy is. He wrote:

> *I just finished a book by Frank Koller, 'SPARK - How Old-Fashioned Values Drive a Twenty-First Century Corporation'*[90] *about Lincoln Electric, the world's largest manufacturer of welding equipment and products, headquartered in Cleveland, Ohio. The book was published in 2010 and contains the latest data (from 2009).*

He goes on to describe Lincoln, which he says is mentioned in almost every HR text as an example of a profit sharing system through sharing of cost reductions with employees. The company also has a no-lay-off policy, even in times of economic downturns. Founded by John Lincoln in 1895 it adopted the guaranteed employment strategy in 1954 and has kept it even during the latest recession. Instead of lay-offs, it used shortened working hours and wage and salary reductions to overcome these dire times.

LE employs 3,300 workers and has another 6,000 in 19 countries. Yearly bonuses range from 45% to 100% of annual compensation. In its history it introduced some breakthrough policies:

1923 - paid vacation

1925 - stock ownership plan for employees

1929 - employee suggestion program

1934 - profit sharing

1950 - cost of living multiplier

1954 - guaranteed employment

LE's average growth per year from 2005 to 2009 was 19%, with an average annual return on investment of 16%, a long-term debt-to-equity ratio of only 9%, a bank balance of $406 million in cash (2009), and a larger global market share than any of its competitors.

For at least 60 years, no worker at Lincoln Electric who is covered by the guaranteed employment policy has been laid off due to a lack of work. Furthermore, for 75 uninterrupted years starting in 1934, the company has paid out a merit-based profit-sharing bonus that has almost always exceeded 60 per cent of each employee's basic earnings. In a number of these years, it has exceeded 100 per cent. In 2008, the average bonus paid out was $28,873. Lincoln Electric's employment policies have proven healthy for the company's bottom line, its customers, its employees and its shareholders.

Lincoln has been able to sustain a truly unusual relationship between its employees across every level of the company. The firm's perennially robust profit margins (driven by consistently innovative technology), the dramatically heightened job security and quality of life enjoyed by its employees and the benefits that accrue to the local economy should give the rest of the business world cause to think.

Bob Tita wrote in the Wall Street Journal[91] that;

> *James Lincoln's ideas about changing the dynamics between labor and management were born out of the calamitous environment of U.S. manufacturing in the late 19th century, when companies were beset by frequent strikes and high levels of employee absenteeism and turnover, often caused by deplorable working conditions and low wages.*
>
> *Mr. Lincoln's older brother, John, started Lincoln Electric in 1895. He brought James onboard in 1907 and promoted him to general manager in 1914. From James's earliest days with the company he was determined to forge a more cooperative relationship with workers than was the norm on most shop floors. 'I knew that if I could get the people in the company to want the company to succeed as badly as I did,' he once wrote, 'there would be no problem we could not solve together.'*
>
> *To create the teamwork he had in mind, James Lincoln relied on four organizational pillars that remain in place to this day:*
>
> - *a management advisory board made up of employee representatives*
> - *wages based on piecework, so that the quality and quantity of individual workers' output can be monitored*
> - *annual performance-based bonuses*
> - *guaranteed employment.*
>
> *Although the no-lay-offs pledge would be formally adopted as a policy only in the late 1950s, the company began the practice, de facto, as far back as the mid-1920s. James Lincoln, who died in 1965, considered the guarantee essential for getting employees to trust management and accept the inevitable wage cuts, reduced work hours and job transfers that were necessary to keep people working when orders slumped.*

By the way, in his book Frank Koller stresses that Lincoln Electric's motives are nothing to do with socialism nor are they related to the religious beliefs which created Bournville[92] for example. They are a hard headed search for profitability. As Tita writes:

> *In exchange for a no-lay-off guarantee, Lincoln's 3,300 U.S. employees are subjected to rigorous performance and productivity standards to keep them*

from becoming complacent. Workers who don't meet the company's expectations receive smaller bonuses or end up getting bounced out entirely.

Professor Schwin remarks that the LE approach to HR policies is:

... an interesting alternative to the currently popular HR systems in most companies. Of course, it would require a major change in those companies' corporate culture and management philosophy, an unlikely possibility.

WHY DON'T OTHER COMPANIES DO THIS? THE XILINX STORY

Let us review the story of Peg Wynn, former vice president for the semiconductor chip company Xilinx Inc., and now Vice President, Director of Human Resources and Assistant Secretary at Granite Construction Incorporated. Ms. Wynn was part of the team who in the 1990s implemented a no lay-offs policy at Xilinx. In 2002, she received the *Honoring Excellence Award* from the *HR Symposium in California*.

The Xilinx policy did not last. Why? Well Peg Wynn said that the company's leadership ultimately found that just doing what everybody else does was easier and that avoiding lay-offs really requires great managers.

One cannot be sure that her exit from Xilinx was peaceful. She made a presentation to Silicon Valley Women in Human Resources, not a body one might think of as a hot bed of radicalism but Xilinx's legal team forced the removal of her presentation from the website. Member Marcia Stein wrote[93]:

This is a real shame. Peg was their VP WW HR and made this presentation in 2003. She ran a great department at a very well-regarded company, and she noted her team's HR strengths, their values, how they avoided layoffs in a tough economic situation, and how they transformed their HR function. There was NOTHING in her presentation harmful to the company and she did not reveal confidential information. The company was public and any details regarding tough economic times - which we all faced then - were public knowledge.

Hey ho! I guess that being told that one is not a *'really great manager'* is tough to take.

WIM ROELANDTS

It is a great pity, especially when one reads of the company's massive achievement during the earlier dotcom crisis. Alexander Kjerulf, author of *Happy Hour is 9 to 5*[94], wrote an account (*The seeeeeeriously cool way out of a downturn*[95]) of Xilinx's successful survival under the leadership of Wim Roelandts. Now this is a story of real leadership.

Kjerulf tells us that for the December 2000 quarter Xilinx's revenue was $450 million. Just 9 months later their revenue was down to $225 million. While their competitors fired a large percentage of their staff to cut costs, Wim Roelandts came up with a plan for his organization and called it *'Share the pain.'* (We are all in this together?) Though Xilinx was careful not to promise that there would be no lay-offs, the company got through the crisis - note this - without laying off a single employee.

> *1: Cut salaries, not jobs*
>
> Wim felt strongly that if they laid off people, they'd just need to rehire them when business improved. So they instituted a pay cut that was progressive and voluntary. Progressive meant that your pay cut depended on your salary; the higher your salary, the higher your pay cut. Voluntary meant voluntary. Everyone volunteered.
>
> *2: Communicate openly*
>
> Wim aimed to keep communicating. This is not easy, as Wim says: 'I didn't know any more than anybody else what was coming and so the tendency is to close your office door and not talk to anybody because if you talk with someone, they can ask questions that you don't know the answers to. But that's actually the wrong thing to do; you have to get out there.'
>
> *3: Involve employees in decisions*
>
> They involved people in all new initiatives by consulting with focus groups of employees. They'd get 20 employees together, tell them about what they were planning to do and get their honest feedback.

It worked. Except for one quarter, and there were technical reasons for that, Xilinx was profitable every quarter during the recession. The company gained 15 points of market share during the crisis because they kept their people and thus could keep momentum. They had the time and the people to develop new products, essential in their industry.

Wim faced a lot of resistance to his approach. Some board members and financial analysts wanted to know why he didn't just lay off 10% of the employees when everyone else was doing it. They would have been much more comfortable with the traditional approach. ('Just doing what everybody else does' was easier, as Wim's successors chose.) However, Wim was a leader, not a follower of the herd.

The positive effect was also felt outside the company. About two years after the crisis when the company was back on track, Wim was approached by a female employee who happened to arrive at work the same time he did. She told him:

> *My husband got laid off and so yesterday evening we had a family meeting with the children. We had to tell them that their father had been laid off and that they had to do some savings and we had to be very careful how we spend money, to make sure that we get through this tough time until our Dad finds a job again.*
>
> *One of my children asked, 'But Mom what is going to happen if you get laid off?' I was so proud to say that I work at Xilinx and Xilinx doesn't lay off people.*

When Wim stepped down

Wim stepped down as Chairman of the Board in February 2009. On 15 April, 2009, Xilinx issued a press release:

> *Xilinx, the San Jose maker of programmable chips, said Wednesday it expects to cut 200 jobs, or about six percent of its total workforce. The move is expected to cost anywhere from $11 to $13 million in charges during its current quarter, mostly to cover severance pay, and estimates that it will save the company somewhere between $4 and $5 million per quarter.*

Comments on the web show a rather different reaction from 2001:

- *Wow that is indeed a surprise, coming from a company which was one of the best places to work for.*
- *Many excellent employees were laid off by new management who didn't even know what they were working on, and with no input from their own managers.*
- *If you are a software engineer at Xilinx that is caught in the current lay-off, please drop me an email with your resume. Several of the companies I'm involved in locally – including Rally Software and Grip – are actively hiring experienced software engineers.*

Of course, the lay-offs were not for cost reasons! As the company said, it was announcing (in PR-speak):

> *... a corporate reorganization into functional areas to better serve its customers and improve its operating performance. As a result of the reorganization, Xilinx will eliminate approximately 250 positions, or about 7% of the Company's global workforce. The workforce reduction is expected to be completed by the end of the next fiscal quarter.*

The proper response is to laugh. The rider to the press release contains some black humour in the light of research that lay-offs rarely if ever produce a financial benefit.

> *This release contains forward-looking statements and projections. Forward-looking statements and projections can often be identified by the use of forward-looking words such as 'expect,' 'may,' 'will,' 'could,' 'believe,' 'anticipate,' 'estimate,' 'continue,' 'plan,' 'intend,' 'project' or other similar words. Undue reliance should not be placed on such forward-looking statements and projections, which speak only as of the date they are made. We undertake no obligation to update such forward-looking statements.* ***Actual events and results may differ materially from those in the forward-looking statements and are subject to risks and uncertainties.***
>
> (Emphasis added)

The no-redundancy policy

Whether or not you have a formal 'no redundancies' or 'no lay-offs' policy, recognise that what damages your chances of gaining employee engagement most are redundancies and lay-offs. I am sorry to have to tell you that employee engagement and avoiding lay-offs really do require great managers. However, the company's leadership may well find that just doing what everybody else does is easier. (Do you think the word 'leadership' is appropriate in that sentence?)

While it might be comforting to say that talk of a no-redundancy policy (and indeed employee engagement) is just idealistic nonsense and not true of real life, and while one really does not wish to cause further pain, it is also incumbent upon me to point out that companies as varied as a department store and supermarket group, a steel company, an airline and a manufacturer of welding equipment have all implemented such policies, formally or otherwise with great success.

On 12 May 2011, the UK Chancellor of the Exchequer, George Osborne, announced that the government planned to remove sections of employment law so that companies could get rid of staff more easily and have a 'flexible' approach.[96]

Employee engagement? It would be funny if it were not so tragic.

* * *

4

TOWARDS UNDERSTANDING I: THE CONTEXT — NOT A PILL YOU CAN TAKE

The problem with focusing on 'employee engagement' is that makes it sound as though employees were disengaged because of the lack of employee engagement programs. But engagement programs treat the symptom not the disease. The real disease is poor management - and that's you, buck. Employees don't need programs and engagement strategies. They need managers with vision, an understanding that employees want and need to work to the best of their abilities. Employees don't need to be engaged - managers need to be improved. Employee engagement is about having a well-run enterprise based on consistently applied values. Do that, and engagement follows.

Paul Herbert writing in *Business Week*[97]

Trust, leadership, management style, organisational culture, values, true grit, involvement, engagement, empowerment, self-sacrifice, motivation, self managing teams; all these concepts and more are interrelated and all are part and parcel of employee engagement. This should give us pause when thinking about employee engagement programmes.

Indeed, UK research by Stephen Wooda and Lilian M. de Menezes[98] found that high involvement processes, with the exception of TQM, have *no effect whatsoever* on engagement. The only positive correlation with employee engagement is a company culture which genuinely prizes involvement. If the company really believes, *and always acts upon the belief*, that employees really matter and that their involvement in all decision making and creativity is genuinely important, then employee engagement will occur.

So to speak of an employee engagement programme is dangerous. It implies that engagement is the result of a set of processes quite detached from leadership. Some pill that employees or management can take perhaps? Worse, it implies that it is a programme that someone (HR?) can take care of while line management get on with the job (which would be what exactly?)

OPINION SURVEYS

While surveys can give some measure of change in opinions, employee engagement is not the result of opinion surveys. The problem is that surveys are almost always about matters tangential to engagement. In his 1994 Harvard Business Review article, *Good Communication That Blocks Learning*, Chris Argyris writes:

> *... when corporations still wanted employees who did only what they were told, employee surveys and walk-around management were appropriate and effective tools. They can still produce useful information about cafeteria service and parking privileges.*

The aim of opinion surveys is to identify discontent and by removing it to produce contented people. However, as Argyris goes on:

> *... there is nothing wrong with contented people, if contentment is the only goal. The key is a system of external compensation and job security that*

> *employees consider fair. In such a system, superficial answers to critical questions produce adequate results, and no one demands more.*
>
> Opinion surveys are about Herzberg's hygiene factors and not about motivating factors. This does not mean that they are useless. After all, we can expect attrition and absenteeism if hygiene factors are below what is acceptable but if engagement is about *'employees' emotional and intellectual commitment to their organisation and its success'* as the Work Foundation says, data on 'contentment' is not much use. Cows are said to be contented.

In summarising the research, Professor Rick Roskin writes for *The Working Manager*:

> *This research, though complex, warrants some reflection, because in the end, stand alone programmes seem to do little for a company except give employees a (not necessarily justified) feeling of job security.*
>
> *Therefore, with the exception of a company-wide and sincerely meant TQM type programme, deeply rooted within the company culture that drives employee involvement and which guides all the company's judgements and behaviour, there may be little effect on productivity.*

The relevance of TQM to employee engagement is that it is independent of capricious management decisions. So let's recognise that the attempt to re-engage employees in their work is not a process isolated from management and leadership. It *is* management and leadership. It is (primarily) *what managers are for.*

Understanding employee engagement

To understand employee engagement, you really have to understand the context in which it exists. The world of management is replete with programmes, buzz words and fashionable phrases. Before employee engagement we had employee involvement and employee empowerment. All these programmes were based on the same idea, enabling employees to take responsibility and accountability. The route to all of these has been seen as a reversal of the traditional top down relationship between management and staff.

A genuine intention to engage employees must be based on a real understanding of its context. Yes, such an understanding takes effort. Yes, it requires some understanding of the development of management and management theory and, no, it cannot be set out in 160 characters.

THE TRADITIONAL TOP DOWN RELATIONSHIP

It goes all the way back to French mining engineer, Henri Fayol, who famously said that it was the job of management to *Plan, Organise, Direct, Co-ordinate* and *Control*. A better definition of top-down management cannot be given. What he said sounds so apparently rational. In his 1916 work, *Administration Industrielle et Générale – Prévoyance, Organisation, Commandement, Coordination, Contrôle*[99], he wrote of:

- *Prévoyance*: examining the future and drawing up a plan of action

- *Organisation*: building up the structure, material and human, of the undertaking

- *Commandement*: maintaining activity among the personnel

- *Coordination*: binding together, unifying and harmonizing all activity and effort

- *Contrôle*: ensuring that everything occurs in conformity with established rules and expressed commands

He called for:

> *Unity of direction* - the overall direction of the enterprise must be one single controlling mind which generates the plan for all to follow. 'One head and one plan for a group having the same objective.'

> *Order* - there must be a logical structure and the presence of any employee justified by this structure, for 'when ambition, nepotism, favouritism or merely ignorance, has multiplied positions without good reason or filled them with incompetent employees, much talent and strength of will and more persistence ... are required in order to sweep away abuses and restore order.'

Specialisation of labour – work should be reduced to its elements so that it can be studied and the best way of carrying it out analysed and taught to the workers.

Authority – vested only in managers is 'the right to give orders and the power to exact obedience.'

Formal chain of command - which must run seamlessly from the top to the bottom of the organization. For any one employee there must be one and only one boss who gives the employee orders. 'For any action whatsoever, an employee should receive orders from one superior only. ... Should (this rule) be violated, authority is undermined, discipline is in jeopardy, order disturbed and stability threatened.'

Discipline – the prevention of slacking and the enforcement of rules. Employees and managers must think only about work during working hours. Their own ambitions should be strictly controlled.

Despite being written about 100 years ago, Fayol's views still sound so apparently rational. In fact, they form the way that so many people still think about management today.

COMPLEXITY

Contrast what Fayol wrote with what Rob Cross and Andrew Parker write in *The Hidden Power of Social Networks: Understanding How Work Really Gets Done in Organizations*[100]:

> *Employees are less constrained than before by formal reporting relationships or overly bureaucratic processes and procedures; important work in most organizations now gets done through networks of employees.*

Contrast Fayol with what Jonas Ridderstrale and Kjell Nordstrom write in *Funky Business*[101]:

> *The most critical resource wears shoes and walks out of the door around 5 o'clock every day.*
>
> *The boss is dead. No longer can we believe in a leader who claims to know more about everything and who is always right.*
>
> *True entrepreneurs and entrepreneurial organisations offer us the opportunity to take a bite of an apple from the tree of knowledge. Then, there is no way back. Why else did God expel Adam and Eve from Paradise?'*

Goodness knows what Henri Fayol would have made of that! Such language is tough enough for most managers today, let alone someone writing around the time of the First World War. Actually, you could win several bets by predicting that most managers working today would agree more with Fayol than with Cross, Parker, Ridderstrale and Nordstrom. Top down management is the enemy of engagement but we have been so imprisoned by old thinking as to believe that it is normal for the boss to command and to make the decisions.

THE STAR EXERCISE

We tend to think that we work to satisfy our boss and that our team members are those in the same department as us. Actually, most of us work more with people from other departments than we do with people in our own. See if this is true for you.

1. Take a sheet of paper and draw a circle in the centre. Enter your name in the circle. This is the centre of the star. Here is a simplified example:

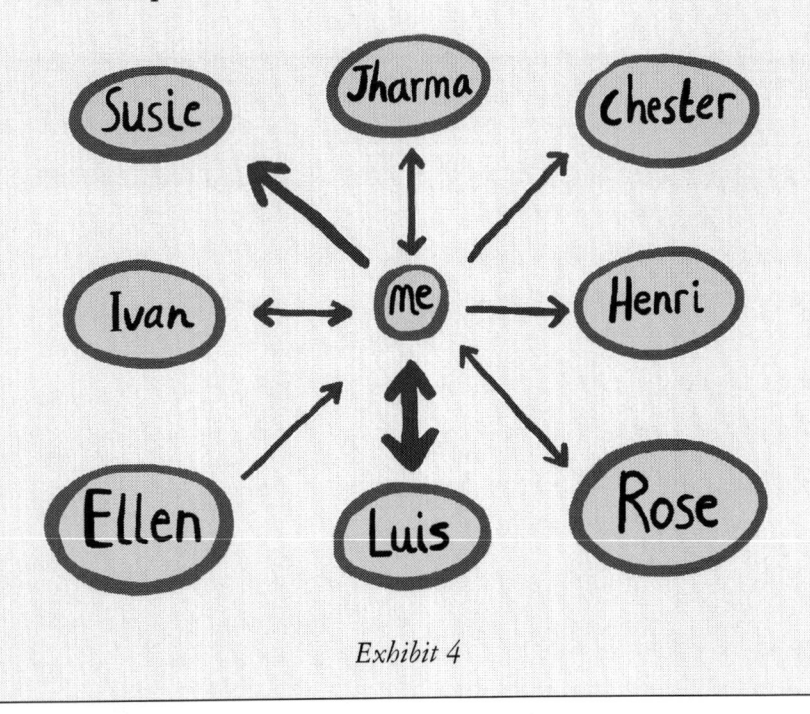

Exhibit 4

THE CONTEXT – NOT A PILL YOU CAN TAKE

2. Add circles around your circle containing the people, departments or areas who you deal with in doing your job. Most of these will be outside of your department.

3. Draw an arrow between each of these circles and your circle.

4. If you receive things (instructions, materials, information, paperwork and so on) from this person or department, draw the arrow with the tip towards yourself.

5. It you give things (instructions, materials, information, paperwork and so on) to this person or department, draw the arrow with the tip towards that person.

6. Select the two or three relationships that are most important to your job. Highlight these with bolder lines.

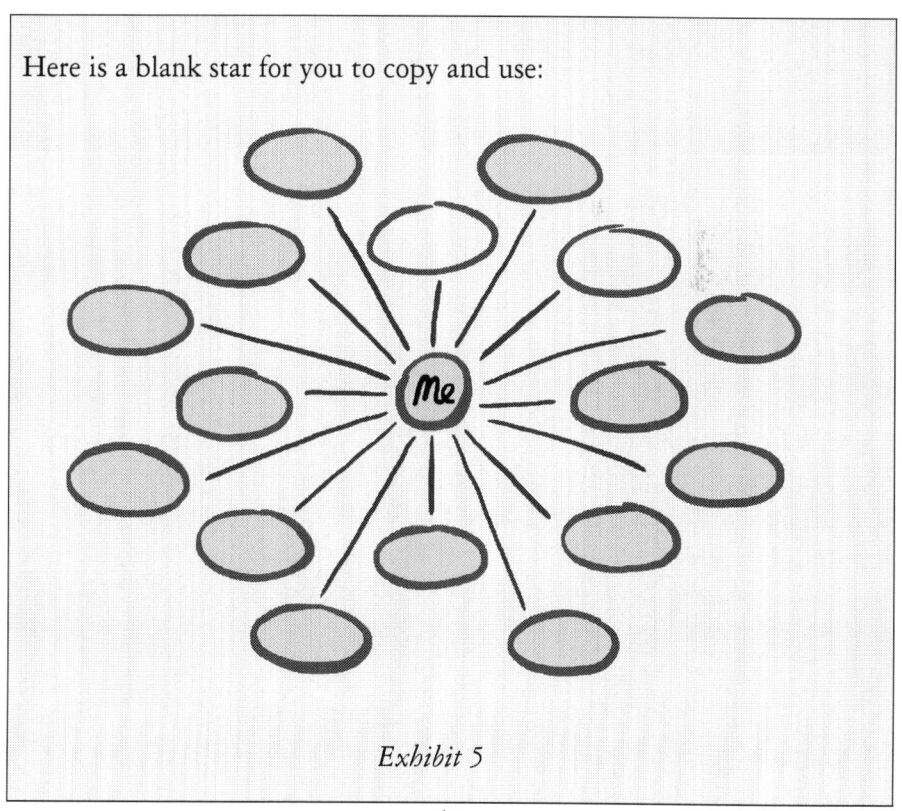

Here is a blank star for you to copy and use:

Exhibit 5

> It is not uncommon for people to find that they have 12 to 20 lines on their star, even in jobs which appear straightforward. This exercise shows just how complex everyone's job is and how many people we deal with daily. It shows how often we are internal customers ourselves and how often colleagues are internal customers of ours.

All firms and companies are complex. They are messy, complicated systems. Good employees learn how to cope with the mess and think ahead. Good team members think about the result of their actions. *'What will happen elsewhere, if I do this - or I don't do this?'* Good team members take responsibility for their part of the system. If one of the links in the system breaks down, then something will not happen. When we have problems, the cause of it is often somewhere else in the system. When other people have problems, it may be that we caused it - from a distance.

What Fayol says, for example *'the right to give orders and the power to exact obedience'*, is much easier to take and sounds so much more rational than *'work gets done through networks of employees.'* It is as if, while we recognise that the latter is true, we believe that it really shouldn't be and that if the organisation ran properly, it wouldn't be. But it is, and when you try to stop it, you stop the organisation.

ENGAGEMENT AND COMPLEXITY

Burke Pease, of the University of California at Monterey Bay, provided this diagram for *The Working Manager*. The vertical axis shows degrees of engagement while the horizontal axis indicates complexity of manager/employee relationships.

THE CONTEXT – NOT A PILL YOU CAN TAKE

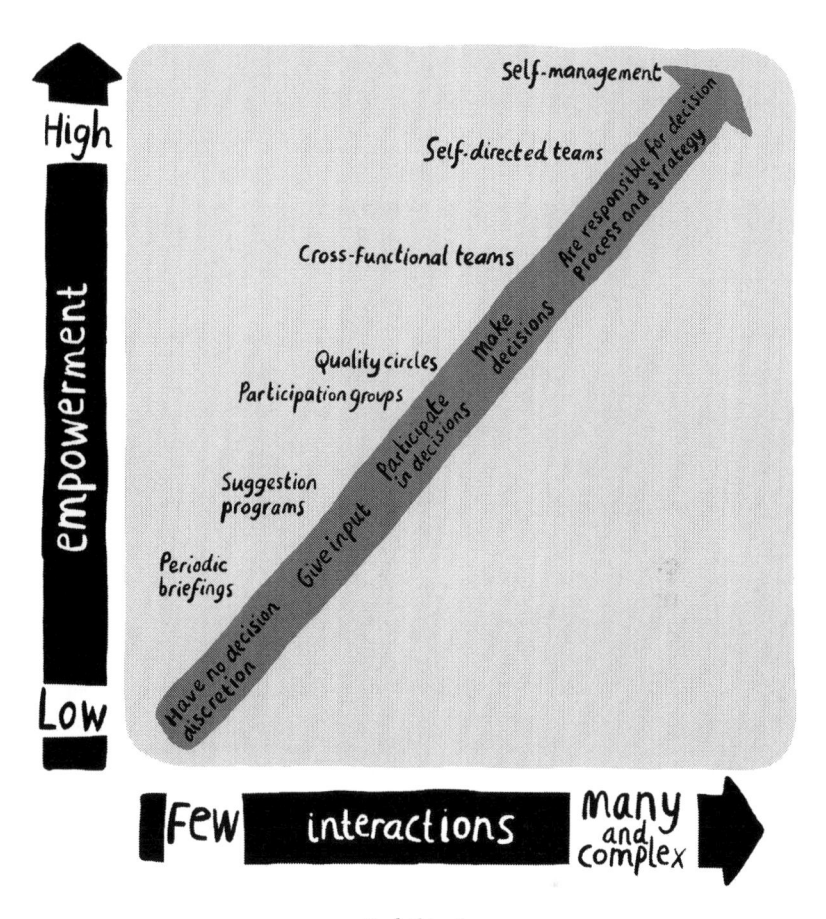

Diagram: A two-axis chart with "empowerment" (Low to High) on the vertical axis and "interactions" (Few to many and complex) on the horizontal axis. A diagonal arrow runs from bottom-left to top-right, showing progression:

- *Periodic briefings* — Have no decision discretion
- *Suggestion programs* — Give input
- *Quality circles / Participation groups* — Participate in decisions
- *Cross-functional teams* — Make decisions
- *Self-directed teams*
- *Self-management* — Are responsible for decision process and strategy

Exhibit 6

As the horizontal axis shows, it is apparently easier to manage top down than to cope with the complexity of involvement. As empowerment increases, so interactions become many and complex. Why allow complexity if you can (or at least think you can) manage with simplicity?

Take another look at the diagram. What it also shows is that the degree of involvement / engagement / empowerment is correlated with complexity. If you wish to keep things simple and avoid giving employees discretion over decisions, then you will get very low involvement. You will find yourself giving orders while they bunk off!

Fayol's words form a prison for thought and unfortunately for those who hunger after the apparently rational simplicity of the Fayol world, the formal structure of jobs and hierarchies is rarely the way that a real life, successful organisation works today.

> ## AN ASIDE - ORGANISATION CHARTS
>
> Have you ever thought what the lines mean on an organisation chart?
>
> *When he (the manager) tells you to pick up a pig and walk, you pick it up and walk, and when he tells you to sit down and rest, you sit down. You do that right through the day. And what's more, no back talk.*
>
> These are Taylor's words[102]. His theory of scientific management was about intelligent people analysing the best way to do a job of work, breaking it into constituent parts and then instructing unintelligent people in how to do each part. The lines of Taylor's organisation chart, had he drawn one, would have meant *'tells'* and *'obeys'*.
>
> (You don't think that happens today? Not in a sophisticated company? I once listened in amazement to an HR manager in a major retail company who said, *'We want creativity in head office but obedience in the field.'*)
>
> If the critical resource, as Ridderstrale and Nordstrom argue, can leave when it wants, if the boss does not know the answers (or perhaps even the questions) and if most work in organisations is done through networks of employees, presumably not in the presence of the boss, then Taylor's words have little relevance. The lines on any organisation chart cannot mean *'tell/obey'*.
>
> Perhaps the most famous exponent of Taylor's ideas was Henry Ford. The problems Ford Motor Company encountered in the attempted transition from the Model T to the A and the V-8 have been attributed to Ford's authoritarian management style. Alfred P Sloan became President of General Motors in 1923 and his ideas on organisation, while not exactly participative, were some distance away from 'command and obey.'

> He recognised that the large company needed a different structure from that which had hitherto existed and set up the now familiar *corporate*, *division* and *plant* structure, with directives of a more general nature emanating from the top and being translated to the more specific as they passed down through the organisation.
>
> Maybe it is here that the words *'reports to'* stem from. The more junior level reported to the higher level what they had done to implement in detail the general directives given earlier. A manager was indeed *'responsible for'* translating and meeting the more general objectives.

MANAGEMENT STYLE AND COMPLEXITY

As management style adapts to the changing demands of the market and company complexity, so the meaning of the lines on the organisation chart shifts - or should do. However, it seems that echoes of the old command and control, *'tell/obey'* meaning of the lines still seeks to return. The nature of the boss seems to be built firmly into our corporate consciousness, often to our detriment. In many organisations, such a boss exists and in many organisations (not always the same ones) he or she should exist. Simpler organisations call for simpler solutions. Less simple organisations call for less simple solutions, as Alfred P Sloan recognised but Henry Ford did not.

A sophisticated organisation today has complex products, major investment in R&D, a global marketplace, the need to recruit and retain people with brainpower, a desperate need for creativity and innovation and a pressing need for speed in bringing new products to the market. It exists in highly competitive markets, not only for its products but also for its best staff. Its customers are readily drawn away by a competitor who makes a better offer. Price competition is fierce. It has to take account of a large number of pressure groups and legislations. It has safety, equal opportunities and environmental concerns that Frederick Winslow Taylor never dreamt about - even in his specially designed bed that assuaged his fear of falling out at night.

In the complex world of the modern organisation, responsibility has to be a shared matter, an organisational one. Decisions are not made by one person but by a consensus of many people, experts in one or more fields of knowledge and endeavour.

Staff may well be more skilled and have more knowledge through the recency of their education. Thus, the thought that the boss should be able to make decisions that he or she can impose on the rest of the organisation and that everyone who reports to him or her can be expected to keep quiet and obey, is a plain nonsense if only from the point of view of risk management and retention of rare and highly skilled staff.

Forms of engagement

To show what is meant by complexity, take a look at some easily identifiable forms of employee engagement. Employee involvement, engagement and empowerment have meant many different things – some formal and many not. However, all forms run counter to Fayol's dictums. Here are some illustrative examples of the more formal approaches.

Co-determination

A legally required form of employee involvement is at the heart of the German system of co-determination (*Mitbestimmung*) involving works councils (*Betriebsrat*). In co-determination, the HR or Personnel Director *(Arbeitsführer)* is elected by the workers themselves and works councils have statutory rights to participate in and vote upon the appointment of the CEO (*Geschäftsführer.*)

Intrapreneurship

In its most sophisticated form, this form of engagement was given impetus by Rosabeth Moss Kanter in her 1990 book, *When Giants Learn to Dance*[103]. She spoke of the need for *'corporate entrepreneurship'* (known to most other writers as *'intrapreneurship'*) as a significant factor in the survival of the company. This form is about delegating decision making as far down the organisation as possible, so empowering people to make decisions which otherwise would have had to be referred to higher authority. The objectives of such programmes are both motivational in a Herzbergian sense and organisational - to speed up decision making especially at the customer interface.

An outstanding example of this is the airline SAS and its turnaround under the leadership of Jan Carlzon who became CEO of SAS in 1981. At that time, the airline was losing $17 million a year and had a terrible reputation for punctuality. By the end of 1982, SAS had made a profit of $54 million and had become the most punctual airline in Europe.

Part of this success was the result of a programme entitled *Putting People First*; delegation to enable customer-facing staff to resolve customer issues without delay. Jan Carlzon argued that problems should be solved on the spot, as soon as they arise. No front-line employee should have to wait for a supervisor's decision or permission. Not just a programme, it was a real change in values and management philosophy.

> Listen to what Jan Carlzon said[104]:
>
> *The real value a company has is in those customers who were so very satisfied with what they got last time they used the company and its services. We questioned companies. We asked them about different things: What is your perception about our head office? What is your perception of our technical and maintenance station? What is your perception about our aircraft and so forth? What is your perception about meeting with people? We found out that the only perception they really had was the meeting with people.*
>
> *I just came from a long journey to Asia where we stayed at the Oriental Hotel in Bangkok. That hotel is famous, and it's absolutely breathtaking how they develop services in the smallest item. It so happened once that I was in Singapore and I read in the paper that the Oriental Hotel had become elected the best hotel in the world for the 10th consecutive year. I called the general manager and said, 'Tell me, what is the truth? What do you really do to become the best hotel in the world year after year?'*
>
> *And he said, 'I can't pinpoint anything special, but there could be one thing, Jan. And that could be that we have not given the authority to our frontline people to say 'no' to our customers. We have only given them the authority to say 'yes' to our customers' demands and requests. If, for any reason, they have to say 'no' - because that happens, of course - then, but not before then, they have to ask for permission from their own managers.'*

> *I promise you that if we go to Western European or the Western part of this world, I would say that the rule is the opposite. You have only the authority to say 'no' for any special request. You must follow the service standard exactly. If you want to exceed or do some special favours, then you have to ask permission from your general manager. I think that's the whole difference.*
>
> *Those companies who really understand the necessity of being customer-driven and business-oriented, will end up with a flatter organization, not as a tool but as a consequence of that, because, if you really want to be business-oriented and customer-driven, you understand that you must give the responsibility not to the top management of the company, not to the middle management but to every individual person managing those moments of truth out there in the front line.*
>
> *Create an environment where people are prepared to take on risks, because to take responsibility means that you take on a risk. There are two forces that control every step in our lives. The one is fear, and the other one is love. I don't use the word, 'love,' when I talk to business people. I say, 'respect and trust,' but it is love. If you create a fearful environment, you can forget about delegating responsibility to frontline people. Why should anybody take on any risks or any responsibilities if there is a fearful environment and I feel that I can get a penalty if I make a mistake? But if you can create an environment where people feel that there's such a respect and trust in me, that as long as I do my best and I'm not making sabotage, nothing bad will happen to me if something goes wrong.*
>
> *I say, 'Don't send out instructions. Communicate to people so that they understand what their responsibility is.' Many people in many companies believe that they can let people in the front line, for example - or in the factory - perform the service or develop it or finish the product but in a very controlled way, where management has developed service standards, for example, or product standards down to very individualized forms. However, I'm afraid that you can't define, for example, a good service.*

TQM

The Total Quality Movement (TQM) - Deming[105], Juran[106] and Crosby[107] - has had several forms. Very often, employees were organised into Quality Circles using statistical quality analysis techniques, such as Ishikawa (fishbone) charts and Pareto charts, to study the causes of quality failures and to identify solutions. This work resurfaced in *Six Sigma*[108] which also involves employees in studying system issues around quality and service.

The relevance of TQM to employee engagement is that it is a rational arbiter of decision making. Western management seems obsessed with cutting costs as opposed to managing present and future profitability. Unless there is an independent and rational arbiter of the resources needed to do something properly – and indeed a rational definition of what counts as 'properly' - decisions will always be at the mercy of a manager who wants another 10% reduction.

Kaizen - change to become good

This is the Japanese approach of continuous improvement, related to TQM. In kaizen, all employees are encouraged to come up with ideas however small that could improve their particular job activity and to implement their ideas themselves. Indeed, suggestion schemes are integral to kaizen. They offer an opportunity for worker self-development, make employees kaizen-conscious and provide an opportunity for the workers to speak with management. The number of workers' suggestions is an important criterion in reviewing the performance of supervisors and managers. Kaizen thus serves as a barometer of leadership. Kaizen users have been described by Edward de Bono and Robert Heller[109] as:

> ... *'half-way-to-the-wall' school of practitioners: every year, managers are expected to improve operations on key parameters by half the distance between the present position and the wall - that is, zero cost or time. As keen mathematicians will spot, you never reach the wall.*

Japanese managers appear to have more freedom to implement employee suggestions than their Western counterparts who, the Japanese commentators believe, have an almost exclusive concern with cost. According to Masaaki Imai, author of *Kaizen: The Key to Japan's Competitive Success*[110], Japanese managers evaluate a change by whether it contributes to any one of the seven goals:

- Making the job easier
- Removing drudgery from the job

- Removing nuisance from the job
- Making the job safer
- Making the job more productive
- Improving product quality
- Saving time and cost

The problem with many if not most Western companies is that they consider only the last item, unless you consider Health and Safety as always directed at making the job safer. (It certainly has been so in the construction industry. Elsewhere it often gives the impression of institutionalised paranoia.)

Six Sigma

Six Sigma was first formulated by Bill Smith at Motorola and is based on TQM. (*Six Sigma* is a registered service mark and trademark of Motorola, Inc.) Processes that operate with Six Sigma quality experience defect levels below 3.4 defects per million opportunities. Six Sigma's goal is to improve all processes to that level of quality. A defect is defined as anything that could lead to customer dissatisfaction.

According to Dr. Howard S Gitlow[111], Six Sigma aims to produce sustained improvement in both defect reduction and cycle time. He says that when Motorola began their Six Sigma effort the rate they chose was a 10-fold reduction in defects in two years along with a 50% reduction in cycle. To explain this, Dr Gitlow applies it to banking:

> *For example, a bank takes 60 days on average to process a loan with a 10% rework rate in 2000. In a Six Sigma organization, the bank should take no longer than 30 days on average to process a loan with a 1% error rate in 2002, and no more than 15 days on average to process a loan with a 0.10% error rate by 2004. Clearly, this requires a dramatically improved/innovated loan process.*

Six Sigma requires a company to commit the entire organization, particularly top management, to achieve sustained quality improvement. Success depends upon the provision of strong and passionate leadership.

Skunk works

A fairly extreme version of employee engagement is the skunk works, an almost anti-establishment and revolutionary (in the civil disobedience sense) attempt to increase the speed of creativity and the development of new products.

Made famous by Lockheed in the 1940's, a skunk works is essentially an informal, quasi-legal, off-line entity set up to create and pilot new ideas and products without the restraining and cold hand of bureaucracy. The very name - connoting smelly, down-home, good old boys - implies that a skunk works is never on the main site, is not subject to normal rules of behaviour, reporting or control, is usually under-funded so that its members have to make do and mend, has often a temporary existence and is protected from the bureaucrats by a powerful champion.

The Lockheed skunk works, under the direction of Clarence 'Kelly' Johnson, was responsible for most of that company's airplane innovation in the 40's and 50's including the P-38 Lightning, the P-80 Shooting Star, the F-104 Starfighter, the C-130 Hercules, the U-2 and the SR-71 Blackbird.

Apparently, the name is taken from the Li'l Abner cartoons popular at the time. The hillbilly family in the cartoon series brewed moonshine which they called, *'Kickapoo Joy Juice.'* Someone in Lockheed asked what Kelly Johnson was doing and received the reply, *'I guess he's stirring up a little kickapoo joy juice,'* and the name resulted.

Kelly's *Fourteen Rules* for managing a skunk works included:

- The manager must be delegated complete control of his program in all aspects.
- The number of people having any connection with the project must be restricted in an almost vicious manner. Use a small number of good people.

- A very simple drawing and drawing release system with great flexibility for making changes must be provided.

- There must be a minimum number of reports required, but important work must be recorded thoroughly.

- There must be mutual trust between the customer project organization and the contractor with very close cooperation and liaison on a day-to-day basis.

In another rule which anticipated TQM, Johnson said it was vital to:

- Push more basic inspection responsibility back to subcontractors and vendors. Don't duplicate so much inspection.

There are many more forms of employee engagement. These are just some of the most easily identifiable. All are about employees doing a great deal more than obeying orders. In fact all are about employees managing. They are contrary to the mantra of *Plan, Organise, Direct, Co-ordinate* and *Control*.

A FUNNY OLD BUSINESS

Maybe Fayol's views sound so apparently rational because management is such a funny old business. Whenever we look at any part of it - be it decision making, recruiting, assessing promotion, project management, new product introduction, pricing and so on – we find that there is a carefully designed and apparently logical process for doing it. The funny thing is that such processes are rarely followed.

Decision making is a very good example. Dr Adrian Banks, of the University of Surrey, says[112] that a good decision process is usually taken to be:

> ... a matter of understanding, retaining and weighing up all the information relevant to the decision.

He says that in making decisions we are advised to ask:

- *What are the options?*

- *What are the potential outcomes of each option?*

- *How good or bad are the outcomes?*
- *How likely are the outcomes?*

We are then supposed to weight each potential outcome according to how likely it is and how desirable the outcome is and choose the best-weighted outcome – except, of course, we don't.

- *We frequently limit our decisions by not considering all the possibilities.*
- *We often evaluate the consequences of an outcome inaccurately.*
- *Our judgements of the likelihood of outcomes are often inaccurate.*

The reality, Banks says, is that information gathering is too complex to do exhaustively and all too often the information required cannot be gathered or cannot be gathered in time. We may lack the imagination to list all the options, or indeed we may reject options or refuse to consider some. The evaluation of outcomes is notoriously subjective and subject to error.

In organisations, the facts can be few and far between - especially with the big decisions. Sure, there are usually enough to indicate possible paths but never to make the visionary decision. Thus, very many decisions in organisations are made on a basis of *other-than-fact*. The so-called decision making process is rarely if ever used. It is one of those oh-so-logical processes in management which turn out to be carefully described but never used.

How do we actually make the decisions? Well, we often rely on heuristics; rules of thumb that give us pretty good decisions most of the time only requiring part of the information to be used. (For example, some people say that a good rule of thumb for property investment is to buy the cheapest house in an expensive road.)

Banks concludes that genuine decision making - decisions we actually make in contrast to the 'logical' ideal - is really a matter of evaluating known alternatives based on largely subjective evaluations of outcomes using estimates of likelihood of the outcomes.

EMOTION IN DECISION MAKING

We may argue that effective decision making requires us to avoid any emotional involvement. However, with no emotions involved, it turns out that decisions become impossible. People who have experienced certain kinds of brain damage such that their emotional life is severely reduced, remain quite capable of (and even rather good at) setting out alternatives, researching outcomes and likelihoods but are totally incapable of making a decision.

There is a wealth of evidence showing decision making to be impossible unless emotions are engaged. For example, as Jharna Sengupta Biswas writes for *The Working Manager*:

> *The brain centre, the amygdala, regulates responses to emotions ... Experimental studies including subject patients with amygdala damage whereby the emotional component is eliminated reveal that such people performed poorly on gambling tasks to 'win' or 'lose' money. They failed to implement a winning strategy because, although intellectually they could understand the game, they were quite unable to build up motivational energy to initiate the appropriate action.*

Researchers have concluded[113] that:

> *... there appears to be a collection of systems in the human brain consistently dedicated to the goal-oriented thinking process we call reasoning, and to the response selection we call decision making, with a special emphasis on the personal and social domain. This same collection of systems is also involved in emotion and feeling, and is partly dedicated to processing body signals.*

To make a decision it is necessary to evaluate; to see some outcomes as more valuable than others. We know that our emotional life is very much tied up with what we value; that we become proud, upset, angry, defensive and so on only when the focus is something that matters. If nothing matters, then no emotion - and it turns out, no decision. Pure logic means nothing. It is an empty process of deduction. Only the premises give it life. Without values we cannot make evaluations.

MAKING DECISIONS IN THE REAL WORLD

How should we make decisions then? The logical process is not an ideal. If followed it would make all decision making impossible. However, we can use it to help our decisions as long as we do not beat ourselves up in failing to do things perfectly.

We cannot list all options in complex situations. We can do better on simple decisions but even then, option listing is a matter of imagination and knowledge. What we can do depends upon the importance of the decision. We can ask other people; we can run a brainstorming session; we can read widely about the subject – all attempts to discover more options.

What we actually do, and this is totally rational, is to invest such time in option listing as we think the decision warrants, given time constraints. Remember that people who cannot make decisions are often those who are never satisfied that they have the full facts. (They don't and cannot have but this is no reason to become obsessive about it.)

To evaluate outcomes is to care about them. We need criteria to decide whether an outcome is good or bad. What is good for one person may be bad for another. Of course, in business, we often have financial criteria but even then, we need to ask whether these are short term or long term, for the management or for the shareholders (not at all always the same), for the employees or for the share price and so on. Much decision making falls down simply because we do not know what we want or cannot agree on what we want. This is often where organisational politics come in.

People who cannot make decisions are often those who have nothing riding on the outcome. The advice to toss a coin when faced with two competing decisions and if disappointed with the result, ignore it, has some sense! So there are four bits of advice. Remember that:

- facts that go against what you want will tend to get ignored, while facts that support what you want will be given extra weight.

- powerful people present facts and have them accepted even if they are not strong facts.

- the likelihood of the implementation of a decision is as important as the correct decision. If you need others to implement, then at the very least involve them in the decision making.

- decision making is a human endeavour, not purely a matter of process or logic.

Intuition

Dr Banks says of decisions that,

> *Typically it seems that we have an implicit feel for good and bad choices - and for good reasons.*

Intuition, frequently called a hunch, a gut feeling, a burst of genius and even luck, is usually a superior source of knowing to reason. However, it is well to be careful of the meaning of the word.

In his book, *Blink*[114], Malcolm Gladwell recounts a series of examples of how people do things, decide things and recognise things apparently without thinking about them. Many people seem to be able to act skilfully on the basis of very little information at all. The success that some people have, in recognising art fakes, speed dating, marriage guidance counselling and even basketball, seems to be superior to those who try to work it out logically.

This is not a matter of guesswork, some magical non-rational ability or telepathy but study and practice. As Gladwell says:

> *Basketball is an intricate, high speed game filled with split-second, spontaneous decisions. But that is possible only when everyone first engages in hours of highly repetitive and structured practice ...*

The fact of the matter is that our ability to make decisions depends upon our knowledge of the field and our confidence in our knowledge. If you want to be a good management decision maker, then an artificial process is far inferior to studying and practising management.

Rationality and Management

So do recognise that feelings play a far larger part in human life than do facts. Emotions drive most of our behaviour, if only because they are rooted in our values and our perception of the world. Facts ultimately are uninteresting. *Other-than-fact* values are what matter to us. After all, the French intellectual Albert Camus was capable of saying:

> *It hurts me to confess it, but I'd have given ten conversations with Einstein for a first meeting with a pretty chorus girl.*

As Professor Robin Stuart-Kotze has written (for *The Working Manager*):

> *The concept of rationality haunts most discussion of individual and group behaviour. Few organisations can be run on a purely rational basis, devoid of any concern for the feelings, emotions, needs and desires of the people in them. However, there is still a strong current of opinion that when things get tough, hard decisions of a purely rational and objective kind are all that matter. One important saying in management is that it is good to make the right decisions but it is better to make the decisions come right.*
>
> *This is an allusion to the fact that making decisions in organisational life is a chancy business. Rarely are the facts available and so often it comes down to personal judgement. The history of bad decisions at senior level is long and colourful. The Harvard Business Review reported in the 1980's that fewer than 20% of mergers and acquisitions achieved any business success at all.*

If people are committed to making decisions work, if they support their bosses, are motivated by them, believe that they are doing their best, believe that their own efforts are respected and rewarded and that they are valued, then they are all the more likely to get behind decisions and work to make them come right.

HAWTHORNE AND LORDSTOWN

The Hawthorne experiments took place in the Hawthorne plant of the Western Electric Company during the years 1927-1932 and were important in showing that a top down and impersonal concentration on routines and procedures was inadequate. No single study has had the effect on subsequent management thought and practice that the Hawthorne research has. It represents a cataclysmic break from the traditional theory (of Taylor and Urwick.) For the first time, man's social and individual nature was seen as important to the functioning of organisations. All of a sudden it was discovered that people worked for something other than just money. Man's emotional and social sides were seen as major determinants of organisational behaviour.

The most famous part of the research involved a series of experiments on the effects on production of various levels of illumination. Six female employees were placed in a separate room from their colleagues with the same production equipment and carried on working as the experimenters varied their working conditions. To the amazement of the researchers (remember this was in the early days of work research), no matter what they did, production went up.

The conclusion was that the changes in production had nothing to do with changes in lighting and other conditions but were due to the fact that the employees were being treated as special people. They were being involved. No longer just workers, they were selected people trying to help the company with production research.

Further research was carried out in the bank wiring room of the same company with a group of fourteen men. The discovery here was that the group set its own production targets; that it had a form of solidarity and that incentives had little impact on production.

The Hawthorne studies are taken to be the beginning of the human relations movement in the study of management. As the introductory story in this book shows, in 1972 General Motors demonstrated how little had been learned since 1927. Remember that Joe Kelly, in *How Managers Manage*[115], reports that:

> ... the union proposed that team assembly be used. This was rejected by the management. Unfortunately, management's effort to increase productivity through classical means mobilized the young assembly line workers to full scale confrontation with management.

The Lordstown fiasco was happening while Volvo under Pehr Gyllenhammar was introducing a team based approach to manufacturing which improved productivity and quality and was instrumental in Volvo's sales increasing by 70%. Gyllenhammar said at the time:

> Young people coming into the labour market will not take jobs which don't provide them with a sense of achievement and personal satisfaction. They are seeking some purpose to their labour beyond mere economic survival. We are trying to create small groups of workers who develop into skilled and proud craftsmen who set their own work pace.

Spontaneous leadership

Too often, what is called 'job enrichment' or 'employee empowerment' has been a sneaky way of headcount reduction. As the number of staff is reduced, employees are given more and more to do in the same amount of time. Empowerment can be abdication in place of delegation as employees are given responsibility without adequate training. The word can actually be a euphemism for *command* as in the not infrequent statement, *'I am empowering you to do this,'* when no change in boss-subordinate relationship is even contemplated. (What it really means is, *'Do this.'*)

The simple and simplistic idea of asking people to participate without any change in management style is doomed to failure. Involvement depends upon organisational values, culture and management style.

Jack Welch[116] holds that a 'telling' style actually hurts the business. It not only interferes with autonomy and self-confidence, it shows up managerial weaknesses:

> *We are constantly amazed by how much people will do when they are not told what to do by management. In the new knowledge-driven economy, people should make their own decision. Managing less is managing better. Close supervision, control and bureaucracy kill the competitive spirit of the company. Weak managers are the killers of business; they are the job killers. You can't manage self-confidence into people.*

There is a strong school of thought that much management is unnecessary. Jim Stroup, author of *Managing Leadership*[117], is a follower of Mary Parker Follett[118] who, he says,

> *... taught that the group would naturally tend to generate its own leadership and develop its own management regimes ... She argued that the role of senior executives is to observe and coordinate these expressions of self-leadership ... and keep them pointed toward the organization's goals.*

The role of management is to communicate these goals so that:

> *In an organization characterized by the spontaneous leadership from within, the consistent communication of the organization's goals provides a basis upon which that leadership can form itself.*

Indeed, according to Follett, the real role of managers is to manage - not suppress - these instances of leadership from within the organization. They should facilitate, develop, direct and coordinate them. They should not shut them off and arrogate management to themselves.

AUTHORITY AND RESPONSIBILITY

Jim Stroup started his career as a soldier. He joined the Marines as a private, was promoted to sergeant and was later commissioned, serving in the first Gulf War in 1990 and 1991. (He later gained a BA and MA, learned Arabic and now lives and works in Turkey for half the year.) His view of the nature and purpose of the military is unvarnished and straightforward:

> *The military is an organization that generates, delivers and applies deadly force in a manner specifically calculated to kill human beings who are in the service of the enemy. Any military activities that do not do this are intended to facilitate the doing of it.*

For this reason, he expresses extreme caution about applying leadership lessons from the military world to the civilian world. However, he does report the research of Brigadier General Samuel L.A. Marshall, published in his book *Men Against Fire: The Problem of Battle Command*[119], which he says, '*has become a classic study of the behaviour of men in combat units.*'

The fundamental military doctrine for small unit offensive operations is the concept of fire and movement - essentially the mutually reinforcing and alternating actions of firing upon and moving toward the enemy objective. Marshall argued that the soldier who fires his weapon (and it may seem surprising but many do not) will also move forward. The shooter is always looking for a better vantage point or line of fire and thus moves forward to find it. Marshall's discovery was also that non-shooters move up alongside the shooter so that action causes further action and movement further movement.

> *The shooter ... does not naively fire and advance independently of what the rest of his unit is doing. He identifies the firing position ahead that offers ... advantages over his present position and that is not too far forward of and isolated from ... his fellows ... Upon this, the non-shooter is disquieted by the*

sense that friendly soldiers have shifted forward. His instinct is to move up alongside them (though) ... he still may not fire.

In this way, quite without movement orders, the unit moves forward. Once the non-shooters have moved up, the shooters, encouraged by the presence of their colleagues, move forward again and thus the process repeats. The key insight here is that the shooters are practising leadership of the type that Stroup refers to as spontaneous leadership.

A DAZZLING GLIMPSE OF THE OBVIOUS

It is not exactly news that good management breeds organisational success. For example, a research report by Peter Doskoch in *Psychology Today*[120] shows that a mere 25% of the differences between individuals in job performance has anything to do with IQ. The other 75% comes from other factors which one might term 'grit' - and an organisation which encourages grit is one that:

- seeks to enable people to have ambition, feel optimistic and to be passionate about their work.
- encourages self-discipline and acts as a role model in this regard.
- encourages and rewards stickability. Grit pays off in the long term.
- has a consistent long term outlook. A company that changes its values, aims, strategies and personnel as often as it changes its socks or tights is not a company where perseverance pays off.
- avoids short term management which inspires opportunism and political activity, not grit.
- prevents vices leading to success.

Take a look at the perennially successful steel company, Nucor. What are the elements of its success?

- Strong culture and vision
- Exemplary values

- Massive investment in people
- Careful recruitment
- Total trust
- Extreme delegation
- Minimal controls
- Focus on creativity in the workplace
- Great rewards for achievement
- The understanding and use of group processes
- Minimal bureaucracy - management as support, not control
- Massive sense of ownership
- Frequent and mutual praise
- Strong sense of belonging
- Great happiness
- Local people, local business

If that seems too way out for you, take a look at the UK National Health Service. The Ipsos MORI study for the UK National Health Service indicated that employee commitment in that organisation depended upon agreement with the statements:

- I've got the knowledge, skills and equipment to do a good job
- I feel fairly treated with pay, benefits and staff facilities
- I feel trusted, listened to and valued at work
- My manager (or supervisor) supports me when I need it
- Senior managers are involved with our work
- I've got a worthwhile job that makes a difference to patients
- I help provide high quality patient care
- I have the opportunity to develop my potential

THE CONTEXT – NOT A PILL YOU CAN TAKE

- I understand my role and where it fits in
- I am able to improve the way we work in my team

The way that management thinks of employees matters as well. Frederick Taylor, the father of scientific management, said:

> ... the workman who is best suited to handling pig iron is unable to understand the real science of doing this class of work. He is so stupid that ... he must consequently be trained by a man more intelligent than himself into the habit of working in accordance with the laws of this science before he can be successful.
>
> When he (the manager) tells you to pick up a pig and walk, you pick it up and walk, and when he tells you to sit down and rest, you sit down. You do that right through the day. And what's more, no back talk.

By contrast, the highly successful retail organisation, John Lewis, says on its website:

> At the John Lewis Partnership, employees are Partners, which means we are all owners of the business and share in its success.
>
> Being a Partnership is about much more than sharing the profits: it defines our approach to what we do. With ownership comes responsibility, and the knowledge that our success depends entirely on providing the best quality products and services to our customers so that they come back to us again and again. Our democratic network of elected councils, committees and forums gives Partners a real say in our decision-making processes, and allows us to challenge management on performance and have a real say in how the business is run. This sense of collective responsibility extends to everyone we deal with - from customers and suppliers to the communities we're part of.
>
> Our Constitution states that: 'The Partnership aims to employ and retain as its members people of ability and integrity who are committed to working together and to supporting its Principles. Relationships are based on mutual respect and courtesy, with as much equality between its members as differences of responsibility permit. The Partnership aims to recognise their individual contribution and reward them fairly.'

Motivation

There is clearly a close relationship between the engaged employee and the motivated one. Films and TV programmes seem to tell us that motivation in management is something that people do to others. Sports coaches and others may be seen as good motivators. Unfortunately, this has often led to a simplistic view of what motivation is. Fear, excitement and Ra! Ra! may be short term motivators but motivation is a complex concept.

People are motivated to do things when they want to do them and will do them without further or constant prompting. Motivation can come and go. There are days when we feel highly motivated and days when we feel like staying in bed. People can be helped to feel motivated. They will feel better about doing things if they feel that the effort is worth it. What is worth it will differ by person and by moment.

David McClelland[121] speaks of three basic needs: the need for achievement, the need for power and the need for affiliation. Abraham Maslow[122] shows that the needs we seek to satisfy change as we become safer, more appreciated, and more independent. In his seminal book, *The Motivation to Work*[123], Frederick Herzberg distinguished between *hygiene* factors - those that will not increase motivation as such but will certainly decrease it if standards are too low - and *motivating* factors.

Hygiene factors include working conditions, salary, job security and company policies. Get these wrong and motivation will decline but add to them over a certain standard and there will be no more effect on motivation.

Motivation, said Herzberg, derives from people having a sense of achievement, recognition, responsibility and opportunities for personal growth. Herzberg also shows that the nature of the job may itself be motivational. He criticises management for ignoring the motivational factors and trying to motivate through hygiene factors like money and benefits - expensive and not successful.

Edward L. Deci, in his book, *Intrinsic Motivation*[124], provides invaluable insights into the difference between motivation from within and from outside.

- *Intrinsic* - the motivation to complete a task for the sake of the interest that it holds for the performer
- *Extrinsic* - the motivation to complete it for external rewards

His discussion of whether extrinsic rewards decrease intrinsic motivation is worth the cost of the book on its own.

> *(It) is not that extrinsic rewards are not effective motivators, but rather that they have some unintended negative consequences ... Rewards can motivate behaviour extrinsically but at the same time they will very likely be decreasing intrinsic motivation.*

In an echo of Argyris, Bennis and others, he says:

> *... if one is seeking more creative work or learning, intrinsic approaches without the interference of external rewards seem more appropriate.*

Deci correlates extrinsic motivation to McGregor's Theory X which, he says:

> *... assumes that a person will perform effectively to the extent that his rewards are made contingent upon effective performance ... piece rate ... sales commissions and bonus plans are ... examples.*

Writing with Marylène Gagné of Concordia University, Deci reported findings in *Self-determination theory and work motivation*[125], that:

> *... contingent tangible rewards and other extrinsic factors such as competition and evaluations can be detrimental to outcomes such as creativity, cognitive flexibility, and problem solving, which has been found to be associated with intrinsic motivation...[Researchers] found monetary rewards to decrease cognitive flexibility in problem solving ... monetary rewards decrease performance on a complex task with difficult goals.*

We are all aware of what President Kennedy said,

> *My fellow Americans, ask not what your country can do for you. Ask what you can do for your country.*

Professor Mark van Vugt of the University of Kent at Canterbury has studied what makes individuals sacrifice their own needs for the benefit of a group. In his research article, *Follow the leader*, first published in *The Psychologist* 2004, van Vugt writes:

> *There are important drawbacks associated with (extrinsic) incentive strategies. Firstly, they are costly to operate. Promotions, pay rises, tax breaks and the like all place a heavy burden on the group's resources. Threat tactics are also expensive because they require extensive surveillance and monitoring*

(although they may also generate new income, as in the example of parking and speeding fines.)

Leaders must often rely on other individuals to monitor, prosecute and punish people for being disloyal. However, whether these others can be trusted to remain loyal themselves and do their job will always be a problem. Quis custodiet ipsos custodes? (Who shall watch the watchers?)

Secondly, leaders who employ such tactics may effectively drive out any intrinsic motivation as Deci notes. The activity becomes a means to an end (the reward) rather than the end itself. Threats may erode social cohesion within a group because they signal to people that they can no longer trust each other to work for the group voluntarily.

Engagement has a great deal to do with intrinsic motivation.

WORK AND BELIEFS ABOUT PEOPLE

People's attitudes towards management and motivation are very often derived from their idea of what work is and why people work. Douglas McGregor[126] argues that people who hold Theory X beliefs about man will tend to see extrinsic motivation as necessary to make people do what they do not want to do. Those who hold to Theory Y beliefs will tend to see motivation as a matter of helping someone do what they want to do anyway - that they are intrinsically motivated to do.

McGregor put forward the concept that people's management behaviour is dependent upon their view of human beings and work. People who espouse Theory X will believe that the average human being dislikes (all) work and will avoid it if they can; that because of this, people must be coerced to put in the required effort, offered inducements and threatened with punishment. Theory X goes on to hold that the average human being seeks to avoid responsibility, is not ambitious and seeks security before advancement.

People who hold to Theory Y, on the other hand, believe that for most people work is as natural as play; that people have capacity for self-control: that motivation also arises from the higher order needs such as self-esteem and achievement and that people, if properly managed, will be more than willing to take on responsibility. Finally, Theory Y holds that people can be creative and team spirited and that few organisations make use of the abilities that people have.

In their research report, *A Little Creativity Goes a Long Way: An Examination of Teams' Engagement in Creative Processes*[127], Dr Lucy Gilson and C. E. Shalley found that the most creatively engaged teams shared a similar profile:

- a belief that the job required creative solutions
- shared values and mutual trust
- a belief that a better outcome would occur by harnessing the ideas of all members within a supportive environment
- encouragement of good tries

The real test of commitment comes not from how success is treated, but rather from how failure is interpreted. In the most successful firms, good tries are rewarded almost as great successes - Theory Y again. One has to say that there are very many managers alive and kicking today who appear to have a very profound belief in Theory X - to the detriment of their companies and their customers.

MANAGEMENT IS NOT EASY

Management is hard work and demands study. As Drucker[128] wrote:

> *Management is what tradition used to call a liberal art – 'liberal' because it deals with the fundamentals of knowledge, self-knowledge, wisdom, and leadership; 'art' because it is also concerned with practice and application. Managers draw on all the knowledge and insights of the humanities and the social sciences – on psychology and philosophy, on economics and history, on ethics – as well as the physical sciences. But they have to focus this knowledge on effectiveness and results.*

In *The Management Myth*[129], Matthew Stewart follows Drucker's view of management. It is, in his view, a neglected branch of the humanities. Stewart writes:

> *A good manager is someone with a facility for analysis and an even greater talent for synthesis; someone who has an eye both for the details and for the one*

big thing that really matters; someone who is able to reflect on the facts in a disinterested way, who is always dissatisfied with pat answers and the conventional wisdom, and who therefore takes a certain pleasure in knowledge itself; someone with a wide knowledge of the world and an even better knowledge of the way people work; someone who knows how to treat people with respect; someone with honesty, integrity, trustworthiness, and the other things that make up character; someone, in short, who understands oneself and the world around us well enough to know how to make it better. By this definition of course, a good manager is nothing more or less than a good and well-educated person.

Managers so rarely get the education and training their roles demand. While data on training has always been poor, Cappelli (for *The Working Manager*) reports that, in 1995, the average annual amount of management training per manager was 1.6 hours (that does read 'hours' and not 'weeks') and that from 1986 to 1991, 3 in four young adults in companies received no training of any kind. Are you willing to bet that the *'average annual amount of management training per manager'* has increased since then?

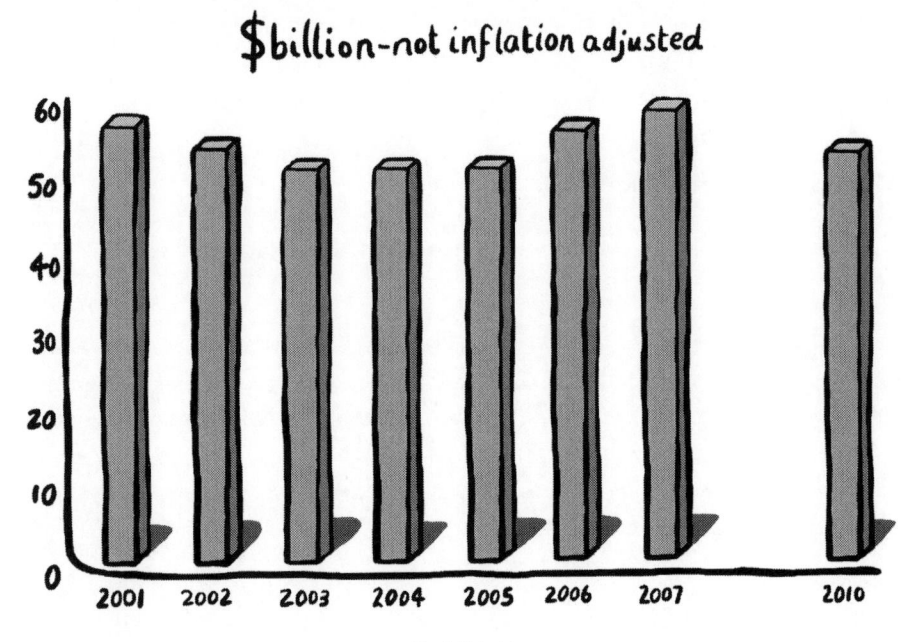

Exhibit 7

Training expenditure in the USA. Source: Training Magazine's annual Training Industry report

The absolute amount spent on training of all types in the USA was actually a bit lower in 2010 than it was in 2001 despite inflation and an increase in working population. The 2005 CIPD Training and Development survey showed that 60% of respondents believed that line managers took training seriously but only 48% believed senior management did.

* * *

5

TOWARDS UNDERSTANDING II: THE CULTURE AND THE PARADIGM SHIFT

In a modern company 70 to 80% of what people do is now done by way of their intellects. The critical means of production is small, gray and weighs around 1.3 kilograms. It is the human brain.

Ridderstrale and Nordstrom

Oddly enough, given the general expectation of redundancy or lay off (you will remember that 74% of US companies instituted lay offs during the recession), many people still seem to think that sticking in a job is (morally) right and that job hopping is wrong. An HR assistant is likely to mark down a candidate who has had, say, three jobs in four years. On one of those agony aunt websites I read this advice, offered to someone who had experienced several jobs in a fairly short time:

> *I think you should consider getting some job counselling to see if there's a way to create more stability in your work life. It might be that a different career would suit you better, and therefore you would hold down a job longer. Or perhaps there are some workplace issues that you need help with. I'm not saying your short-term job history is your fault, but it does take two hands to clap so you must be playing a role in this pattern.*

Amazing, isn't it? Another said that a reply to the question, *'You've moved around a lot so how long would you stay with us?'* needs preparation. If you have moved around, then, this agony aunt says that something along the lines of *'I'm seeking a long term opportunity, where I can learn and develop. Does this come with the position we are discussing?'* should set the interviewer's mind at ease. Actually, the real answer is,

> *I will stay for as long as I am learning, being offered opportunities for development and paid properly. If I am, I will stay until you make me redundant. If I am not and I find a better job, I will leave.*

It is indeed true that job hoppers show far less interest in any psychological contract. Research has indicated that employees in Singapore, where many are on short term contracts, have a far lower sense of obligation to employers. Does this mean that job hoppers need counselling? Given the realities of employment today, job hopping may be a rational response to the threat of redundancy.

Mind you, not everyone is brave enough to do it. The best are. Penelope Trunk, writing *Why Job Hoppers Make the Best Employees* for BNET, says:

> *... if you think job-hopping is bad, change your thinking. Job hoppers are not quitters. In fact, they make better co-workers and better employees and I bet are generally more satisfied with their work life.*

She says that job hoppers:

- have more intellectually rewarding careers. In almost any job, the learning curve is very steep early on. And then it goes flat. So hop when you have nothing more to learn.
- have more stable careers. The corporation doesn't provide stability for its employees. The only people who think it does are really old and out of touch. The stability you get in your career comes from you.

- are higher performers. If you know you are going to leave your job in the next year, you're going to be very conscious of your resume and how its gets improved —skills, achievements, experience, expertise.
- are more emotionally mature. It takes self-knowledge to know what you want to do next and to go get it rather than stay someplace that for the moment seems safe.

CAREERS

As Ridderstrale and Nordstrom argue in *Funky Business*[130], the days of continuity and predictability in jobs have largely gone. People joining the world of work today can only rarely expect to find a safe job in a safe company, work their way up the hierarchy and retire rich 40 or so years later. So in a sense everyone is self-employed. Everyone has to maintain a set of skills which are in demand, honing those skills constantly, ready to sell them to the next bidder, the next employer.

The knowledge worker is rather better placed to do this than the company man or woman. As Ridderstrale and Nordstrom might say, their brains are more in demand. Such independence brings value changes. The company man or woman has to obey the culture of their employer and if they are to stay in the company they need to internalise these values. This is increasingly out of tune with the times. As Jeff Immelt, President of General Electric told an audience of financiers, executives and entrepreneurs at the Montana Economic Development Summit 2010:

Be the contrarian. Everyone is mad today. Be happy.

KNOWLEDGE WORKERS AND INDEPENDENCE

Joseph A Raelin, in his book *Clash of Cultures*[131], talks about professional people who work in companies: 'salaried professionals' as he calls them. Raelin was writing in 1986 and today we are more likely to refer to such people as knowledge workers. (I will substitute this term in quoting from his work.)

As Drucker argues in *Management Challenges for the 21st Century*[132]:

> *Knowledge worker productivity is the biggest of the 21st century management challenges. In developed countries it is their first survival requirement. In no other way can the developed countries hope to maintain themselves, let alone maintain their leadership and their standards of living.*

Knowledge workers need and to some extent can demand specific treatment and if they do not get it, they can and will job-hop. This is not a matter of morality but of expediency. Raelin says of such knowledge workers that they:

> *... need to keep moving. It is important continually to nurture new contacts and to stay professionally active.*

Because the stock-in-trade of the knowledge worker is obviously knowledge and the ability to handle it, they have only a:

> *... marginal loyalty to the organization, preferring instead to align themselves for purposes of recognition and evaluation with their professional colleagues and associations.*

Raelin argues that such people are interested:

> *... in jobs that tap their creative instincts, that treat them in a personal way, that emphasise professional standards and that allow them to operate without excessive supervision.*

and that they:

> *... need to be viewed as highly skilled potential contributors who work best when given considerable autonomy combined with a sense of corporate purpose.*

Raelin says that a manager's home base is the company while the knowledge worker's home base is his or her profession. Therefore:

> *... there is a natural conflict between management and knowledge workers because of their differences in educational background, socialization, values, vocational interests, work habits, and outlook.*

Managers, according to Raelin, have a career ethic. They are concerned about other people's opinions of them. They are ambitious and into marketing themselves. The knowledge worker has a craft ethic. Craftsmen are most satisfied when they control their own work. Their ethic is marked by self-sufficiency, independence and autonomy.

A CASE IN POINT

A little while ago now, Professor Robin Stuart-Kotze and I were engaged in a change management programme with the research arm of a telecoms company. Their main laboratory in Europe had a long tradition of exemplary but rather academic research. The then CEO of the research arm told us that the company wanted to change the focus of the lab from *'Big R, little d'* to *'little r, Big D'*. In other words, the company wanted to stress product development more than original research.

The people in the laboratory, which in fact was a site with over a thousand people employed, were all knowledge workers. In the main they were scientists and engineers. Earlier attempts at change had failed because they had been rather traditional approaches with re-training, extrinsic motivation, and exhortation. Managers had been given targets for product innovation; which is rather like asking Picasso to knock up a painting in pink to fit the space over the fireplace by Friday! The more that people were exhorted to change, the less they did so.

In fact, effective management in the labs turned out to be very different from the modern manager's self-image. The most effective management style turned out to be facilitative and supportive. We used to express this, somewhat irreverently, as the *white rat* style of management.

Says Raelin:

> *Managers, as careerists, and professionals, as craftsmen, come into natural conflict ... managers threaten the professional's autonomy, while professionals impede the manager's progress towards his or her goals.*

The manager, typically, wants things done quickly and at least cost and makes demands that threaten the knowledge worker's ability to get things done properly; which may involve research, the learning of new tools and technologies. Effective management in the research labs needed to be based upon this recognition.

> White rats? Oh, yes. Well, we got the point over to managers by telling them that all they had to do was to ensure that the scientists and engineers were comfortable and not distracted from what they wanted to do anyway: solve problems.
>
> > *Are you sitting in a draught? Did you park the car OK? Do you have enough white rats?*
>
> We hasten to add that rats of any colour were not used in experiments in the labs. It was just a joke. Rats may be able to run mazes but not inside telephone cables.

The change programme became a success when managers started explaining the company's situation to the people and showing them new, and indeed very interesting, problems that if solved would lead to immediate product enhancements. In place of exhortation, explanation; in place of targets, tempting problems to work on. Simple really.

A MESSAGE FOR GARCIA[133]

Elbert Hubbard (1856–1915) is best known for his fable *A message for Garcia*. **This is an extract:**

> *When war broke out between Spain and the United States, it was very necessary to communicate quickly with the leader of the insurgents. Garcia was somewhere in the mountain fastnesses of Cuba - no one knew where. No mail or telegraph message could reach him. The President must secure his co-operation, and quickly. What to do? Someone said to the President, 'There is a fellow by the name of Rowan will find Garcia for you, if anybody can.'*
>
> *Rowan was sent for and was given a letter to be delivered to Garcia. How 'the fellow by the name of Rowan' took the letter, sealed it up in an oilskin pouch, strapped it over his heart, in four days landed by night off the coast of Cuba from an open boat, disappeared into the jungle, and in three weeks came out on the other side of the island, having traversed a hostile country on foot, and delivered his letter to Garcia - are things I have no special desire now to tell in detail.*

> *The point that I wish to make is this: McKinley gave Rowan a letter to be delivered to Garcia; Rowan took the letter and did not ask, 'Where is he at?' By the Eternal! There is a man whose form should be cast in deathless bronze and the statue placed in every college of the land. It is not book-learning young men need, nor instruction about this and that, but a stiffening of the vertebrae which will cause them to be loyal to a trust, to act promptly, concentrate their energies: do the thing - 'Carry a message to Garcia.'*
>
> *I have carried a dinner-pail and worked for day's wages, and I have also been an employer of labor, and I know there is something to be said on both sides. There is no excellence, per se, in poverty; rags are no recommendation; and all employers are not rapacious and high-handed, any more than all poor men are virtuous.*
>
> *My heart goes out to the man who does his work when the boss is away, as well as when he is at home. And the man who, when given a letter for Garcia, quietly takes the missive, without asking any idiotic questions, and with no lurking intention of chucking it into the nearest sewer, or of doing aught else but deliver it, never gets laid off nor has to go on a strike for higher wages. Civilization is one long, anxious search for just such individuals. Anything such a man asks shall be granted. His kind is so rare that no employer can afford to let him go. He is wanted in every city, town and village - in every office, shop, store and factory.*
>
> *The world cries out for such: he is needed, and needed badly - the man who can carry a message to Garcia.*

Hubbard's moral seems simple enough: that the person who simply does his job well and without complaint will be sought after and wanted in every city, town and village in every office, shop, store and factory. Actually Hubbard's moral is somewhat more complex and centres on the phrase *'without asking any idiotic questions.'* In a curious passage with a curious example, he writes:

> *You, reader, put this matter to a test: You are sitting now in your office - six clerks are within call. Summon any one and make this request: 'Please look in the encyclopaedia and make a brief memorandum for me concerning the life of Correggio.'*

Will the clerk quietly say, 'Yes, sir,' and go do the task? On your life he will not. He will look at you out of a fishy eye and ask one or more of the following questions:

- *Who was he?*
- *Which encyclopaedia?*
- *Where is the encyclopaedia?*
- *Was I hired for that?*
- *Don't you mean Bismarck?*
- *What's the matter with Charlie doing it?*
- *Is he dead?*
- *Is there any hurry?*
- *Shall I bring you the book and let you look it up yourself?*
- *What do you want to know for?*

And I will lay you ten to one that after you have answered the questions, and explained how to find the information, and why you want it, the clerk will go off and get one of the other clerks to help him try to find Corregio - and then come back and tell you there is no such man. Of course I may lose my bet, but according to the Law of Average I will not. Now, if you are wise, you will not bother to explain to your assistant that Correggio is indexed under the C's, not in the K's, but you will smile very sweetly and say, 'Never mind,' and go look it up yourself.

Hubbard clearly approves of those people: knowledgeable enough to know about Correggio, able to research an encyclopaedia and write a synopsis of the artist but who do just what they are told without question.

(For those of you unable to live up to Hubbard's standards, Antonio Allegri da Correggio, 1489–1534, was a painter who lived and worked in Parma, Italy. His work is often erotic. Correggio is hardly a name likely to crop up in everyday conversation.)

By contrast, here is some sound advice given by *The Working Manager* on how to receive instructions, which would have really upset dear Elbert:

Ask yourself:

- *Are you sure you know what the boss means?*
- *Have you asked questions about the meaning?*
- *Are you sure that you can do the job?*
- *Do you have the necessary skills?*
- *Have you discussed these with the boss?*
- *Can you contact the boss during the process if things go wrong?*
- *Do you know how much room you have to make your own decisions?*
- *Do you have the time? Do you have the resources?*
- *Can you make a plan of action?*
- *Can you discuss this with your boss?*
- *Have you decided with your boss what counts as success?*

The more you ask, the more clear you will be. Take on an unclear instruction and you may be asking for trouble.

The truth of the matter is, of course, that both these approaches give problems. There was a time, perhaps, when unquestioning obedience was prized. Such behaviour has had infamous consequences. Today, 'because I was told to do it' is not taken as an excuse for immoral acts. Today also, the world is too complex for unquestioning obedience. However, no doubt asking the boss a series of questions every time drives him or her mad.

HAVE PEOPLE CHANGED?

People talk about Millennials, Generation X, Baby Boomers and The Silent Generation. There may be some truth in what Diane Thielfoldt writes for *The Learning Cafe*[134]:

> *Just as events and social influences create preferences, attitudes and values which in turn shape personality, so social history influences generational characteristics and workplace behaviour. There are real differences to manage across generations.*

In a 2010 BNET article, Peterkin, owner of Head Games Salon in Portland Maine, complained that:

> It seems impossible to find good hires from the generation of 18-to-25-year-olds today. With the huge pool of unemployed people, it's just shocking to me that there aren't hard-working people available to choose from. Right now, we have 10 employees and we're hiring for nine positions. (Our sales were more than $500,000 last year and we're expecting about $700,000 for 2010.)
>
> I think parents have spoiled these kids so much over the last decade. They've taught them that everybody has a Gucci bag. I haven't found anything that helps if you hire someone of that mindset. I think we may just have a whole generation of people on unemployment, because there's nothing that seems to inspire them to work.

Is it that people have become lazy and uninterested in earning a living? Or is it that they are more choosy about what they do to earn that living? Is the answer in what John Adams (1735-1826, the second President of the United States), wrote:

> I must study politics and war that my sons may have liberty to study mathematics and philosophy. My sons ought to study mathematics and philosophy, geography, natural history, naval architecture, navigation, commerce, and agriculture in order to give their children a right to study painting, poetry, music, architecture, statuary, tapestry, and porcelain.

Or is it a large part of the problem that companies no longer offer people what they want and so where people have a choice, they choose something else? Peter Shadbolt has written, for *The Working Manager*:

> In a large company, the brightest and best are constrained. They find their creative input restricted and cannot adjust to their working environment. They leave, weakening the talent pool for succession.

Is it simply a matter of indifferent management? As Roberta Chinsky Matuson, author of *Suddenly in Charge!* wrote for *Fast Company*:

> If you think it's tough being a manager these days, try being an employee. Most are in the position of having to go with the flow because of the current economic conditions. But that doesn't necessarily mean they do so with a smile on their face.

> *Employees are happy to have a job but that doesn't necessarily mean they are happy in their job. Big difference. People who are happy in their jobs act a lot different than those grateful to have a job. They are highly engaged and will do whatever it takes to delight the customer. The other group simply floats along praying for the day they can tell you really what they are thinking. Most likely they will do this as they hand in their notice. That is if they even give notice.*

She goes on to give ten things employees wish managers knew about them. Here are four that seem most relevant:

> *We are no longer going to take one for the team[135] especially after the senior team has just awarded the departing CEO an exit package that certainly could have been used to restore salary cuts.*

> *We are tired of picking up the slack from the non-performers. We know who is not pulling their weight and so do you. Do something about it before we throw ourselves on top of the dead weight pile.*

> *Stop wasting our time with surveys. You already know what's wrong. Now start fixing things before we find a work place that is willing to take action.*

> *Stop micromanaging us. Micromanagement is a sign of mistrust. You've hired us for a reason. If you don't trust (us to) get the job done, then by all means either find people who you think will or leave us alone to do our jobs.*

Orders

No doubt generational change has something to do with it but there is also something else afoot, something rather more dramatic. One might argue that the days of giving orders and indeed obeying them, Rowan-like without question, have passed. Partly this is to do with the recognition that the saying, apparently common at one time in the UK police force, that rank implies knowledge is untrue. It has partly to do with the fact that not every giver of orders can be trusted.

In the article, *The dark side*, Rick Roskin reviewed (for *The Working Manager*) the causes and effects of leadership gone wrong and in particular the work of Katherine A. DeCelles & Michael D. Pfarrer[136] in this area. He wrote that the very attributes of the charismatic leader provide an Achilles heel.

The supreme self-confidence that anchors their personality means that they rarely suffer from internal conflict. So:

> ... if these leaders never experience self-doubt, they might not experience a distinct moral sense of right and wrong.

The skills of the charismatic leader enable him or her to lie with great effect, both to themselves and to stakeholders and impression management skills means the façade is hard to detect. Compliance of followers minimizes dissent and produces 'groupthink', even if they thereby participate in corrupt behaviour. The more dynamic and complex the environment, the greater becomes the likelihood of corruption.

Arnaud de Borchgrave[137] says of the sub-prime crisis, for example, that even the so-called experts did not and could not understand the market complexity and interconnectedness of instruments such as derivatives, sub-prime mortgages, CDOs, and asset backed commercial paper; but they did know that the house of cards would collapse. The only question was when. Yet few blew the whistle and even fewer paid any attention.

> Too clever by half, complex debt instruments clogged the engines that produced gargantuan paper profits. The gravy train was running out of gravy ...

So complexity, greed and charismatic leadership assured the end result and lacking the courage to admit the forthcoming doom, no one spoke up. Most did not want to know in any case. That is a management problem.

Duncan Glassey, founder of Wealthflow[138], blames the financial crisis on the inability of senior management to understand what the employees were doing, how they were doing it and why. He puts it down to a clash of generations:

The people who made the strategy in the banks are of the baby-boomer generation born from 1945 onwards. They are a generation of grand visions, optimism and high ideals about combining individual empowerment with social values. They are the big talkers and the people with the vision and mission statements.
The generation who have managed us into the present situation, Generation X, are the thrill seekers. What's important to them is individualism - choice, self-reliance and immediate gratification.

> *Those who created the financial products, which have so disastrously failed, constitute Generation Y. Highly techno-savvy and street smart but naïve, they are self-obsessed and narrowly focused.*
>
> The belief systems of the three groups – the strategists, the managers and the traders – are entirely different. They don't really understand one another at all. Everybody was locked into the Nick Leeson scenario; no one asked questions so long as everyone was making money. That's senior management's problem.

OUT OF DATE

While the dark side has much to do with this change, many observers believe management today to be out of date. In his book, *The future of management*[139], Gary Hamel points out that most of what most managers consider to be the essential tools of management *'were invented by individuals born in the 19th century.'*

> That's quite a thought. Indeed, Hamel challenges us to think of any management practice of significant importance that was invented in the last 20 years. It is quite tricky. What about these? Surely one of these will pass the 'Hamel test'
>
> - TQM
> - Process re-engineering
> - E-commerce
> - Competencies
> - Just in time
> - Empowerment
> - 360 degree feedback
> - Futures markets
>
> It turns out none will.
>
> *Total Quality Control was the subject of Armand Feigenbaum's Quality Control: Principles, Practice, and Administration - published in 1951.*

Michael Hammer's book, *Re-engineering* the Corporation may have been published in 1990 but you could argue this was simply an extension of the work of Frederick Taylor (1856 -1915.)

Electronic Data Interchange (EDI) and Electronic Funds Transfer (EFT) were introduced in the late 1970s. ATMs and telephone banking arrived in the 1980s. Boston Computer Exchange, an electronic marketplace for used computers was launched in 1982. ARPnet was invented in 1968 and the internet's first five nodes arrived in 1970.

The competency approach to training originated in the 1960's when the USA was worried about standards in education and training across the country.

The technique of *just in* time was first used by the Ford Motor Company and was described by Henry Ford in his book *My Life and Work* published in 1922.

Empowerment? Well, take a look at the work of Mary Parker Follett (1868-1933.)

Clark Wilson developed the first 360 *feedback* survey instrument in 1973. It was called the *Survey of Management Practices*™.

The first *futures contract* on record was made on March 13, 1851. It specified that 3,000 bushels of corn were to be delivered to Chicago in June at a price of one cent below the March 13th cash market price. Futures contracts on the currency exchanges stem from 1970.

Today, what we see is a bifurcation with management still determined to go down old routes:

- money
- control
- command
- short-term
- impersonality
- best practice

while employees, at least those with a brain and education, are seeking something else:

- honesty
- relationships
- creativity
- openness
- responsibility
- recognition

Oh sure, employees will go along with the old methods if they have to and for as long as they have to; but they will jump ship when they can. The old verities of management seem to be under pressure. Why so? Well, think paradigm shift.

Paradigm shift

In his book, *The Structure of Scientific Revolutions*[140], Thomas Kuhn explains that all communities work with a set of received beliefs. These beliefs derive from education and from the accepted norms people grow up with. Such received beliefs he calls paradigms.

Kuhn said of scientific research that it is *'a strenuous and devoted attempt to force nature into the conceptual boxes supplied by professional education.'* When facts start to rebel, start to refuse to be forced into existing boxes, a paradigm shift occurs. Such a shift is what Kuhn describes as a scientific revolution. We are forced to think of things in a different way.

Kuhn talks about the scientific community but paradigms are true of all communities, including the business and management community. Our business training so to speak licenses us for professional practice. Our learning ensures that the received beliefs are firmly fixed in our minds. We know the right way to do things. We understand best practice and we resist novel approaches that do not seem to fit in.

Kuhn said that a paradigm shift occurs when the facts start to rebel and many thinkers argue that we have reached such a point in management; that we need to change many of the assumptions we have lived with over the last 50 years. It is increasingly difficult, to paraphrase Kuhn, to force management into the conceptual boxes of existing ways of thinking about it.

REBELLIOUS FACTS

My first job on leaving university was with Ford Motor Company. My role was as a buyer for a production line manufacturing plant. It was an experience I would not have missed. Much of it I enjoyed; all of it was educational.

Sixty percent of the Ford car was bought in and my job was to source the smaller metal pressings such as engine mounts, grilles, clips and fastenings. I learned a fair amount about the pubs of the Black Country (the UK's West Midlands) and a fairly poisonous drink known as 'Rum and shrub', a great deal about negotiation and a lot about metal pressings, much of it from wandering through Ford's own press shop where I got to know many of the foremen and operatives.

One thing that struck me was the recruitment and training method employed for people on the line at that time. Very basically, Ford's own recruitment bureau maintained a list of people who had applied for production jobs. When a vacancy occurred, the bureau called the next person on the list and asked them if they wanted to start work. If they were not ready there and then, the bureau went on to the next person on the list.

Soon enough they found someone who was available and that person was told to get to the plant right away - whereupon they were given 20 minutes induction and put on the line. If they came back the next day, the recruitment was deemed a success. Indeed, Henry Ford is said once to have exclaimed, *'How come when I want a pair of hands, they come with a brain attached?'*

The saying is variously quoted but, whatever he actually said, the sentiment was certainly apposite to working in Dagenham UK in 1964. Management made the decisions and told the workers what to do. The turnover rate was

THE CULTURE AND THE PARADIGM SHIFT

high although some people stayed a long time. The job suited some – and that was that, as far as talent management went.

You may find this a bit inhuman and in many ways it was. The management paradigm at Ford's in 1964 had not really changed since the days of Taylor and one might argue that the shift has not yet occurred in many of our organisations despite the rise of Toyota, the failure of Lordstown, the successes of Apple, Nucor and the near death of General Motors and Chrysler to say nothing of the failure of a large number of banks.

A CHANGE IN 'SEEING'

Paradigm shifts are sudden changes in the way we see things. An analogy of this is the double-aspect picture, first studied by Edgar Rubin (1886-1951). While you can see either a candlestick or two faces, you cannot see both at the same time. One is always the 'figure' and one the 'ground' as Rubin put it.

Exhibit 8

In science, a few examples of such switches are:

- From the earth-centred universe to the sun-centred solar system to the big bang
- From pantheism to Aristotlean nature to Newtonian physics to string theory
- From creation by design to survival of the fittest to genetics

If we take the word 'paradigm' to mean the dominant beliefs in management then the old paradigm consists of beliefs that Elbert Hubbard and Henri Fayol might have approved of:

- Organisational life should be free from emotion
- All processes should exclude human intervention
- All decisions should be made entirely on the facts
- Employees should be loyal to their employer
- Planning is the basis of all management actions
- Control must be maintained at all times
- Management is planning, organizing, directing and controlling
- Targets should be set for all activities and employees
- Pay for performance produces the best results
- Managers must motivate employees
- We must follow best practice
- Equity and fairness is the essence of employee relations

These beliefs go back a long way. Many of them are rooted in Theory X and all, I dare say, are taken to be common sense. Nevertheless, in the eyes of many commentators, while such beliefs are common, they are not sense. Management is at a crossroads and success will only come from switching away from this dominant paradigm. In its place, we need:

THE CULTURE AND THE PARADIGM SHIFT

- Idealism
- Tough love
- Creativity
- Caring
- Opportunism
- Empowerment
- Risk taking
- Shared vision
- Initiative
- Imagination
- Ethics
- Innovation

Let's try a little experiment here. I am going to bet that you agreed with almost all of the statements described as the old paradigm - and that you also agreed with the need for almost all the characteristics listed as the new paradigm. Am I right?

In management today, we are living in transitional times. It appears that we seek to hold a number of contrary beliefs at the same time. It is as if we are constantly switching between the faces and the candlestick. This does not mean that both are right. It means that we are confused and this accounts for many of the problems in management today.

Some of us want it both ways: to maintain control, to be in charge but at the same time to have empowerment, creativity and initiative in others. (Remember my example of the HR manager who said, *'We want creativity in head office but obedience in the field.'*) Of course, you cannot hold two paradigms at once. The new paradigm drives out the old. As Kuhn said:

> ... *because it is a transition between incommensurables, the transition between competing paradigms cannot be made a step at a time ...*

Maverick

In 1993, Ricardo Semler published *Maverick!*[141] a book about his own company Semco.

> '*I think everyone should set their own salaries. ... We've implemented the Round Pyramid,*' Paulo said. '*We've eliminated rules and cut the bureaucracy. We've tried to make our company transparent, to let our people be free. Why can't we trust our employees to decide how much they should be making? Is that really such a big step?*'

Semler calls his account of his company an invitation:

> *To forget socialism, capitalism, just in time deliveries, salary surveys ... and to concentrate upon building organisations that achieve that most difficult of all challenges: to make people look forward to coming to work.*

This is an account of a real company in what might seem the most unlikely place (Brazil) that did some things which most (i.e. 99%) of managers elsewhere would only contemplate during a Tom Peters seminar supposing they ever got to one. They would certainly forget it all, or at least ignore it all, when they got back home. Is it true? Well, it so happens that I know someone who knows Semler very well. And he says that it is all true. Difficult to believe but there it is.

In the introduction, Semler sounds almost ordinary. Not very ordinary, but almost.

> *What we do is strip away the blind, irrational authoritarianism that diminishes productivity. We're thrilled when our workers are self-governing and self-managing. It means that they care about their jobs and about their company, and that's good for us.*

But look at the results.

> *Semco has grown sixfold despite withering recessions, staggering inflation and chaotic national economic policy. Productivity has increased nearly sevenfold. Profits have risen fivefold. And we have had periods of up to 14 months in which not one worker has left us. And in a poll of recent college graduates conducted by a leading Brazilian magazine, 25% of the men and 13% of the women said that Semco was the company at which they most wanted to work.*

In the chapter, *The Inmates Take Over The Asylum*, Semler talks about how they (that is the workers) chose the new factory and installed the machines in it.

> *They designed the layout. Instead of a series of lathes and then a series of welding operations and so on the workers formed small groups of different machines. The idea was to have, at each of these clusters, a team whose members would fashion a product from beginning to end.*

Does Semco have an appraisal system? Yes it does. Twice a year the workers evaluate their managers. Does Semco have a recruitment and an interviewing system? Yes it does.

> *In a plant where everybody has a stake in success, the idea of asking subordinates to choose future bosses seems an utterly sensible way to stop accidents before they are promoted.*

Semler took over Semco from his (authoritarian) father in 1982. In 2003, Semco had annual revenue of $212 million, up from $4m in 1982 and $35m in 1994; a startling annual growth rate of up to 40 per cent. It employed 3,000 workers in 2003, as opposed to 90 in 1982.[142]

MANPOWER PLANNING

Peter Cappelli says, in his 2008 book *Talent on Demand*[143], that what used to be called manpower planning (and which he calls talent management) doesn't happen anymore.

> *By the mid-1960s, a study of personnel departments found that 96% had a dedicated talent planning function. Virtually every company had an executive ('the manpower planner') ...*

By the mid 1970s, as Cappelli reports:

> *Technology companies like Hewlett-Packard and medical companies like Medtronic reported that about 90% of their profits came from products less than one year old.*

Massively reduced product life cycles, the rise and fall of new companies and even markets, record levels of mergers and acquisitions and their opposites, divestitures, the rise of outsourcing, opportunistic decision making and downsizing - all combine to make classical planning, and classical manpower planning in particular, impossible.

As late as the end of the 1970s, survey evidence from the Conference Board indicated that management's priorities in setting employment practices were to build a loyal, stable workforce. But a decade later, that priority had shifted to increasing organizational performance and reducing costs. So what do you do? You hire outside.

But you can't go on doing that can you? Anecdotes about employers poaching talent from one another are legion. There is a story about townships on the New Jersey shore poaching lifeguards from one another during the summer, of nurses receiving job ads faxed directly into operating rooms. It is also said that in 2007 a Gulf state tried to hire the entire Singapore urban planning department.

The Accel Team[144] site says of Manpower Planning:

> *Planning staff levels requires that an assessment of present and future needs of the organization be compared with present resources and future predicted resources ... the first step is to take a 'satellite picture' of the existing workforce profile (numbers, skills, ages, flexibility, gender, experience, forecast capabilities, character, potential, etc. of existing employees) and then to adjust this for 1, 3 and 10 years ahead by amendments for normal turnover, planned staff movements, retirements, etc, in line with the business plan for the corresponding time frames.*

This sounds so logical, doesn't it? Indeed, Lawrence Klein won the Nobel Prize for Economics for his work in building planning techniques like this. Well, rather more complex ones, perhaps. In 1980, he was working on

> *... modeling the centrally-planned economies of the world (especially the U.S.S.R.), introducing modern econometrics into the People's Republic of China.*

Now, please don't laugh! The world that Professor Klein inhabited disappeared about the time his Nobel Prize was awarded.

So what now?

You have to decide one thing first. Are you committed to the planning, organizing, directing and controlling paradigm or not? If you believe that what is happening today is a passing phase and that the world will get back to stability, logic and order quite soon, then there is a vast array of planning models – and indeed talent planning models – available to you. You will believe that manpower planning and management is about:

- Identifying jobs required
- Writing job descriptions
- Identifying skills required
- Quantifying the number of people required for each job / skill set
- Identifying ways of measuring potential for such jobs / skills
- Implementing the necessary recruitment tools
- Interviews
- Ability Tests
- Psychometric Tests
- References
- Work experience
- Simulations
- Intray exercises
- Assessment Centres
- Biographical Analysis
- Bio-data
- Hand-writing Analysis
- Reviewing progress through performance appraisal
- Appointing the talent to the target jobs

You will also continue to observe job hopping with distaste. On the other hand, if you believe that the idea of planning the skills the company will need in 1 or 3 years, let alone 10, is wildly funny then you have almost certainly crossed the bridge towards the new paradigm. Remember what Kuhn said:

> *When facts start to rebel, start to refuse to be forced into existing boxes, a paradigm shift occurs.*

Laughter may be a sure sign that a paradigm shift has occurred. The new world, the one that Lawrence Klein could not plan, is not a world in which management knows and employees obey. It is a world in which the idea of control, job descriptions and skill sets are about as useful as an investment in sub-prime mortgages. If you are willing to accept the new paradigm, then you will accept the need for development and growth and factor this into your management. You will accept a degree of job hopping but seek to make this happen within the company.

How do you do this?

Well, first, you can remember the motto of the CEO of Nucor.

> *Hire the right people, give them the resources and tools to do the job, and then get the hell out of their way.*

Who are the right people? Let's look at some of the things Nucor supervisors say:

> *My job is to foster thought processes in order to run the lowest cost production team. To do that, we ask questions and experiment. Questions and experiments are at the heart of production improvements and efficiencies. If we see what might be a better way and design the improvement, the company will pay for the experiment — and if we're right, they'll pay for the improvement. I have two in my line who designed improvements that cost $500,000 and $750,000 respectively.*

> *Besides, figuring out how to solve problems and improve things, well, there isn't much that's more satisfying than that. We come to work and people value us, our ideas, efforts, and contributions. We get paid well, and improvement is not only part of the job it is one of the best things about it.*

> *The key operating assumptions are that people are self-regulating - that observation skills, habits of innovation and being articulate elicit and strengthen conversation, initiative, community, pride, kindness, and confidence.*
>
> *Teamwork is contagious and people want to work together, share the ideas and successes. Yet it can be fragile. So I have to do what I say I'll do, pay close attention to every idea, and follow up. If I tell the team, 'If you see a better, safer, more efficient way to do something, let me know and I'll follow up' they'll believe it when I act on it.*

The skills that Nucor seeks are not specific to a job. They are more what we might call personal skills or even what Stephen Covey[145] might call habits. The people Nucor seems to be looking for can:

- foster thought processes
- ask questions
- experiment
- solve problems
- improve things
- value ideas, efforts, and contributions
- be self-regulating
- observe insightfully
- innovate constantly
- be articulate
- take initiative
- have pride in the community
- show kindness
- exude confidence
- excel in teamwork
- share successes
- do what they say they'll do

- pay close attention to every idea
- follow up

You see, the specific job skills that people have today may well be relevant today. They are unlikely to be as relevant next year and will quite possibly be irrelevant a year after that. If you stick to job skills and job descriptions, redundancies are almost inevitable. However, the mental skills of asking questions, experimenting, problem solving, improving, observing, taking initiative and the personal attributes of idealism, creativity, caring, imagination and ethics are always relevant.

If you think that the change rate will continue; if you think that control is no longer the be-all and end-all; if you think that training is out but learning is in; if you think that planning is a joke but opportunism is where it's at, then you have to find enquiring minds with strong ethics. That's talent.

Don't worry

For those of you committed to the old paradigm, please don't worry. It is alive and well. A recent job ad in the UK Sunday press called for someone to:

- Drive performance improvement initiatives across the finance function
- Develop 3 year plans
- Drive KPI-driven benchmarking
- Drive adoption of best practice

Lot of driving in the job, obviously. One may not be too surprised that the return address was a box number.

In fact, my own fear is that the way management happens (or doesn't) in the West today may be stifling the arrival of the new paradigm. We seem to seek obedience, seek control and avoid originality of thought. The more we do this, the less we gain employee engagement (although gaining a great deal of lip service in its place) and the less and less competitive we become.

* * *

6

TOWARDS UNDERSTANDING III: CONTROL AND CREATIVITY

In my philosophy of management it follows that if the strategic objective has been worked out together and agreed, and the right conditions have been created in which people can be switched on, the 'how' of what is to be achieved is a matter for delegation.

John Harvey-Jones, *Making it happen*[146]

Britain's leading businesses are innovation flops, a report says, with just one company in a worldwide top 100, leaving the country ranked alongside the tiny principality of Liechtenstein. And that one company, Unilever, is half Dutch.[147]

Source: Thomson Reuters

Frederick Taylor and Fayol placed control at the very heart of management while today many people call for creativity, innovation and continuous improvement in its place. The issue of the need for control is at the centre of the paradigm shift that we seem to have difficulty in making. Control and creativity are polar opposites; the one drives out the other.

SITUATIONAL DEMANDS

When Fayol was working and writing (*he died in 1925*), the industrial and commercial world was very different from today. Education was not widespread; change was relatively slow by today's standards; business was essentially local and communication and decision-making were more leisurely affairs.

Since these factors are determinants of management style, management was quite top down at that time. In fact, Fayol's own break-through was to argue for the replacement of a pure top down, almost capricious style by something more bureaucratic (which was not then a negative word); a more systematic approach to management. Fayol's book was published only five years after the publication of Frederick Taylor's famous (and infamous) *The Principles of Scientific Management*.

Management style has to change to reflect the demands of the management situation, which is why Reddin, in his book *Managerial Effectiveness*[148], referred to the demands on a manager as *'situational demands.'* The situation must be analysed to ascertain which style is most appropriate.

Thus, a style appropriate to soldiers on a parade ground - simple commands that all have to follow - is not appropriate to managing research workers in a laboratory - individual work of high complexity. In fact, one can easily argue that the more complex a task and the more individual it is, the less likely that any form of command and control style of management will be appropriate.

One might argue that the best leaders do not seem that interested in control but manifest power by delegation, inspiration and communicating vision. Yes, some leaders have been controllers - Geneen at ITT being the most famous - but others are quite different. Take the example of John

Harvey-Jones, the chairman of ICI and the author of the quote at the beginning of this chapter. Take also the examples of world leaders such as Churchill, Kennedy, Ghandi and Mandela. Winston Churchill certainly gave direct commands *('Action this day')* but he was famous for wanting reports on one side of a sheet of paper. He appointed field commanders and government ministers who he believed would take on and achieve tasks. He did not try to control what they did, though he was quick to change them if they did not succeed. Kennedy, although we experienced only a short period of his leadership, sought to inspire, to excite and motivate achievement. Ghandi appears to have led by example and Mandela similarly - both gaining most power when they actually gave all control away.

FAILURE OF CONTROL

Those leaders who have seemed to want to control everything have often (but not always) been evil. Perhaps their need for control stems from the fact that without fear, no one would follow them. Stalin used Beria and his secret service, seeking to control through the knowledge of everything that people did and said. The problems and relative failure of the Soviet Union might be put down, to a large extent, to the time it took to get rid of this culture of fear and failed attempts at control. Hitler, famously, would not allow the Panzer regiments to become involved in defence against the D-Day landings without his direct command. Thank goodness he was in a drugged sleep at the time.

One might argue that the attempt to control inevitably leads to failure as the organisation or entity gets bigger. Modern leaders in China, inspired perhaps by Deng Xiaoping, have recognised that central state control has to be (gradually) relinquished if economic and development gains are to be made. Perhaps Mao Zedong's Cultural Revolution was the last gasp of a refusal to recognise this and perhaps Deng's genius was in enabling a slow change away from control without economic and social collapse. (Perhaps Gorbachev would have been able to effect a more gradual transition, had he been allowed to.)

There are no doubt times when management style has to emphasise control - but there are more times when it should emphasise delegation and inspiration. One of the most important phrases is *'loose-tight'*, as used by Peters and

Waterman in their first book, *In search of excellence*[149]. Management has to be tight (controlling) on a few things that really matter and loose (delegating) on everything else. How do you do this? Well, the delegation is controlled by the value system inherent in the culture.

Remember, the first task for any manager is to get things done through other people. Maintaining control is not an objective in itself - nor is protecting your ego! New York Professor Dale Zand says[150]:

> *Traditional methods of leadership were designed for supervision of factory workers. They emphasize regularity, measurement, orderly appearance, predictability and control. When leaders attempt to enforce traditional leadership in the new knowledge organization, they impede the flow of information, discourage creativity, inhibit adaptation and undermine productivity.*

Some of us recognise the need for change but are not (yet) willing to switch away from the old paradigm. As Ed Schein says[151]:

> *We all know of groups, organizations, and societies in which certain beliefs and values work at cross purposes with other beliefs and values, leading to situations full of conflict and ambiguity.*

At *The Working Manager*, we once received a question, *'Does lack of creativity affect organizational growth and development?'* This is one of those questions where the answer is contained in the question itself - like *'Are vegetables good for you?'* or *'Does ice cream taste good?'* However, the fact that the question is asked is serious.

MUDDLING ALONG

Part of the difficulty that many people have with modern writing on management is that they find it difficult to relate to their everyday lives. They live in one of those many organisations which seem to muddle along without trying. Such organisations have:

- no inspiration
- top down management
- lots of theory X

- indifferent customer service
- poor or at least ordinary quality
- inward looking advertising often with no connection to the real world
- alienated staff
- managers who seem to believe that status comes before effectiveness

- and so on and so on and so on. I sometimes wonder whether managers are actually interested in management. Many managers seem actually to reject thinking about management. The fact of the matter is that there are so many companies out there who are getting by but not making anything like the money they could or should; not growing as they might but muddling along somehow.

Now, many of them have been muddling along a lot worse than they have let on. Much of the scandal (and the damage done to the world economy) has been the firms, big and small, whose only creativity has been in their accounting. They have not been growing. They have not been profitable. They have fooled the markets for a while with their reporting but have met their come-uppance in the end. (You can fool some of the markets all of the time. You can fool all of the markets some of the time ...)

So we have to take a deep breath and remind managers that they can do better - and that if they do not, someone else will. Japan has not been doing so well lately but surely we have not forgotten all the drama of those revelations of the incompetence of western companies as their markets were simply taken away from them by new Japanese competition? It is still happening today. It may not be Japanese competition but it is still real.

CREATIVITY AND EVOLUTION

Creativity is not necessarily about product. It can also be (perhaps more importantly) about other areas of business life as well. Creativity leads to dramatically reduced costs (Ryanair). It can lead to dramatically improved service (Virgin Atlantic). It can lead to both together (John Lewis). It can lead to new ways of selling and buying things (Xerox and Dell).

The real point is that for each of these examples, there is another company who was not so creative. In very many instances, they have failed or survived only by the skin of their teeth. So, yes, lack of creativity kills.

How does it happen? Well, as Seth Godin says in his book, *Survival Is Not Enough*[152], it's all down to evolution; the survival of the fittest. The business environment changes all the time. Now animals do not choose to evolve. Evolution just happens.

> *Evolution works among animals for two reasons: (1) There are lots of animals (2) They've got plenty of time.*

Pterodactyls did not suddenly decide it would be a neat idea to fly, anymore than T-Rex decided to go down to the gym to build some muscles. Evolution is just the way it happens. However, in the case of organisations, to evolve or not to evolve can be a conscious decision. Most of the time, you evolve or you lose out. As conscious beings, we have an ability to respond to changes. Seth Godin writes:

> *As long as there are entrepreneurs willing to take risks, sources of capital willing to fund them and employees willing to give it a try, there will always be chaos in the markets ... Your choice is to respond to it, by beating the turbulence at its own game, or to react to it, by getting frantic when it's too late to make any difference.*

Creativity is the one way that we can respond and it is not necessarily a matter of big changes. As Tom Peters says in his book, *Thriving on Chaos*[153]:

> *... I have long observed that one of the primary distinguishing characteristics of the best leaders is their personal thirst for and continued quest for new/small/practical ideas ... Governor Don Schaefer of Maryland and Roger Milliken are voracious note-takers. Certainly neither one, nor their kindred spirits, ever turned their back on a so-called breakthrough idea. It's just that they long ago gave up on believing in miracles; instead, they depend upon a mass of small innovations - from everyone - to raise every element of their operations to stratospheric levels of performance.*

Don Schaeffer, before becoming Governor of Maryland was Mayor of Baltimore for more than 15 years and is credited with dramatic improvements in a city hitherto close to being the pits. Of Roger Milliken, Chairman of Milliken and Co., Peters says,

> *His genius in 1980 was to see that the answer to competition in the mature textile market was unparalleled quality attained largely through people.*

In both cases - Baltimore and textiles - most people would have thought success was impossible. Peters goes on:

> *The reality is that millions - literally an unlimited number - of innovation/ improvement opportunities lie within any factory, distribution center, store, or operations center. And you can multiply that by more millions when you can involve the factory and distribution center and store working together as a team. And multiply that again when you add in involvement in innovation by suppliers and customers.*

A virus

Note what Peters says,

> *... they depend upon a mass of small innovations - from everyone.*

Such improvement does not come from tired old management, clinging to their status and saying, *'Look! We pay you to do the job. Now get on with it!'* What it requires is a culture where lateral thinking and new ways of looking at processes are normal - accepted, encouraged and supported.

There is a virus in management. This virus makes us think of 'manager good' and 'employee bad'; as 'manager knows' and 'employee doesn't know'; as 'manager responsible' and 'employee irresponsible'; as 'manager company oriented' and 'employee selfish' and thus to the need for the view of manager as controller and employee as controlled.

The virus also gets us to think that creativity is the job of the senior management, but as Godin says:

> *Except that the job of the CEO is not to be right. That's impossible. No company has consistently been smarter than the market place. The job of the CEO is to organize the company to jump on board a winning strategy and at the same time, to organize the company to evolve often enough to find the next strategy before today's strategy disappears.*
>
> *While we'd all like to believe that we're smarter than the market, we're not. The track record of every entertainment, manufacturing and services company*

CEO demonstrates that while markets morph and change around us, no one has a perfect track record in determining what's going to happen next.

A Manifesto

We need a manifesto for management. We have to get away from the dire, ignorant and thought-avoidance behaviour of so many managers. In fact we need a new set of beliefs about what the enterprise is for.

The Chilean thinker and teacher, Professor Luis E Bastias, argues (for *The Working Manager*) that the organisation can be considered as a living entity that is born, grows, interrelates with its environment, takes actions, has motivations, faults, duties and responsibilities. Thus, for Bastias, an organisation is more than the people who work within it and more than the sum total of what he calls their 'conversations', that is their actions and behaviours. It can be said to have an independent life beyond the life of the people who pass through it as employees.[154]

An implication of what Bastias says is that the identity of an organisation includes its past and future actions and thus an organisation cannot be made anew in an instant. Perhaps most importantly, an organisation cannot be truly said to belong to its current shareholders or current management. In fact, Bastias might argue that management has stewardship of the entity and a responsibility for its future existence and well-being.

So an organisation is not for making CEOs feel good and rich. It is not for short term gains - which may or may not be genuine. This attitude has brought capitalism to a crisis point. An enterprise is of course about profitability but more importantly the organisation is the way that, in this world, we bring together people, investment and raw materials to create economic growth, products, jobs and equally important human well-being and satisfaction. Profitability is the health that enables this social purpose to be fulfilled.

A manifesto has at least been started in a book by Max McKeown and Philip Whiteley with the title *Unshrink*[155]. Here the authors set out to show that the old, bad ways of management are neither necessary nor as successful as management based upon the development of the human psyche. They discuss research showing that differences in the way that people are treated explains 19 per cent of the variation in profitability while differences in investment into research accounted for only 6 per cent and technology just 1 per cent. They report the Hay Group research that shows that the people skills of a leader contribute up to 70 per cent of the factors that determine organizational climate and that this climate in turn can add 25 per cent to business returns. They also analyse the Watson Wyatt's human capital index that indicates that good management of people can add up to 30% to shareholder returns over 5 years.

THE CUBAN HEALTH SERVICE

Their most surprising example of a successful organisation is the Cuban health service. Most people from outside that country would see Cuba as the source of no more than some remarkably good music, cigars and rum.

> *Figures from the World Health Organization show that the Cuban population has mortality and morbidity patterns similar to those of a developed country. For such a poor country to achieve this was one of the most impressive achievements of human endeavour of the 20th century.*

The authors add:

> *One detail about the service embarrasses the capitalist and the communist simultaneously: it is one of Cuba's biggest export earners. It is a successful business. It employs cutting-edge technology and displays all the features of the classic business clusters like the Japanese motor industry or Silicon Valley, with close cooperation between research establishments, the state and the enterprises.*

What is interesting about this example is that it demonstrates vividly what we all know really, that the best motivation is not an extrinsic matter of individual reward. The best motivation stems from being part of an endeavour which matters - whose values one shares and whose management demonstrates those values in action. It is intrinsic.

Yes, creativity matters but more importantly, the creation of an organisational culture in which creativity can flourish matters even more. Those companies, large and small, which remain firmly committed to their blinkers through ignorance, lack of energy, fear of loss of managerial status or just plain stupidity will evolute out.

The dinosaurs lasted a very long time and so has old management. The dinosaurs went and so will those organisations that refuse to accept the new realities. (Perhaps if T-Rex had been more into employee engagement ...)

As Ridderstrale and Nordstrom say in *Funky Business*:

> ... there will be many more questions with fewer and fewer universal answers. Einstein was wrong. No single theory can guide us. Diversity rules. Questions rather than answers fundamentally drive the future. And along the way do not expect much help from technology because as Pablo Picasso once pointed out, 'Computers are useless. They can only give us answers.' But if you ask smart questions, in a unique way, faster than anyone else, you will be momentarily ahead of the game. Enjoy it. Seconds later you have to think of the next question. Then the next.

THE NATURE OF CREATIVE PEOPLE

Creative people will not respond to command and control. As Gavin Kotze wrote for *The Working Manager*, creative people tend to share certain traits.

- *They have an interest in the abnormal, accepting oddities and abnormalities as intriguing, not repulsive.*
- *They cast aside existing assumptions and look at things from new perspectives.*
- *They are open to different ideas and perspectives, always being willing to change tack to find a new route to success.*
- *They subscribe to the notion that security is for sissies; a leap of faith can land one in a whole new realm.*
- *They exhibit endurance and perseverance, accepting the struggles and strife that litter the road to success*

A list of traits that characterize creative people can be as long as one's thesaurus allows. However, perhaps the essential characteristics of creativity are summed up by just two beliefs:

- *A willingness to embrace problems*
- *A belief that destruction and creation go hand in hand*

For creative people, success and failure are not seen as opposites. Failure is an essential component on the road to success and should be accepted as a positive aspect. Failure is better regarded simply as practice and as an attempt. This does not sit well in a world of targets, performance appraisals and monthly reports.

We know this. It is not rocket science to say it. But still, the old paradigm rises up to haunt us. In his article (for the *Working Manager*), *Freedom from command and control*, John Seddon writes:

> *Command and control is the norm. Following the success of Henry Ford's mass production system, its principles and practices have governed the way we think about the design and management of work. Central to the command and control logic is the separation of decision making from work, defining the role of management.*

The problem is that management is still focused on control. It seems that so many initiatives, aimed at freeing creativity, have been subverted by the need, quite probably deep in the management psyche, for control.

MbO

Take the example of Management by Objectives (MbO) which started out as an almost chance remark by Peter Drucker about enabling people to see how and where their work connected with the aims of the organisation. It has now become a way of controlling people by targets. (Indeed, I remember people, in what was then Wang Labs[156], talking about their 'MbOs', meaning the targets they had to reach for their bonuses.) MbO, to hear many managers talk, has become accepted as the only way to manage.

In fact, what is taken to be MbO in most companies is a very watered down version of what was once put forward by consultants as the ultimate break-through in running organisations. The idea that clear objectives could be set and agreed, monitored, trained for, measured and rewarded seemed to bring together both the classical school of management (measurement, process) and the human relations school (involvement, enrichment). In the event, the difficulties of setting down objectives in an objective way, the time consumed in agreeing and indeed constantly altering objectives as the organisation changed, and the sheer impossibility of actually measuring performance against objectives in many jobs, proved insuperable difficulties.

A truism is that what gets measured gets done. One of the problems with MbO is that by concentrating upon specific outputs in a job, other aspects of the role that is filled get ignored - and gradually less well performed. Another problem is that since business statistics can rarely be defined precisely, performance and results get massaged.

MbO and performance rewards

The blind use of MbO particularly when tied to performance pay and bonuses has led to the most dramatic failures, particularly in the banking world. Indeed Richard Lambert, the director general of the Confederation of British Industry (CBI) singled out the bonus culture that has turned thousands of bankers into millionaires, as one of the main causes of the financial problems now engulfing the world's banks. Lambert said the bonuses rewarded success but did not penalise failure and that if bankers had been staking their own capital they might not have taken such big risks. The CBI chief also accused investment banks of being cavalier in their attitude towards risk. He said:

> *At the heart of many of Wall Street's problems has been a serious misalignment between the interests of managers and shareholders. It's clear a number of investment banks overlooked basic risk controls in their drive to increase profits.*
>
> *This pattern of behaviour has been exacerbated by a remuneration structure which has encouraged some employees to take spectacular short-term risks, confident that if things work out well they will reap huge rewards, and that if they don't they won't be around to pay the price. If it had been their own equity at risk, things might have played out differently.*

The bonus culture has turned thousands of relatively mediocre performers in the banking industry into multi-millionaires, while top performers have earned vast sums. (The head of Barclays investment banking, Bob Diamond, was paid £36m in 2008 even though Barclays took a £1.6bn hit from the US sub-prime crisis.)

MbO has had undesirable effects in other spheres as well, in the UK health service and the US education system. Levitt and Dubner[157] report a study of student performance in Chicago from 1993 to 2000. In an attempt to do something about under-achievement in the education system, the Chicago Public School (CPS) system started to hold schools accountable for the results of their pupils and test for achievement using standardised instruments - so called 'high stakes testing.' They set targets. As Levitt and Dubner say:

> *Schoolchildren, of course, have had the incentive to cheat for as long as there have been tests. But high-stakes testing has so radically changed the incentives for teachers that they too now have added reason to cheat. With high-stakes testing, a teacher whose students test poorly can be censured or passed over for a raise or promotion. If the whole school does poorly, federal funding can be withheld.*

How do you discover which teachers have been cheating?

> *To catch a cheater, it helps to think like one. If you were willing to erase your students' wrong answers and fill in the correct ones, you probably wouldn't want to change too many wrong answers ... nor, in all likelihood would you have enough time, because the answer sheets are turned in soon after the test is over.*

So what you might do is select a string of eight to ten consecutive questions and fill in the correct answers for, say, one-half to two-thirds of your students. Data was available for every CPS student from 3rd to 7th grade for seven years in the form of summary answer strings. Levitt and Dubner give the example of students in two classes who took an identical maths test.

> In the data, a letter (a,b,c,d) indicates a correct answer while a number (1,2,3,4) indicates a wrong answer and a 0 indicates the answer was left blank. Levitt and Dubner present two sets of strings, one set from each class which at first appear to be a just a sequence of letters and numbers. However, once an algorithm is applied, based upon the assumptions of cheating, certain patterns appear. In one class fifteen of the twenty-two students *managed to reel off the same six consecutive correct answers!* Or did they?
>
> - *those questions, coming near the end of the test, were harder than the earlier questions*
> - *these were mainly sub par students ... few of whom got six consecutive right answers elsewhere*
> - *up to this point in the test, the fifteen students' answers were virtually uncorrelated*
> - *three of the students left at least one answer blank before the suspicious string and then ended the test with another series of blanks*

In case you think this was a long while ago and in another country anyway, I am afraid that such practices are commonplace where targets are used and schools rewarded for meeting them. Penny Haslam writes[158]:

> *Teachers blame constant testing and the importance placed on league tables for the pressure to improve results - which for some teachers has led to cheating. Some teachers admitted telling pupils what to write in coursework. One unnamed teacher from Leeds said ready-made answers were kept in a filing cabinet. These were used by teachers to fill in missing gaps in pupils' coursework without the students' knowledge. Another teacher told the BBC how he pointed over pupils' shoulders when they made mistakes in an exam. A survey by the Teacher Support Network, a teachers' welfare charity, found the majority of respondents thought cheating was commonplace in England.*

The Finnish education system is consistently to be found at the top of educational rankings. While this is not the only factor, it is at least noteworthy that there are no centrally set targets, no system of national testing, no league tables nor any school inspections in the Finnish system. Speaking of Finnish teachers, Professor Jari Lavonen, of the University of Helsinki, said,

'They are academics and well trained, so we trust them. The teachers are trusted to assess their own pupils.'

SMART

I am sure that you have heard that all objectives must be smart.

- Specific – What is to be achieved?
- Measurable – How will achievement be measured?
- Achievable - Are the objectives achievable and attainable?
- Realistic – Can the objectives be realistically achieved with the resources available?
- Time – By when must the objectives be achieved?

Actually, no SMART objectives meet the criteria for being SMART. Here are some objectives claimed by their authors to meet the criteria. They are all taken from websites which preach SMART and are given as examples to follow.

- To achieve attendance of at least 150 guests at the national conference on 31 March 2008 by sending a promotional email to all relevant professionals by 30 November 2007.
- Organise and provide administrative support to national committees, including the development and distribution of agendas and minutes at least 2 weeks before and after the meeting.
- Achieve a 20% return on capital employed by August 2019.
- Gain 25% of the market for sports shoes by September 2018.
- Survive the recession.
- Increase the revenue of the Brazilian operation from $200,000 to $400,000 by 2018.
- Ensure full compliance with Equality & Diversity policy at all times.

- Reduce water use in 2009.
- Ensure all staff are trained to required standards by end March 2009.
- Ensure all core Health and Safety requirements are met on an ongoing basis.
- Run 3 skills workshops each for 30 members of staff by 1 March 2009.
- Hold one team meeting a month for all team members.

None of these objectives fits the criteria for SMART. None can actually stand alone.

To achieve attendance of at least 150 guests at the national conference on 31 March 2008 by sending a promotional email to all relevant professionals by 30 November 2007.

> *Which? Achieve attendance or send a promotional email? The latter might well be insufficient to achieve the former.*

Organise and provide administrative support to national committees, including the development and distribution of agendas and minutes at least 2 weeks before and after the meeting.

> *Minutes part of the objective is time bound but what (more) is the administrative support to national committees? How is this to be measured? Are there qualitative measures?*

To achieve a 20% return on capital employed by August 2019.

> *ROCE measures return against the value of assets in the business. Decrease the assets and for the same revenue, the return increases. This may be artificial (sell plant and rent it back), a matter of depreciation (depreciated assets with same revenue) or inflation (revenue goes up with inflation while assets may have been depreciated.) None of these are a matter of performance.*

> To gain 25% of the market for sports shoes by September 2018.
>
> *What is included in the market? (adults, children, fashion sports wear, football boots?) Where? (home or global?) Is there a constraint on methods? How about a dramatic price reduction?*
>
> (If you want to work through the rest of the objectives, look in the footnotes here.[159])

OK, you might think I am being picky. But that is what SMART is about! It is supposed to be totally objective, needing no interpretation; even to be machine like. It is supposed to be phrased so as to measure performance exactly. In fact, no objective can ever live in isolation from its environment - the culture of the company, ethics, other parts of the job, priorities, the needs of other people and so on.

You might argue that each of these objectives could be made more detailed, and indeed you can try. You will find that no matter how much detail you add, there will still be uncertainties and you will also find that the objective grows exponentially in length such as to be quite unusable. As a manager, instead of wasting your time on creating ever more detailed and ever less readable objectives, seek to gain mutual understanding of what you, the employee, the team and the company are trying to do. Systems and processes don't manage. You do!

BACK TO CONTROL

MbO is essentially top down. The objectives are set so that the subordinate knows what to do. The boss's job is either to set the objectives or at least to ensure that they are consistent with the objectives of the team, his or her own job, the department and company at large. As such, MbO can be seen as one step up in an order of complexity than management by command - where the boss tells the subordinate what to do.

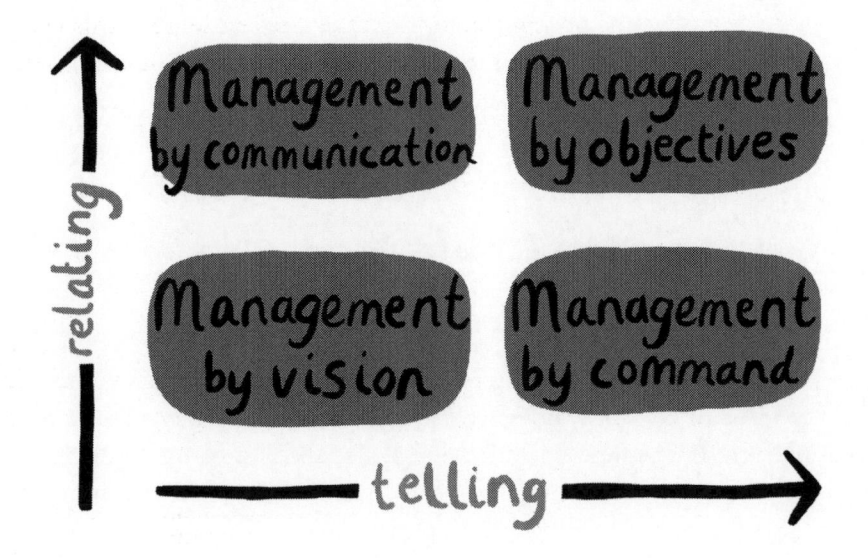

Exhibit 9

A 2×2 matrix with axes "relating" (vertical) and "telling" (horizontal):
- Top-left (high relating, low telling): **Management by communication**
- Top-right (high relating, high telling): **Management by objectives**
- Bottom-left (low relating, low telling): **Management by vision**
- Bottom-right (low relating, high telling): **Management by command**

Exhibit 9

- *Management by command* is about telling, with little support or encouragement. It is appropriate at times, for example on a soldiers' parade ground.

- *MbO* is still about telling but aims also at a form of participation. The boss controls the objectives but leaves it up to the subordinate to decide how to achieve them.

- *Management by Communication* assumes that people know what to do, can set their own objectives and recognise their own outputs. The manager concentrates upon maximum support, communication, feedback and information giving.

- *Management by Vision* assumes fully competent experts who create their own roles, the manager concentrating upon facilitating their abilities and decisions.

Control reduces work to smaller tasks if only because the manager has to do the controlling – and many managers have simple minds! Control is thus the enemy of creativity. It is also the enemy of commitment and motivation which, in the knowledge industry at least, go hand in hand with creativity.

However, the absence of any control, even in the weakest sense of this word, is anarchy and few companies can risk that. So the enigma, particularly for the knowledge industry, is how to keep people focused in the same direction while maximising their ability to be creative, different, opportunist and to use that 1.5kg tool, the brain.

STATION X

Perhaps the most successful knowledge organisation, certainly of its time and perhaps ever, was Station X, located primarily at Bletchley Park, in England from 1938 to 1945. We can measure its success not in terms of profits but in terms of an even more valuable commodity, human life.

For a time in 1942, Station X was unable to read Nazi naval codes. As Michael Smith writes, in a book you absolutely must read if you are interested in motivation, *Station X – the codebreakers of Bletchley Park*[160]:

> During August and September, the U-boats located twenty-one of the sixty-three convoys that sailed, sinking forty-three ships. They destroyed 485,143 tons of shipping in September, and, in October, when there were more than a hundred U-boats at sea, sank 619,417 tons ... At the same time, the number of U-boats sunk dropped to just five in August and three in September ... (and) by the third week of November, only two U-boats had been sunk while the number of Allied ships lost that month was rising steadily towards the one hundred mark.

Once the ability to read the codes was re-established, the situation was reversed.

> On 23 May, after hearing of the loss of the forty-seventh U-boat that month, Doenitz ordered the wolf packs to be withdrawn from the Atlantic, giving the Allies the respite they needed to get supplies across to Britain in preparation for the invasion of mainland Europe.

The primary target of Bletchley Park's endeavours was the *Enigma* machine, actually first invented in 1919 by a Dutchman. This machine took plain German text and - through a system involving a choice of wheels, varying the order of them, altering the connections between the keys and the output by a plugboard and finally by setting the start point of any wheel in any position - enciphered the message so that only an identical machine, set up in an identical manner, could read it. As Smith says:

> *There were sixty possible orders in which the wheels could be placed in the machine, with a total of 17,576 different position settings for each wheel. The plugboard allowed 150 million million changes of circuit. The total number of possible settings for a basic German Enigma machine was, therefore, 159 million million million.*[161]

That's 159,000,000,000,000,000,000 and this was the size of the task. This was in the days before computers although the first practical application of a large scale program-controlled computer was eventually part of the solution. However, *Colossus*[162], as this computer was called, was not installed until December 1943 and even then it had a limited function. The work for the first years, certainly from 1938 to March 1940, was all by hand.

For example, it involved the hunt for *Cillis,* named after one of the enemy operators' girlfriends whose name frequently appeared in the Enigma settings. As Mavis Lever says:

> *One was thinking all the time about the psychology of what it was like in the middle of the fighting when you were supposed to be encoding a message for your general and you had to put three or four letters in these little windows and in the heat of the battle you would put in your girlfriend's name or dirty German four letter words. I am the world's expert on German dirty four letter words!*

It involved looking for cribs or *kisses* and what was called *gardening*:

> *The RAF dropped mines in specific positions in the North Sea so that they would produce warning messages that would give us a crib. The positions were carefully chosen so as to avoid (some) numbers, especially 0 and 5, for which the Germans used more than one spelling.*

It involved *Banburismus*: sheets of paper 10 inches wide and several feet long, used to check for turnover points of the wheels on Enigma to find repeats and thus a way in to the message. More than anything, it required enormous imagination, fantastic creativity, a vast number of people and total dedication – what one might call employee engagement on the grandest scale.[163]

It required the invention of the *Bombes*: electrical machines with many reels simulating possible Enigma settings (by the end of the war there were 2,000 Bombe operators) and eventually the computer, all stemming from Turing machines, named after the genius Alan Turing.

In so, so many ways, it was the reverse of the command and control culture. One of the leaders was Dilly Knox:

> *He said the most extraordinary things. He was a great admirer of Lewis Carroll: 'Which way does the clock go round?' And if you were stupid enough to say clockwise, he'd just say: 'Oh no it doesn't; not if you're the clock. It's the opposite way.' And that's sometimes how you had to think about the (Enigma) machines. Not just to look at them how you saw them but what was going on inside. That was the only way in which one was really trained. But trained is a bad word because that was the one thing you mustn't be.*

SURFACE CULTURE

When you read about Bletchley Park, you are struck by what at first appears to be a culture of amateurism.

> *Admiral Sinclair had bought the mansion at Bletchley Park in the Spring of 1938 ... acting entirely on his own initiative ... Frustrated by his inability to get a government department to pay the £7,500 (several million today) asking price ... Sir Hugh dipped into his own pocket to buy it. 'We know what he paid for it,' said one former intelligence officer. 'We are not sure if he was ever re-paid. He died soon afterwards so he probably wasn't.'*

and

> *I had read classics – Latin and Greek – at Glasgow. By way of ancillary to that I had taken a short course in German mainly because many of the best texts and commentaries on the Latin and Greek classics are in German. As a result of that very minimal knowledge the Army posted me to Bletchley Park.*

and

> *When the shifts changed over at 9 am, 4 pm and midnight, swarms of people descended from a variety of vehicles, many of them driven by young female Motor Transport Corps volunteers, young society women who had no need to*

> be paid for their war effort ... They were usually quite wealthy and had to buy their own uniforms which were beautifully cut and they were all very pretty.

The conditions were appalling at times.

> It was even colder in the huts, which were bleak ... Bare concrete floors disguised with a coat of red tile paint, windows with blackout curtains, wooden trestle tables, light bulbs with no shades, and inefficient electric heaters, or worse, cast iron coke stoves with metal chimneys going up through the asbestos roof ...They were awful. When the wind was high, long flames would be blown out into the room frightening anyone nearby Alternatively, the fire would go out and smoke would come billowing forth filling the room with a thick fog.

So how, with such an apparently amateurish approach and such appalling conditions, did Station X manage to be so successful? Perhaps the conditions were primitive (although less so by the standards of 1940 than by those of today) but motivation was not:

> I can remember quite well showing Harry some of the sorting and how delighted he seemed when he began to recognise the different types of signals. He joined up with Miss Bostock working on frequencies and call signs. I then had to pass to Harry any strange, new or unknown signals. If I was in difficulty, I knew I could go to Harry. It was a great pleasure because he was always interested in everything and took great pains to find out what it was and why. They were enjoyable days indeed. We were all happy and cheerful, working in close cooperation with each other.

and

> The transmitter itself has a sound ... and the man who is actually transmitting the Morse, he has his own particular way of sending letters ... It is like a voice ... So if they changed frequency and we lost them, we would go looking for them and we would listen first for the sound of the transmitter and listen for the operator ... As soon as we heard the sound of our man, the way he sent the letters, he was our man.

and

> Sometimes we had a very quiet shift and not an awful lot happened ... hour after hour waiting for the station to open. It was a bit like a cat sitting outside

> *a mouse hole ... Then suddenly we'd hear (him) transmitting again and then all your adrenalin was running and it didn't matter how tired you were, how sleepy or bored you felt, the minute that station came alive again, you would be alive too, tearing pieces of paper off the pad and scribbling away like mad.*

ECCENTRICITY

Genius is usually unusual. People who look and act as they are supposed to are rarely the most original thinkers. Station X, as one might expect, had more than the usual number of eccentrics.

> *My arrival was unforgettable. As I saluted, I stamped the wooden floor in my Army boots and came to attention with another shattering noise. Tiltman (head of the hut) turned, looked at my feet, and exclaimed: 'I say old boy. Must you wear those damned boots?' I became the only other rank at BP in battledress and white running shoes, much to the disgust of the adjutant.*

> *On my first day there, I saluted this captain and he turned to me and said: 'Excuse me,' – which is not the language normally used by captains to privates - 'Excuse me,' he said, 'What is that noise?' To which I replied, 'That is the air raid siren, sir.' That gives you the impression of what kind of place Bletchley was. Mad people on all sides.*

Ann Lavell was PA to Josh Cooper:

> *He was absolutely mad, frightening really ... But when I got to know him I got quite fond of him ... He was on another plane I think. He'd get awfully embarrassed and worried when he felt he wasn't acting like an ordinary human being. Once (we) were beside the lake and Cooper had finished drinking a cup of coffee ... he stood there with the empty cup and was clearly slightly embarrassed by having it in his hand. So he just threw it in the lake.*

Alan Turing was perhaps the ultimate genius of Station X.

> *He had all sorts of crackpot notions based upon the fact that he didn't think the currency would stand up to a substantial war ... and he put a lot of money into silver bars. Having extracted them from his bank with the utmost difficulty, he ... buried them somewhere. He had a very elaborate set of instructions for how to find them after the war. But he never did find them.*

If eccentricity can be amusing, genius is the coin it often mints.

> *I thought of this imaginary German fellow with his wheels and his book of keys. He would open the book and find what wheels and settings he was supposed to use that day ... and the next thing he would have to do would be to choose a three letter word for his first message of the day. So I began to think, how would he choose that indicator ... Then I had the thought, suppose he was a lazy fellow, or in a tearing hurry ... and he were to leave the wheels untouched in the machine and bang the top down and look in the windows, see what letters were showing and just use them ... What about the rings? ... Then I had a flash of illumination ... He would, as it were, be sending in clear.*

I have missed a lot out here and you would need to know how the Enigma works to understand the implications but the key is the flash of illumination. The idea did not work for some time but in May 1940 it did and the Nazi Red enigma was broken as a result.

Taking responsibility

> *I was so convinced that 'Robinson' (an electro-mechanical precursor of the first computer) would never work that we developed the new machine on our own at Dollis Hill. We made the first prototype in ten months (starting February 1943), working day and night, six-and-a-half days a week, twelve hours a day ... The purpose of Colossus was to find out what the positions of the code wheels were at the beginning of the message and it did that by trying all the possible combinations ... then having found the starting positions of the cipher wheels you could decode the message ... It had about 1500 valves in it, which horrified Bletchley ... the first day they got it, (they) put a problem on it to which they knew the answer. It took about half an hour to do the run.*

and

> *As I studied that first collection of decodes ... I began to see that ... we were dealing with an entire communications system ... these call signs came alive as representing elements of ... forces, whose commanders ... would have to*

> *send messages to each other ... No one seemed to be doing anything about this potential gold mine so ...*

and even

> *I took the day off, went up to London, connected with a priceless office keeper in our peacetime quarters and returned with two furniture vans of loot. I can well imagine the army of civil servants who are still searching for those tables, chairs, desks, card indexes etc. ...*

> *We were a heterogeneous crowd ... worth their weight in gold. If we did strike a dud it was my business to sell him or her. I am told that I once swapped a small and incompetent typist for a large and priceless card index.*

Organisation

So did this array of motivation, commitment, genius and creativity really stem from a delightfully amateur management process? Well, of course not. What it stemmed from was an almost hidden, certainly behind the scenes, management process which was perhaps of greater genius than the codebreaking itself. It was management, which in a totally self-effacing way (not a word too common on management lips today) set out to enable the genius to work.

Put hundreds of geniuses together and while you will certainly generate many ideas, you will equally certainly generate no cohesion. The genius of Station X management was to create an underlying process, to tolerate and even encourage eccentricity, to strive against the interference of formality and bureaucracy and to allow the natural commitment to flourish: the commitment of people fighting for the survival of their country, ideals and themselves.

There were no big ideas, no mission statements, no change programmes, and precious few motivational addresses: certainly no company newspaper. This was life or death. However, there was a management process.

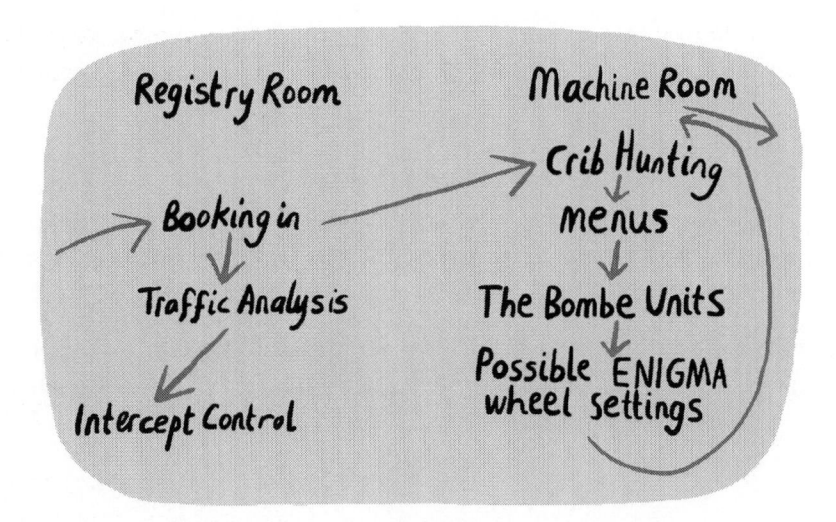

Exhibit 10

Each section was organised into areas, often known as 'huts' after the wooden buildings they were mostly housed in. Each hut was headed by one person, usually a brilliant codebreaker. The huts were arranged such that material passed from one to the other in a series. But it was not all linear. Cross-fertilisation of ideas was achieved by the leaders getting together and seeking new and more creative ways of using the data that became available. Change was, of course, constant.

With such a group of oddballs, inter-personal management was not only difficult but extremely important. For example, in 1941, Dilly Knox, one of the most brilliant codebreakers and a major Greek scholar and Egyptologist, took grave exception to the process. He wrote:

> *As a scholar ... to concede your monstrous theory of collecting material for others is impossible. By profession and in all his contracts a scholar is bound to see his research through from the raw material to the final text.*

The head of Station X, Alistair Denniston, replied:

> *If you do design a super Rolls Royce, that is no reason why you should yourself drive the thing up to the house of a possible buyer, more especially if you are not a good driver ... You are Knox, a scholar with a European reputation, who knows more about the inside of a machine than anyone else ...*

CONTROL AND CREATIVITY

and persuaded him of the benefits of the process. Within days, Knox had worked out the internal mechanisms of a radically different Enigma machine used by Nazi military intelligence.

Peter Hilton on Max Newman:

> *He realised that he could get the best out of us by trusting to our own good intentions and our strong motivation ... For example, he gave us one week in four off. We would just be encouraged to do research on our own cryptographical methods.*

and

> *I was taken to Dilly Knox's section ... It was very much a research section ... When I arrived, he said: 'Oh hello, we're breaking machines, have you got a pencil?' That was it, I was never really told what to do ... I think looking back on it that was a great precedent in my life, because it taught me to think that you could do things yourself without always checking up to see what the book said.*

Of course, at the truly highest levels of creativity, in codebreaking, business or elsewhere, there is no book.

Many of the people were in theory subject to military discipline and many of the senior ranks outside of Bletchley Park were unhappy about the informality.

> *Some people were group-captains, some were lieutenants and so on. So for a longish period we all wore civilian clothes and we were perfectly happy about it, uniforms were uncomfortable. Then some wretched admiral came down and said, 'Where are my Wrens (WRNS - Women's Royal Naval Service)?' and there were these girls in skirts and jumpers and he said, 'It's disgraceful. My Wrens should be jumping up, hands down seams of skirts.' So we were all made to wear uniform.*

MOTIVATION?

Idiots like that Admiral still exist today, of course, but the story serves to show that there was another world impinging on Bletchley Park, a world where people were supposed to obey orders first – command and control – and get the codes broken second.

How then did those who were working outside the codebreaking itself feel so involved? Part of the answer was that there was a very active, if unique, social life. Revues, parties, twice weekly dances, a drama group, musical and choral societies, rounders (similar to baseball) and even Scottish dancing. There was also a *'lot of romance going on.'* Even if there was some demarcation in the work, there was none in the social side. There were few if any signs of rank. There was no executive dining room, no executive car parking spaces, no executive washrooms.

The primary motivation was the knowledge that together they were doing a job, a really valuable, tough, job and something well worth doing; and they were kept aware of just how important and how successful their work was.

> *He tried to explain to me exactly what my contribution had been ... I just didn't understand. I'm not a mathematician, I'm not a linguist. I'm just somebody who's given instructions and does funny little calculations with a slide rule and bingo! A few days later a smiling Shaun comes in. I don't know what my contribution is but OK, it must be satisfactory.*

The story is its own conclusion. Chaotic? Yes. Successful? Yes. In line with views on performance appraisal, target setting, activity measurement and competencies? No. The success was not due to command and control but to creativity, working together, concentrating together on an amazingly important job, valuing eccentricity, playing together and always thinking of another way to look at things. As the late Anita Roddick said in her book, *Business as Unusual*:

> *There aren't many motivating forces more potent than giving your staff an opportunity to exercise and express their idealism.*

LESS MANAGEMENT IS MORE

You know the feeling: once you have read about something, examples of it keep appearing wherever you look. For me, it was Mary Follett and her notion of self-managing groups. Once I had read what she wrote, I started seeing self-managing groups all over the place. I do wish that more managers would see them too.

> *When there is identification with organizational goals, the members tend to perceive what the situation requires and to do it whether the boss exerts influence to have it done or not. In fact, he need not be present or even aware of the immediate circumstances.*

Mary Parker Follett was primarily a management thinker. What she says is not always easy to grasp, but what she is saying here is that there are times when less management is more, specifically when the group of employees knows what to do, why it is important and is willing to work to get it done.

EARLS COURT

It was a while ago, probably sometime in the 1990's, when I was working with Earls Court on customer service improvement, that I came across a bunch of men collectively known as the *'heavy gang'*. Their job was to clear away the vast amount of rubbish that building an exhibition causes, to keep the aisles clean during the show and then to return the halls to normal once the exhibition had been 'knocked down', as the phrase is.

They did it very well but what was even more important, they generated a great deal of good will from the exhibitors. They were indeed assiduous in their cleaning but were also friendly and helpful. There appeared to be little management control over them. They knew what to do, worked well together and delivered the goods. Management largely let them get on with it and to good effect for the title *'heavy gang'* was one worn with pride by its members.

In the end, it all fell apart; not from any reasons to do with the heavy gang itself but because an accountant felt that savings could be made. The gang was privatised, in the sense that the cleaning was contracted out to an external company and the gang was transferred as part of this arrangement.

This external company felt that it had to get more productivity to make a profit on its deal with Earls Court and thus started setting targets, telling the gang how to do their job more quickly, and reducing the time allocated for the tasks. The result? All the members of the gang left, new people were employed, customer service went through the floor and there were constant complaints of dirty aisles, rubbish left uncleared and the halls left in a poor state after exhibitions.

> Earls Court had been dearly loved as a venue. Its main hall was old but revered. However, at that time the National Exhibition Centre opened in Birmingham and, shortly after that, Excel opened in London's docklands. Whether Earls Court could have withstood such competition is open to debate and certainly the absence of the old heavy gang would have been only one part of its lack of competitiveness but people fell out of love with the place and it was sold. It will now be knocked down. As the *Guardian* newspaper says:
>
> *Earls Court is one of London's largest and oldest entertainment venues and it will host volleyball matches at the 2012 London Olympics. But its rich and varied history could come to an end following the games, with new owners planning to demolish the venue to make way for a housing project. The company has revealed plans to bulldoze the Earls Court complex, which covers around 26 acres, and integrate it into a huge residential area that will straddle the two London boroughs of Kensington and Chelsea and Hammersmith and Fulham.*
>
> I think that a large part of the reason for its decline and ultimate demise was a lack of understanding on the part of the then management, who over-managed and under-led, that less management can often be more and that, while costs always have to be watched, cutting the costs that drive the business is usually very wrong indeed. Exhibitions are immensely complicated affairs and anyone who tries to control every variable personally will fail. The business requires extreme forms of delegation, largely based on the saying, common in the theatre world – 'the show must go on.'

As Jim Stroup (*Managing Leadership*) says, glossing Mary Parker Follett:

> *It is important, then, for managers to pay particular attention to the 'group life.' The dynamic interrelationships of its members are its essence, by means of which members continuously refine and reinforce their group loyalty and their identification with group goals. It is also the vehicle for the instigation of specific instances of creativity within the group, and then the dissemination of them throughout it.*

And this is true, even when you are talking about a gang of cleaners.

> ## THE RE-CYCLING CENTRE
>
> What is your image of dustmen, garbage collectors and people who work in re-cycling centres - commonly known as the 'town dump'? Would you be surprised to be welcomed at a re-cycling centre, offered advice on where what goes, given a hand unloading uncle's old wardrobe and have an operative take the used paint tins away for you? Would you expect friendliness, courtesy, efficiency and expertise?
>
> Well, whether you would or not, these are exactly what you get at the Havering Re-cycling Centre, the main, if not only, occupant of the poetically named Gerpins Lane. The people there seem to enjoy their work, to be at ease with each other and ready to help the populace of the London Borough of Havering. So surprised have I been, that I actually asked one of them about the quality of management there.
>
> *They are alright. They don't bother us and we don't bother them.*
>
> How does it work then?
>
> *We are a bit older than some and we work things out for ourselves. We have the occasional wrong'un but they do not stay long.*
>
> Is it a close knit community?
>
> *No. We rub along with each other. We don't socialise out of work but we get on.*

It works, and I suspect it works because the management in this case is intelligent enough to recognise that less management is more; that people can be trusted; that they can work out how to do things and that if they are left alone to do it, everyone will be happy.

The Clean Team

You may think it laziness but I do not clean my car, or indeed my wife's car. I take both to a hand car wash just up the road. To look at the queues, everyone else does as well.

There have been other car washes in the area, some automatic and some, like this one, not. All have failed. Why? The three rules of retailing are location, location and location, they say, and the Magic Car Wash is based on the roundabout (rotary) where several main roads come together. However, I am convinced that this is not the only answer.

My excuse is that my bad back plays up when I try to wash the car wheels but the main reason I go to this car wash is to watch the team in action. The members know exactly what they are doing and no words of command are spoken. Members of the team do their bit on your car, help each other and then move on to the next car – wheels, glass, shampoo, rinse, shampoo again, wash over, dry, collect the money and then out on the road again. Take a hard right at one point and the team is all over the inside as they vacuum the carpets, polish the inside glass, dust the fascia and clean the upholstery. A bit more expensive and takes a bit longer but many folk often choose this option to watch the 'car cleaning ballet' in action.

> I spoke to the manager there. By the way, he is as much a working part of the team as anyone else. He said,
>
> *It took a fair bit of time to work out the system and get the right tools and fluids. We think we have it right now and the main thing is letting the team get on with it. I give a guiding hand now and again but my main management job is really restricted to training any new people who come aboard.*

In all three cases, the essence of the success seems to be management in the background. OK, there is a system at Magic Car Wash, a good one, and there must be some very clear rules at the Re-cycling Centre, if only on health and safety grounds. However, what is equally clear, in all three cases, is that they are self-managing teams.

From what I can gather, they:

- work out their own rota
- discuss how things are done
- initiate changes in work methods
- regulate membership of the team
- help each other

… and cover for each other if someone needs an hour off. In all three cases, staff attrition seems to be very low. Absenteeism is not only virtually zero but is also managed by the team. (If you are absent when needed, the team itself will soon let you know that you are not wanted.) It is not as if cleaning, rubbish disposal and car washing are inherently attractive jobs. What makes the job attractive is the way that they are (not) managed.

Could more efficient methods be designed by a time and motion engineer? Well, possibly, but isn't that the point? If you want a group of people to work well, look after the customers and do a quality job, with low staff attrition and no absenteeism, then it appears that less management is more.

The inner game?

I expect you have heard of Tim Gallwey and his notion of the inner game.

> *In every human endeavor there are two arenas of engagement: the outer and the inner. The outer game is played on an external arena to overcome external obstacles to reach an external goal. The inner game takes place within the mind of the player and is played against such obstacles as fear, self-doubt, lapses in focus, and limiting concepts or assumptions.*
>
> *In simple terms the game can be summarized in a formula: Performance = potential minus interference, $P=p-i$. According to this formula, performance can be enhanced either by growing potential or by decreasing interference.*

Whether on a sports field, at work, or in some creative effort, we have all had moments in which our actions flowed from us with a kind of effortless excellence. Athletes have called this state, 'playing in the zone.' Generally at these times our mind is quiet and focused. But whatever it's called, when we're there, we excel, we learn, and we enjoy ourselves. Unfortunately most of us have also experienced times when everything we do seems difficult. With minds filled with self-criticism, hesitation, and over-analysis, our actions were awkward, mis-timed, and ineffective. Obviously we all would prefer to have more of the first and less of the second.

Think about it. All too often in organisations, the performance reducing *interference*, experienced as *fear, self-doubt, lapses in focus, and limiting concepts or assumptions,* is produced by management.

Examples from the telly

Three TV programmes, two new and one very old, have engaged me in ways we can learn from. All point out the fact that people create change and the system can often be simply interference.

In *Tinker Tailor Soldier Spy* with its great acting (the TV series, not the film, made in 1979, but just as good and twice as relevant today), Smiley (*Alec Guinness*) discovers the mole by patient research and a refusal to be put off by the shenanigans of the hierarchy – which is all too keen to show results whether they are real or not. Oliver Lacon (*Anthony Bate*), the Civil Servant between the Circus and the Minister, appears to be part of the hierarchy but in fact is risking much to enable ('facilitate' we might say today) Smiley to get on with the job.

In *New Tricks* (in its eighth series on TV in 2011), the retired, but hugely experienced, police officers solve cold cases; using modern technology, yes, but more using their experience, common sense and a dedication to working the details. They are led by an active Police Superintendent, Sandra Pullman (*Amanda Redman.*) Sandra is often to be found 'flying the high cover' as I sometimes call it. She spends a lot of time keeping the hierarchy off the backs of the team so they can get on with the job. The hierarchy is more interested in the politics, the appearance of success and its own PR.

I use the phrase 'high cover' as an analogy drawn from fighter operations in the 1939-1945 war. While one squadron attacked the bombers, another stayed high to cover them, ready to intercept enemy fighters: and yes, I do mean that management is often the enemy of success.

FACT NOT FICTION

These two programmes are fiction[164]. They are still important if only as a counter-weight to so many programmes that show management as a matter of shouting at people. However, a really important reality TV series, from the point of view of management, was *'Can Gerry Robinson fix the NHS?'* a programme developed with staff from the Open University. Now, if you have not seen this three part series, you absolutely must find a way of doing so. It has been released on DVD.

Sir Gerry Robinson worked with an NHS Foundation Trust, based at Rotherham General Hospital. The hospital, with an annual budget of £140m, 3,300 employees and more than 400,000 patients a year, is a successful one. It achieved three-star status for four consecutive years. The three episodes form a fascinating insight into the inner workings of the NHS and a large modern-day hospital. The cameras show a hard-working, dedicated staff with the issues and situations that form their busy working lives.

WHAT GERRY DID

I suppose you might call it a form of 'management by walking about' but it was a lot more than this. Sir Gerry went out and about in the hospital looking for what the management thinker, Eli Goldratt[165], would have called the constraints. The real chief executive of the hospital was concentrating on the big picture, not surprising given that his previous experience was in strategy and not operations. What Sir Gerry did was to look for the small but real opportunities for improvement and get the people at the coal face to suggest and create new ideas and processes.

The real CEO still misses the point. In a review, he says:

> *What disappoints me is that the main message seems to be that the chief executive should walk around a bit more and tell staff what they should be doing,*

> *and it isn't like that. It's about finding ways of incentivising staff who are frankly demoralised after years of reform. It's about stopping them being cynical and helping them to do more to look after the people they serve.*

This misses the point in two vital ways. Sir Gerry does not tell people what to do. He finds opportunities and asks questions. He invites, cajoles and encourages people to come up with ideas, to grasp the opportunities; usually ideas they have had for a long while but have felt powerless to implement. He then finds ways to facilitate these ideas; to try them out and see if they will work, right now. (Tom Peters: *'Try it, do it, fix it.'*)

It is not about incentives. We should all be aware by now that extrinsic motivation drives out intrinsic motivation. We must be aware that most people in the health professions don't do it for the money. OK, so they want to be paid a decent salary and one that recognises their qualifications and dedication but, in the main, they enter the health profession to do something useful, to help people and to make a difference.

Motivation comes, therefore, not from paying people more, not from some form of pay for performance and certainly not from management by objectives but from enabling people to do what they know should be done and what they want to do anyway and which the management processes too often prevent them from doing.

The cynicism comes not from a lack of incentives. How could it? It comes from a dissonance between the words of the management and the impossibility of action. Cynicism arises, very frequently, from the obstacles that management put up, the systems that are created and do not work and the resultant doublespeak. In many organisations, what is achieved is done in spite of, not because of the system. Sir Gerry worked at that interface – and made major improvements.

Loose, tight again

It is true that management is not only about intrinsic motivation but I would argue that today it is mainly about it. I would also argue that if you want employee involvement or engagement, then the concept of intrinsic motivation is absolutely central.

CONTROL AND CREATIVITY

Yes, in any organisation there are things which need to be controlled, with varying degrees of strictness. However, there are equally many, and probably more, elements in any organisation that do not and there control will be the enemy of creativity.

Too often management thinks it is all about control. It isn't. It really, really isn't! Management is about enabling people to do good things and that comes from training, facilitation, encouragement, praise and recognition, intrinsic motivation and asking questions.

It is perhaps no coincidence that the most successful hotel company in the UK has *'be yourself'* and *'have fun'* as two of its six core values. Malmasion is tight on lots of elements within its hotels but it really concentrates on making management support their people to deliver its service, rather than command and control.

* * *

7

TOWARDS A SOLUTION I: BEING READY TO THINK DIFFERENTLY

In individuals, insanity is rare; but in groups, parties, nations and epochs, it is the rule.

Friedrich Nietzsche

The March 2009 the *Independent* reported:

Sea levels are predicted to rise twice as fast as was forecast by the United Nations only two years ago ... Rapidly melting ice sheets in Greenland and Antarctica are likely to push up sea levels by a metre or more by 2100.

It is the accelerated melting of the vast, land-based ice sheets in Greenland and Antarctica ... which is now speeding up the increase beyond anything previously forecast. The Greenland ice sheet, in particular, is ... melting

> *'dynamically' – that is, it is collapsing in parts as meltwater seeps down through crevices and speeds up its disintegration ... Professor Steffen said Greenland was losing 200 to 300 cubic-kilometres of ice into the sea each year – about the same amount as all the ice in Arctic Europe.*

The National Snow and Ice Data Center reported, September 2011, that the minimum Arctic ice extent was the second lowest in the satellite record after 2007 and continues the trend of rapidly decreasing summer sea ice happening in this decade.

This is not the place to enter the debate on global warming. However, the structure of the debate may be instructive as a major example of our ability to reject what is counter to our beliefs or wishes. As Cordelia Fine says in her book, *A Mind of its own*[166],

> *Evidence that supports your case is quickly accepted ... However, evidence that threatens (you) is subjected to gruelling cross-examination.*

Fine's book is a lively summary of the experimental evidence on brain functioning. In her introduction, Fine writes:

> *The truth of the matter ... is that your unscrupulous brain is entirely undeserving of your confidence. It has some shifty habits that leave the truth distorted and disguised. Your brain is vainglorious. It deludes you. It is emotional, pigheaded and secretive. Oh, and it is also a bigot.*

OPEN-MINDEDNESS AND FAILURE

The essence of the scientific revolution is open-mindedness. Scientific truth is based upon evidence. If the evidence is contrary to a belief or theory previously held (to put it crudely), then we must be open-minded enough to reject that belief. Maintaining a belief in the face of evidence to the contrary is a failure of open-mindedness and a failure in scientific logic.

The March 2009 newspaper carried an interview with James Lovelock who describes himself an optimist on climate change. That is as may be but some of the answers he gives to questions asked are somewhat scary. When asked whether humanity is doomed, he replies:

> *I hope not, since I have nine grandchildren. We are in for a tough time this century and beyond, but we are the toughest of animals and, more than this, we know how to adapt to change.*

Asked if there is any hope for his grandchildren, he replies:

> *I surely hope so but it may be a tough life enlivened by excitement and fear. Climate change could be deadly by the middle of the century.*

When asked about the world his grandchildren may live in, he says:

> *The post-global warming world, perhaps 100 years from now, may well be like that of the early Eocene period, 55 million years ago. At that time, most of life had moved to the Arctic where conditions were almost tropical. Once the earth settles down a bit, the survivors will have time to adapt.*

In response to a question about population, he replies:

> *When Malthus first warned of the overpopulation of the Earth in 1800, there were only one billion of us. He has been derided ever since, yet I think he was right. One billion is about the right number and I fear we will reach it not by our own choice but by attrition.*

The current population of the Earth is about 7 billion. Thus, the optimist Lovelock projects that there will be 6 billion fewer people living in 2110 and the population of the earth will be about 14% of what it is now.

To put Lovelock's remarks into context, the Eocene period began as a time of global warming. The dinosaurs died out and a great variety of birds, mammals, fish and insects took their place. The climate of Northern Canada and Greenland, for example, was temperate with abundant and varied forests growing right up to the poles. Tropical rain forests extended as far north as what is now Montreal, Minneapolis and Zagreb. At the warmest point, there was no ice anywhere on earth and crocodiles swam off Greenland.

If the Greenland ice sheet were to melt today, sea level would rise by about 7m.[167]

So OK – what was your response to this?

Think about it. Recall your thoughts and feelings. Is this what you thought?

- *That fits with what I have read elsewhere.*
- *That's very interesting - and a little frightening. Can anything be done?*
- *I am not sure about this. What do other experts say?*
- *I think I disagree. Let me evaluate the arguments more.*

Any of these responses are rational. However, suppose your response was:

- *Rubbish! It will not happen.*
- *Lovelock is a scaremonger.*
- *Global warming is exaggerated. Any effects will take thousands, not hundreds of years.*

Such responses are not as they stand rational responses.

Rubbish! It will not happen.

Of course, such an answer *could* be followed by evidence but more often it is not. It may have psychological causes rather than a rational basis. If no evidence is presented, one would like to ask, in these exact terms, 'What <u>makes</u> you say that?' Such a rejection might be caused by the scary nature of the facts. Our minds are protecting us as Fine might say. The rejection may be caused by our own wish-fulfilment; it cannot happen because we do not want it to. Cordelia Fine would say that our (deluded) brains simply deny the possibility of the event.

Lovelock is just a scaremonger.

This answer sounds as if it is capable of evidential proof. We could investigate everything else that Lovelock has said or written and see if he has in the past caused scares, deliberately or not. However, this answer is not usually meant that way. It is another form of rejection - one often termed an *ad hominen* argument. You dislike a conclusion so you attack the person who made it. (Common enough in management is it not?)

Global warming is exaggerated. Any effects will take thousands, not hundreds of years.

Well, this reply seems to be a matter of logic and evidence, of entering the debate. Scientific advance depends upon challenge and the presentation of new theories and evidence. However, is such a reaction based upon carefully sifted contrary evidence or not? Too often, we water down evidence and ideas simply because they do not fit the way that we see the world or want to see the world. This happens in management as well.

Mental filing

There are interesting parallels between the debate on global warming and the disagreements that arise in management. We frequently reject or refuse to get to grips with matters in management just as some people refuse to engage in rational discussion over global warming.

Indeed as Cordelia Fine explains, our minds work largely by filing things in what are called 'schema'. We do not have time to work everything out anew each time and so our minds categorise our perceptions and thereby a range of reactions for us. They then bring out the whole set when triggered. (This explains, for example, the prevalence of stereotypes.) The notion of global warming attacks some deeply rooted schema, possibly:

- buying a house is a very good investment
- grandchildren are highly desirable
- it is the duty of parents to give their children a better world
- the world will continue to improve
- loyalty to our country of birth is a prime virtue

If Lovelock is right, the world will not improve but get dramatically worse:

- buying a house, certainly in the Maldives or other low lying areas, including New York City, will fairly quickly turn out to be a very bad investment indeed
- bringing yet another generation into the world will increase the probability of unhappiness at best and early death at worst
- we as parents will bequeath not greater comfort but catastrophic discomfort and pain

- any attempt to prevent that part of global warming caused by humans will be prevented by the lack of a common world response

There are more simple and personal issues. I don't want to give up my car or my air travel on holiday or my central heating (and I certainly don't want to put on a heavy pullover in the evening.) These are associated with the schema such as, 'I have a right to ...'

No wonder we want to reject any arguments for global warming. The fact that we want to (and thus are often able to) dismiss such arguments as Lovelock's is a tribute to our deluded minds, and to the power of schema.

What we say and what we do

Management is full of schema; preconceived notions that control the way we manage. Much of the new writing is an attempt to break down these preconceptions and get managers to take a fresh look at management. The pity is that our ability to reject (or even avoid seeing) the need for such changes usually implies that we respond to the changes too late and only when they are forced upon us.

The fact that many managers avoid thinking about the need to think differently, is again a tribute to the protection that our minds give us. Unfortunately such protection gives short term comfort but long term pain. Often, our preconceptions are inadequate in the face of changed circumstances. We need to break them down. This is difficult. It requires what Chris Argyris has called *double-loop learning*.

Single-loop learning takes goals, values and strategies for granted. The fundamentals are not challenged but accepted and problem solving is a matter of making things more efficient within existing assumptions. *Double-loop learning* questions assumptions – the goals, values and strategies themselves.

Donald Schön - philosopher, jazz clarinettist and academic - argued[168] that we all seek to maintain a belief in the stable state, *'the unchangeability, the constancy of central aspects of our lives.'* Most organisations have what Schön calls *dynamic conservatism;* a tendency to fight to remain the same. However, technical, market and global change makes the stable state unattainable. Society and all of its institutions are in continuous processes of transformation.

BEING READY TO THINK DIFFERENTLY

Donald Schön and Chris Argyris argue that people have *mental maps* to help them respond to events. It is these maps that control people's actions rather than what they say. What we say is rather different from what we do. They suggest that two theories of action are involved. The theories that are implicit in what we do are 'theories-in-use'. What we like to think we do is 'espoused theory'.

This is an important distinction. Most company reports say somewhere that people are their greatest asset. This is not always cynicism or PR-speak, but espoused theory. Actions that cut training spend are part of the theory-in-use. Any organisation will have a theory-in-use that largely controls its actions no matter what its mission, vision, and strategy statements may say. Organisational learning is a matter of learning to surface and question these theories-in-use. (This is frequently a focus of OD.)

Schön saw that organisations can be (though perhaps not many are) learning systems. Pre-dating the idea of the learning organization[169], Schön emphasises that many companies can no longer feel the comfort of a stable base in the technologies, products or the systems built around them. Thus a company has to create change for itself, not rely on market forces.

Schön dismisses the received notion that decision making is purely rational. He says it needs to be transactional, open-ended, and inherently social. *'How do we know this?'* is an important question and may lead to the recognition that we don't. The inquirer does not stand outside the problem like a spectator; he is in it and in transaction with it.

Schön talks of how the problem or issue is 'framed' and indeed that the framing can be part of the problem. By this he means the assumptions we make in thinking about a problem and a solution. What Schön calls 'reflection-in-action' is the process of seeking to become aware of those assumptions (and what we have called schema.) As he tries to make sense of it, the agent also:

> ...*reflects on the understandings that have been implicit in his action; understandings which he surfaces, criticizes, restructures, and embodies in further action.*

The hopes and disappointment of Organisation Development

Despite the importance of the paradigm shift, or perhaps in reaction to it, today there seems to be an increase in rule-governed behaviour in management. Single loop learning is more and more prevalent. More and more we are governed by the rules of best practice; the rules say that we should do things that way and therefore we do them that way.

How correct are these rules? The rules of best practice are taken from past experience. Some are good and useful; others are not. To accept them all uncritically is to fail in scientific (and management) analysis. The past is sometimes a good guide to the future but, given the amount of change that is occurring today (and will occur even more rapidly if Lovelock is right) the past is a less and less certain guide.

Far from accepting authority and rules uncritically, we need to analyse each situation, and indeed each potential process, on its own terms and in its own time. We need to, but do not seem to be able to, change the paradigm, accept new theories-in-use and break away from the grip of the past.

As long ago as 1969, the great Warren Bennis said he saw a change under way because of new concepts (new theories-in-use):

> of *man*, based on increased knowledge of his complex and shifting needs, which replaces an oversimplified, innocent, push-button idea of man.
>
> of *power*, based upon collaboration and reason, which replaces a model of power based on coercion and threat.
>
> of *organizational values*, based on humanistic-democratic ideals, which replaces the depersonalised, mechanistic value system of bureaucracy.

In the 1960s and 1970s, the practice of OD, led by Bennis, Reddin and Blake and building on the earlier work of Kurt Lewin and Douglas McGregor, did indeed offer a dream of a new organisational world, one in which control was rejected in favour of engagement. Bennis saw management in the 1960s as essentially bureaucratic and showed how such management rarely made genuine responses to problems it faced. Instead, the organisation of the 1960s simply followed established routines, whether or not they solved the problem.

He set out the nine goals of change agents (OD practitioners) in his book *Organizational Development: its nature, origins, and prospects*.[170]

1. *To create an open, problem-solving climate throughout an organization.*
2. *To supplement the authority associated with role or status with the authority of knowledge and competence.*
3. *To locate decision-making and problem-solving responsibilities as close to the information sources as possible.*
4. *To build trust among persons and groups throughout the organization.*
5. *To make competition more relevant to work goals and to maximise collaborative efforts.*
6. *To develop a reward system which recognises both the achievement of the organization's goals (profits or service) and development of people.*
7. *To increase the sense of 'ownership' of organizational objectives throughout the work force.*
8. *To help managers to manage according to relevant objectives rather than according to 'past practices' or according to objectives which do not make sense for one's area of responsibility.*
9. *To increase self-control and self-direction for people within the organization.*

So where are we today? Did Bennis's dream come to reality? Did OD work? In a few places and organisations perhaps. In most Western organisations, it is as if new thinking is considered wrong, perhaps even dangerous. It is as if management actively rejects genuine attempts at creativity and double loop learning, seeing it as disruptive, as a nuisance and even as disloyal.

Management is a serious matter

Management is a serious matter and requires a curious and open mind. To attempt to do a management job on auto-pilot, so to speak, is to really reinforce the power of our pre-conceptions. Successful management (like a successful marriage) does not just happen. It needs thinking about and working at.

We avoid thinking about things we do not find interesting and management seems to be in this category. Perhaps this is a sign of the age, that many people have ceased to find interesting anything serious.

> A number of students at a religious American University were invited to list their interests. Number one was *laughing* and number two, *snowboarding*. Given that this is a religious institution, it may be a surprise to find that *bible reading* ranked only 62nd, below *golf, flying, horses* and *acting*. The activity, if such it be, of being a *friend of God* ranked immediately below *playing with Lego* at 64th. *Politics* do get a mention at 69th while *counter-espionage* the next serious (?) interest - comes in at 169th. *Praying for people* received the same (low) number of mentions as *eBay*.

To find management theory boring is an admission that one is a passenger in the world rather than a player. You just cannot be a good manager unless you take management seriously and this means being ready to challenge your preconceptions and to refuse to let your mind protect you from reality.

- We may wish things will stay the same but they won't.
- We may fear the future but this will not prevent it happening.
- We may wish to lean on authority but authority may well be out of date.
- We may find it comfortable to follow the rules but the rules may longer apply.

We have to recognise the mental filing that our brains indulge in and fight to un-learn and re-learn. We have to accept that the frivolous will not feed a future world or enable our companies to compete. To stick to beliefs appropriate to yesterday is to court failure.

The herd mentality

Friedrich Nietzsche wrote:

> *In individuals, insanity is rare; but in groups, parties, nations and epochs, it is the rule.*

The 2008/11 recession was caused by the inane activities of major banks, not one or two but a whole chorus line of them, all doing the same thing, making the same mistakes, ignoring the same warnings and using the same amazingly amateurish bonus systems. In writing for *The Working Manager*, I quoted the Independent newspaper[171]:

> *Standard Chartered's chief executive, Peter Sands, has become the pin-up boy of the sector. Profits and dividends for last year are up, with the bank having apparently made a stonking start to 2009. What's Standard Chartered got that others haven't? It obviously helps to have no exposure whatsoever to the over-leveraged markets of the West. Oddly for a modern bank, it never allowed itself to forget the basic principles of banking, and, surprise, these have stood it in rather good stead.*

If Peter Sands could get it right, why did the CEOs for other banks get it all so wrong; an almost complete consensus of greed, herd mentality or both?

Why do people follow the herd? Pat Thomas, general curator at the Bronx Zoo, says:

> *... individual members of a herd relate, behave in a similar fashion. And that's so that they don't stand out and appear different from their group mates. If they act too much out of the norm, more often than not they're singled out and identified by a predator - and don't survive very long.*

Fear makes animals run in herds and fear driven herd behaviour probably accounts for an awful lot of management behaviour. It is a bit like the IT manager's saying from the old days, *'No one got fired for buying IBM.'*

Research at the University of Leeds shows that it takes a minority of just five per cent to influence a crowd's direction and that the other 95 per cent follow without realizing it.[172] The findings show that in all cases, the 'informed individuals' were followed by others in the crowd, forming a self-organizing, snake-like structure.

> *We've all been in situations where we get swept along by the crowd, says Professor Krause. But what's interesting about this research is that our participants ended up making a consensus decision despite the fact that they weren't allowed to talk or gesture to one another. In most cases the participants didn't realize they were being led by others.*

So many managers follow the herd. They do things because other managers do; even when there is evidence that what they are doing is bad for their companies.

AVOIDING THE HERD

Writing for *The Working Manager*, Charles Lines characterises management herds as follows:

> *The herd is ... very comfortable with where it is going. It does not want any doubt cast on the direction it has chosen. The team herd has a well mapped out territory. It is its stamping ground. It knows where everything is and how to get there. The territories over the hill are unknown, would take a great deal of effort to get to and could well turn out to be dangerous. So best not go there.*

Note the sentence, '*It does not want any doubt cast on the direction it has chosen.*' Charles Lines goes on:

> *The problem is that the herd, through its repeated, habitual use of the same old tracks, is slowly trampling down the vegetation that provides it with variety and goodness, turning everything dust grey. The stimulating colours of creativity and innovation are steadily being smeared away and trodden under foot. Individuals in the herd are starting to ape each other's behaviour, language and attitudes. What is frightening is that you can feel yourself becoming monochrome grey, picking up the group habits and losing your individual spark.*

To avoid herd behaviour, Charles Lines argues that teams should:

- Question the routine each and every day
- Regularly ask what the team does and what it needs to do
- Regularly ask why the team does what it does and why does it do it that way

However, the real prophylactic against herd behaviour is thought. Arkadi Kuhlmann created ING DIRECT. In Helen Kelly's interview with him for *The Working Manager*, he asks:

> *What is your contribution to productivity? What is your energy level? Your knowledge level? What are you doing to keep yourself current? How much do you read? Do you do anything that actually refreshes the base upon which your knowledge stands - or are you now basically a Blackberry brain during the week who watches football all weekend?*

Of so many employees he says:

> *It's not a fair exchange. We pay a fair wage and create career opportunities and offer to develop personal potential to the fullest in the path they're on. Yet I have to spend my time basically teaching people how to do reading, writing and arithmetic. I ask people to write a page. They go out and get a consultant. Today's world is reactive. You know: 'Don't think; just respond to email.' It has become a total mishmash of actions and reactions so there's no more time for discussion and debate; no time to contemplate and think.*

Perhaps initially surprising for a businessman, he says:

> *I believe the source of the problem is that so few people study philosophy, literature, poetry, and the classics. With philosophy as a basis, people move to psychology, writing, reading, arithmetic, and statistics. It's the level and amount of academics you study, learn and bring as a foundation to a commercial enterprise that's important.*

FINDING TALENT

Who is the talent in companies? Those who follow the herd? Or is it those who get things done; those who make a difference; those with the new ideas? The sort-of-accepted view of talent management in companies is a little disappointing. It seems all too often to be about general staff development. Deloitte's Develop-Deploy-Connect model is about:

- giving employees the opportunity to develop their skills and capabilities
- bringing out the best in their people by understanding what they are passionate about and then deploying them on assignments that align with their skills, interests and growth goals.
- recognizing that personal relationships help bind employees to the organization and create a sense of shared values and purpose.

There is nothing at all wrong with general staff development of course but presumably the idea of talent management is to identify who has the extra talent and fast track them for the good of the company. After all, observers say that the talent is usually no more than 15% of the employees.

Talent may be hidden under the proverbial bushel. So you have to go look for it. The *South Shields Gazette* reported on 21 January 2008:

> *Legendary Liverpool and England winger John Barnes has started his search for the Caribbean's best young footballing talent. Starting in Barbados, the former Celtic manager is hosting a series of soccer clinics in the region, seen as an untapped market in the world game. The region has already produced stars such as Dwight Yorke, Kenwyne Jones and Carlos Edwards.*

Gwyn Williams, the scout who discovered England captain John Terry, said:

> *John Terry? We signed him on his 14th birthday. I saw him playing for Essex county schools. He went training twice a week with them and on a Sunday played for Chelsea schoolboys.*

Talent management cannot be simply a matter of reading appraisal forms. The scout who sits back and just reads newspaper reports would not last long! Gwyn Williams again:

> *I spend almost every night of the week out and about, looking at games at different levels. On a Monday, I might watch Chelsea reserves to monitor how the next generation at the club was coming along. On Tuesday I could go to a lower league club and see who they had got there. Sometimes I would get a tip-off about a player or an agent would ring me to recommend a player. In the space of a week, I would be at an under-20 tournament in Toulon, an under-17 event in Luxembourg and then an under-21 tournament in Portugal.*

Should not talent managers in companies be spending most of the week out and about, looking at people at different levels? We might hear a talent manager say,

> *On a Monday, I might talk to a contact in training to see how the next generation was coming along. On Tuesday I could visit a contact in another company and see who they had got there. Sometimes I would get a tip-off about a person who was 'on the market' or a headhunter would ring me to recommend*

a manager. In the space of a week, I would be at conference in Toulon, an internal event in Luxembourg and then a training session in Portugal.

The talent agent

The movie, *Jerry Maguire*, as the blurbs say, is about:

> ... a typical sports agent, willing to do just about anything he could to get the biggest possible contracts for his clients, plus a nice commission for himself.

While scouts go out to find talent, often the talent has to advertise itself. Agents exist to help that talent, to market it, to exploit it, to make it rich – hence Cuba Gooding Jnr's line, *'Show me the money,'* in the movie. Agents are perhaps even more prevalent in the worlds of stage and film. As the BBC reports:

> Talent agents work on behalf of the 'creative talent' in the entertainment industry. Usually 'creative talent' means actors, directors and writers, but can also include producers, costume designers, lighting, cameramen, choreographers, composers. Basically anyone who has creative input in an entertainment project can have an agent to represent them.
>
> Primarily it is the agents' task to find work for their clients, and negotiate the fees, royalties and credit for the work.

But more than this ...

> Agents also provide moral support, send flowers on opening night, post signed photographs to fans, field enquiries from chatshows and charities, take crisis calls from film sets on the other side of the world, deny everything to journalists, fend off producers, arrange schedules, throw parties and recommend good lawyers.

OK, and that all sounds fun, but more interestingly:

> ... the role of the agent has expanded even further in recent years ... agencies are now closely involved in packaging, script development and film financing ... use their influence ... to get projects financed and made. Often agents will assist in coming up with the initial ideas - say, for a new television series - and will sell the project directly to the channel controllers or commissioning editors.

Retaining talent

Talent is said to be in short supply. Demographics, the oft commented on failure of many education systems, the apparent unattractiveness of life in the big organisation, the continuing unwillingness of many companies to embrace diversity, all seem to conspire to make filling the crucial jobs with the right people more and more difficult.

We have to think differently about talent, finding and keeping it. If the talent manager is to fulfil the objective of supplying the talent gap in a company, he or she has to be able to do – both in terms of skill and permission – more than an HR job. In fact, the roles may be diametrically opposed.

HR is primarily about systems for equity and fairness in compensation and employment. It has little to do with people as individuals but a lot to do with systems and processes. The tools of HR feature job evaluation and grading, competencies, appraisal, recruitment controls, standard terms and conditions and so on.

The talent agent is about uniqueness, individual differences, the special, about 'show me the money.' He or she has no interest in what is fair to all. The agent is interested in the best - and what is right for the untalented has no relevance for the talent he or she manages.

TRY THIS FOR SIZE

Brenda was recruited into the company because it was thought she had a special talent and so it has proved. She has shown that she has an outstanding eye for children's fashion. She works for the head of children's clothing who is a grade above her and she has no interest in management. She is paid at the top of her grade. She has just told her boss that she has been offered 25% more money to move to the competition. Her boss has checked this and it is true.

What do you do?

> *The HR response* is almost certainly to say that it is unfortunate but nothing can be done. There is no job to which she can be promoted even if she was prepared to do a management job. She is paid as much as the grade will allow and no exceptions can be made without damaging the grading system and being unfair to others.

> *The scout's response* is one of horror. He or she has discovered this outstanding talent after an enormous amount of hard work and possibly only after a great deal of persuasion has got Brenda to join the company. Now all that work seems wasted.
>
> *The talent agent's response* is to say 'Show me the money.' The agent has no interest in your personnel systems. He or she is there to find the client the best deal and if you cannot offer it, then someone else will (and has.)
>
> How much is Brenda's special talent worth to the company now and in the future? How much will it cost to replace her in her current job, if this is even possible? How much will it cost to find someone who may lead the company in the future as she may? Pay her what is necessary to keep her if the return on this investment is right.
>
> OK, so no one is supposed to be irreplaceable but at some levels such a remark is plain silly. Brenda may be as irreplaceable as they get. What do you want? A star who will lead the company forward or a bunch of less talented people thinking you are fair? (And will they think you are so fair if the company fails and they lose their jobs?)

PAY AND THE 15%

If talent is about 15% of the company and if finding it and retaining it is going to be as tough as people say, a company may need two sets of employment rules: one for the talented and another for the foot soldiers. Perhaps we need to be a little more hard-headed if we are running a talent management process. After all, as Professor David Dunning reports[173]:

> *The average person claims to be more disciplined, idealistic, socially skilled, a better driver, good at leadership, and healthier than the average person.*

… and as he points out

> *Mathematically, this cannot be right – the average person cannot be above average.*

But make sure the talent is real. In this regard, be sure to read *Fooled by Randomness* by Nassim Nicholas Taleb.[174] The book is about how we delude ourselves into confusing luck with skill and probability with certainty.

Taleb talks about the lucky fool - the individual who has a run of luck but thinks it is skill. When people who should know better take credit for events that they do not actually control, they are indeed fools, fooling themselves and, unfortunately, others.

RECRUITMENT FAILURE

Of all the management practices and skills, recruitment is the single most important. The other management skills will work if and only if the right people have been recruited. Jack Welch said that nothing matters more than getting the right people on the field. If you recruit the right people, then everything else is fairly plain sailing. If you recruit the wrong people, then everything becomes really hard. Recruiting the wrong people will damage a large company and can destroy a smaller one.

If a manager's job is to get things done (willingly) through people then the essence of the managerial job is to inspire, teach, develop and delegate to people of ever-increasing knowledge, skill and confidence. People can be challenged, exhorted, tested, and extended; but all this depends upon having the right people on board first - people ready to take responsibility for themselves, to challenge themselves, to take risks and stretch themselves, and to grow and develop.

Who are the right people? This is less about skills and knowledge and more about values, beliefs and commitment. You can only truly delegate to people who share your values and beliefs. To the degree that the right people are on board, to the extent that people share a common vision and hold values in common, to that degree decisions will be more easily taken and the degree of hostility to any outcome or change will be less.

The problem is that the accepted ways of recruiting don't work. Greg Call, President and CEO of Irvine, California-based Self StorageWorks, made a study of recruitment options for his own firm's purposes. He found that:

- *87% of managers believe hiring the best people should be No. 1 in terms of importance to a company.*
- *79% of managers said their companies did little to make sure hiring was a priority, even though they talked about it a lot.*

- *87% of hiring professionals did not think they were interviewing the best candidates available.*

- *81% of hiring professionals said only one-third of the people they hired performed as well as expected. Another third fell short, and the final third should never have been hired.*

It turns out that even HR managers do not believe in the processes they espouse. The *Personnel Today* magazine headline, 23 May 2006, ran:

> *HR's role in recruitment called into question by shock survey. HR practitioners view every current recruitment method for senior roles as virtually worthless.*

The magazine was reporting the *Recruitment Confidence Index* from the Cranfield School of Management which said:

- 50% of HR people use one-to-one interviews but 68% of these say they are not useful.
- 78% of the HR professionals said competency-based interviews are ineffective.
- Only 10% believed panel interviews are useful predictors of job success.
- Only 10% always use psychometric testing.
- Only 2% say that psychometric tests are very useful.
- 44% say psychometric tests are of no use at all.
- 67% of HR people found CVs poor indicators.
- 86% said written references were not useful.

The Working Manager, reporting these figures, posed readers a question. *In which year do you think the Recruitment Confidence Index was conducted: 1957, 1974, 1988, 1999 or 2004?*

It is a trick question. The *Recruitment Confidence Index* survey was undertaken during each of these years, with the same results. Lack of commitment, poor hiring systems, overvaluing presentation as opposed to performance, and using skill-based and subjective job descriptions that preclude the best people from being considered are the most historically committed hiring mistakes. How come?

Companies seem not to give much or any thought to what they are doing. Indeed the survey also reported that more than half of companies never evaluate the success or failure of their recruitment processes. When a recruitment assignment fails, they use the same (failed) methods again. Back to the herd.

DOING IT DIFFERENTLY — AND SUCCESSFULLY

Nucor, a company that has never had a layoff in over forty years in business, spends an enormous amount of time on its recruitment. Its objective is to ensure that the company hires only the right people. Nucor do not involve HR in recruitment except to process applications.

Paul Watson, a programmer at Vulcraft South Carolina in Florence, said this of interviewing with Nucor. [175]

> *From the first moment you know about Nucor because the people are so friendly. But that friendliness doesn't preclude an impressive, professional, interesting and surprisingly extensive interview process.*
>
> *Before they brought me here, we had two hours on the phone. They'd been looking for the right person for eighteen months, as it turned out, and they wanted to be sure. Once I'd been for the interview, I liked what I saw and I wanted to know more. In other words, I wanted the job.*
>
> *We did the phone interview. The Nucor plant manager interviewing me was warm, polite, and down to earth. He wanted to get to know me, and after a time I wasn't cautious about speaking my mind.*
>
> *Then they brought me here and we talked more about my background. I could see in retrospect that he really wanted to know me; to know what I'm made of. I would have a lot of responsibility to supervise the mill's accounting, purchasing, credit and collections, HR, and Information Systems functions. They were looking for mill controllers who are general managers.*
>
> *The next day I met Jim Coblin and Jim Frias and I thought: 'I'm done.' On the way home I thought: 'The job is mine, and how great that is.' But I wasn't done yet.*

The next day the plant manager called. 'We'd like to get to know you a little bit better,' he said. Better? What more is there? I asked myself. 'And we'd like your wife to have a chance to see the area. If we consider you for a position with this mill, we want to know that your family would feel content to be in this area.' So I went out again, this time with my wife, and while she went with the Real Estate agent I had another half day of interviewing and then met with some long time employees and some who were relatively new to the company.

He encouraged me to ask any questions I wanted to ask, and he told me that the employees would have no compunction about answering frankly. After a few days, the plant manager called and offered the job.

Nucor screens for people who have a strong work ethic, a high degree of intelligence and willingness to learn and grow, mechanical ability, a deep and genuine commitment to the environment, self-sufficiency and a strong sense of common purpose. They hire people who are team players and willing to help even if things don't go your way. They hire people who are articulate, curious, open to learning, and good listeners; and basically, good natured. Nucor gets to know people.

People getting to know people

The point? Think about it. The problem is that too many managers think that recruitment is a process. It seems all too often that they want the recruitment process to be an automatic application of procedures.

Successful recruitment is about getting to know people, not about systems, processes and banks of pre-prepared questions. Above all, it is not an impersonal matter. Recruitment is carried out by people. Getting the right people on board depends almost always, in the end, on a human, subjective judgement.

So how should it work? It is unlikely that the usual gamut of recruitment aids will be of much help. Most of these are designed, after all, with the old paradigm in mind. They attempt to remove the person from the process – to objectify it. Jim Collins[176] advises:

- When in doubt, don't hire - keep looking.

- Whether someone is the right person has more to do with character and innate capabilities than specific knowledge, skills or experience.

- Only with the right team on board can an organisation get to grips with the other aspects of management which will truly bring success.

SO THINKING DIFFERENTLY?

What was your reaction to the figures on recruitment quoted above? Your reaction to what I said about talent? About Nucor? Either you can pause and think about what you are doing in your company or you can simply reject what I say above. If the former, you are at least open to evidence even if you eventually decide not to change. If the latter, then the herd will welcome you as a member.

I was given a book one Christmas, a memoir of Brian Clough[177]. By the way, the person who gave it to me was Reader in Psychology at a major UK university. Now for those of you who have never heard of him let me explain. Cloughie was the legendary manager of, first, Derby County Football Club and later, even more famously, of Nottingham Forest FC.

He managed Derby County, in partnership with Peter Taylor, from June 1967 to October 1973, made them Division 2 Champions in the 1971-72 season, League Champions the following year and European Cup semi-finalists the year after that. He managed Nottingham Forest from January 1975 to May 1993. As with Derby, he took them out of the second division and made them League Champions the following year - again. (That really does not happen!) Thereafter, he made Nottingham Forest European Cup winners two years in succession (that does not happen either!) as well as winning a host of other cups and championships. He died of stomach cancer, brought on by drink, in 2004. (That does happen.)

He was deeply loved by the fans of Derby County and Nottingham Forest – and by many others outside these clubs. Fans thought he walked on water.

> *Walk on water? I know most people out there will be saying that instead of walking on it, I should have taken more of it with my drinks. They are absolutely right.*

How did he do it? Part of the reason, of course, may have been that he had been a great player himself. He had scored 197 goals in 213 games for Middlesborough and 54 goals in 61 games for Sunderland before injury ended his playing career. Both records are absolutely outstanding. Still, great managers are not always great players. Arsène Wenger and Sir Alec Ferguson were no great shakes on the field but both are outstanding managers off it. So how did Clough do it?

Clearly there was little if any management practice. There was little football theory either. He left most of the actual coaching of the players to others, making just the occasional remark. Duncan Hamilton, the author of the book, says of Clough:

> *While he didn't concern himself too much with tactics or training techniques, he did think at length about how an individual's mind worked, his likes and dislikes and how he lived his life. Having bought a player, Clough wanted more to understand the attitude of his new arrival and what made him respond positively, than to fill his head with arid tactical theories.*

The secret of his success was his deep understanding of people.

> *I can tell, from the moment I see someone in the dressing room whether he's off colour, had a row with his missus, kicked the cat or just doesn't fancy it that day. I know who needs lifting. I know who needs to get his arse kicked. I know who needs leaving alone to get on with it.*

> *It only takes a minute to score a goal, and it takes less than a minute to change someone's outlook with a word or two. That's just another form of coaching that you won't find in the manuals ... It's a special kind of coaching done only by very, very good managers – like me.*

He was not what you might call a participative manager. If a player disagreed with his decision, he and the player would

> *... talk about it for twenty minutes and then we decide I was right.*

He recognised the fear and anxiety that players felt before important matches, especially away games. He once took his team to the pub before a match at Anfield, Liverpool's home ground. He spent time making the players feel comfortable:

> *You're in the team 'cos you're good enough son.*

But most of all, he and Peter Taylor could spot talent. Not only could they develop players, they could and did discover talent in the most unlikely places. They invested time – usually their own - in looking for players. They would go to matches all over the place if they heard a whisper. Taylor would call Clough. *'I've found one.'* Clough would drop everything and go to see the player. Unknown player or not, they trusted their judgement – and it worked.

A sorry mess

Recruitment today is a bit of a sorry mess. It is as if we feel it wrong to look for talent. We have to place an advert in the paper or online no matter what. We have to go through the charade of interviewing people because the rules say so, even when we are sure that none of them is any good or that we know the right person already. We have to use external interviewers. We have to ask each candidate the same questions.

Clough and Taylor had no such inhibitions. So if you don't want to follow the herd:

- Take recruitment really seriously. You really do need the right material even if it is a bit raw. Mistakes in recruitment can and do destroy teams and even companies.

- Don't rely on interviews. Get out and see the person in action. Talk to people who know him or her. Make sure they are special.

- Recruit the right people, not just those who pass some sort of test, give a good interview, have great cvs, seem the right sort of person.

- Recruit those who add genuine value to your team: those who truly believe what you are seeking to do and will respond to your management.

- Remember that there are too many ordinary people around with ordinary minds. You are looking for those who can score goals, those with something special to offer. (Remember also that the ordinary ones usually cannot see they are ordinary.)

- Don't just wait for people to respond to job ads. Know your market and seek out those who are good, especially those who are unregarded. Actively go and look for the right people. They may well be in unlikely places.

- Invest your time in understanding what makes the team and its members tick. Understand their real talents and weaknesses. Understand their real emotions and motivations. Understand which recruit will add to that team – and why.

If, of all the management practices and skills, recruitment is the single most important, it is vital to think differently and not just follow the herd.

* * *

8

TOWARDS A SOLUTION II: AT LEAST DON'T DISENGAGE

Leadership for cultural change has passed down the ranks as it is now the local manager who will persuade their own staff to change their behaviours, values or attitudes. People will not change just because it is good for the corporation or because senior managers say so. Our research shows that it is middle managers who carry the burden of translating strategic imperatives of cultural change into persuasive stories to change the everyday behaviours, routines and mindsets of their staff.

Veronica Hope Hailey[178]

Professor Hailey, Director of the Change Management Consortium at the University of Bath, ran a study from 1993 to 2001 in major UK companies on the readiness to change. She reported that over that period employee commitment to the organisation and trust in senior management both decreased while commitment and loyalty to the employee's immediate line manager was either maintained or even increased.

There is a failure of leadership at senior levels in our companies. However, while it sounds a bit odd, it turns out that if senior executives keep well out of the way, it may still be possible for middle and junior management to do something to engage employees. While employees have little if any trust in senior management, they still have some in their immediate managers.

However, it does mean managing, not doing just what everyone else does. Unthinking following of the herd produces management behaviour which actually *disengages* employees. In many cases, it seems that line management has abdicated actual management.

The Emperor's New Clothes

> *There once lived an emperor who thought of nothing but fashion. He had a coat for every hour of the day and spent most of his time getting dressed in the next suit of clothes. He thought of himself as a man of great discernment and an icon of fashion.*
>
> *One day two new tailors came to the city and declared they could make clothes from the finest cloth to be imagined. Their colours and patterns, they said, were exceptionally beautiful but would suit only those of the greatest taste and intelligence. In fact, they would be quite invisible to any one who was unpardonably stupid.*
>
> *The emperor was entranced. He summoned the tailors and ordered them to start at once to create the most wonderful suit of clothes ever made. The tailors set up their loom, shut themselves away and worked late into the night as the emperor paid them by the hour. After a while, the emperor became anxious and wanted to know how they were getting on. He felt a little uneasy because to anyone who was not of the greatest intelligence the material would be invisible. While he was sure that he personally had nothing to fear, he thought it best to first send somebody else. So he sent his oldest and most trusted minister.*
>
> *The tailors welcomed the old minister and invited him to admire the exquisite patterns and dazzling colours, invisible, of course, to anyone who was not of the highest intelligence and taste. The poor man could see nothing but dared*

not admit it because that would be admitting that he lacked ability and discernment.

'Wonderful,' said the old minister, crossing his fingers behind his back. 'Such a beautiful pattern, such brilliant colours! I will inform the emperor at once.'

The emperor was delighted and the tailors continued their work — and continued to receive their bountiful pay. After another while, the emperor's anxiety returned and he sent another courtier to the tailors. Like the old minister, the courtier could see nothing, try as he might. 'Is it not beautiful?' asked the two tailors.

'If I cannot see anything, it must mean that I am not a man of intelligence and taste and if I say this, I will lose my job,' he said to himself. So he praised the cloth which he could not see and expressed his joy at the delightful cut and the fine pattern to which he was blind. 'It is excellent,' he said to the emperor — who continued to pay the tailors.

At last the emperor would brook no further delay and the tailors were told that the suit must be ready in the morning for the emperor to wear in a great procession which was to take place next day. He promised the tailors a magnificent bonus if the suit was ready.

The next morning, the tailors came to the emperor with the old minister and the courtier who they asked to carry the clothes. The emperor disrobed and the old minister and the courtier dressed him in the new suit of clothes. 'Is it not magnificent?' they asked.

'This is terrible' thought the emperor, 'I can't see anything at all. Am I stupid? Am I not a man of discernment? What shall I do?' Swallowing and forcing himself to act calmly, he nodded sagely. 'Your cloth and suit of clothes has our most gracious approval. I shall wear it in the procession.'

'Your majesty,' objected the old minister. 'What if in the crowd there are people who lack intelligence and discernment? Might they not make remarks that your imperial self would find wounding?'

'That is a good point,' said the emperor. 'Issue a proclamation that anyone who lacks the intelligence and discernment to see and admire my new clothes will be beheaded immediately.'

> *The proclamation was therefore issued in the sternest manner possible and the imperial procession was augmented by a dozen huge guards bearing enormous and very sharp axes. So it happened that the procession wound its way through the streets of the town and all who saw the emperor exclaimed, 'The emperor's new suit is wonderful! How well it fits him!' Never were new clothes more admired.*
>
> *Just then a child, who had no important job to lose and who could not read proclamations, cried out. 'But he has nothing on at all. The Emperor is naked.'*
>
> *'Fool!' hissed his father. 'Do you want your head chopped off? Don't talk nonsense!' He grabbed his child and hurried him away. Fortunately for both of them, no one took any notice.*

This story has been told by many people. There are versions in Sri Lanka, Turkey and India, medieval Spain and Arabia. The version best known in the West is that written by Hans Christian Andersen. His ending is different.

> *Around the crowd, one person whispered to another what the child had said. The sound grew, 'But he has nothing on at all,' cried at last the whole people. 'The boy is right! The Emperor is naked! It's true!'*
>
> *The Emperor realized that the people were right but could not admit it. He decided to maintain the illusion that anyone who couldn't see his clothes was either stupid or incompetent. So he marched stiffly in the procession, while behind him a page held his imaginary mantle ... and the chamberlains walked with still greater dignity, as they carried a train which did not exist.*

Much of what happens in organisations is a matter of clothes that people are too scared to tell management do not exist; processes which management itself knows to be rubbish but seem afraid to question. Such processes not only waste time and money but actively *disengage* employees. After all, when you are up to your neck in alligators, being told to fill in another form is not welcome.

Wheels start spinning freely in a broken watch when the cogwheels no longer engage each other or when the engine of a car becomes detached from the transmission. In all walks of management life, there is a risk that wheels will start spinning freely. In management, they start spinning freely when jargon takes over or when the theory becomes an end in itself. As Peter Drucker says[179]:

> ... there is always the danger that the true workman, the true professional, will believe that he is accomplishing something when in fact he is just polishing stones or collecting footnotes.

I am sure you can think of many examples of systems and processes which disengage employees. I describe just four here:

A. Customer service and the 'system'

B. The appraisal process

C. Competencies

D. The planning process

A: CUSTOMER SERVICE AND 'THE SYSTEM'

You just come on then?
Yeah. I'm on 2 till 10. What about you?
Swing shift. I'm off at 2.30.
Lucky you!

Did you hear about Vanessa?
No. What?
She just got fired.
No! Why?
They said she didn't seem interested in the job.
Who is?

I am sure that you've been standing in a queue for the checkout and heard these and similar conversations; bored, disaffected and de-motivated staff discussing their employment issues in front of customers, giving the company a really poor image. Is it just poor quality staff or is it something more?

The truth of the matter so often is that companies who are bad at customer service have an internal focus for their systems and processes. They serve the needs of the company itself and not of the customer.

Gabriella O' Rourke, writing for *The Working Manager*, asks how many organisations truly write their business materials, build their products and deliver their services with the interests and aspirations of their customers in mind. If they do not, then it becomes impossible for staff to truly deliver customer service and employees quickly recognise that. Engagement? No, the talk of customer service becomes a force for disengagement.

The system is the system. You will follow it whether you like it or not. At Alton's Garden Centre in Essex, UK, there is an indoor and an outdoor area for shopping. At the door from the indoor to the outdoor areas there is a check-out with a bouncer who challenges customers trying to exit with items in their trolleys.

> *'Have you paid for those?'*
> *'No. I haven't finished shopping yet. I want to get some things from outside over there.'*
> *'It doesn't work like that.'*

The customer cannot continue shopping outside and pay for everything at once. Instead he or she has to join a long queue to pay at the indoor checkout and then another long queue to pay at the outdoor checkout - assuming they haven't already abandoned their trolley in frustration.

'It doesn't work like that.' Isn't this a wonderful way to treat customers? The system comes first and the customer's needs a long way second. The bouncer's message is the old favourite, *'I don't make the rules. I just enforce them. Don't blame me if you don't like it.'*

Isn't it wonderful that a company employs a bouncer to force customers to obey their system? When the system is inconvenient or irksome for the customer, change the system. If you don't, you have to employ bouncers who can work without empathy or caring for others - and there are a lot of garden centres in Essex.

> Angus Gordon[180] analyses the notice seen on stations in the UK: *Don't take it out on our staff*. He says that what 'it' refers to is left to the reader to work out. And there are a lot of different ways to fill in the gaps in this sentence, none of them very flattering to the railway company.
>
> > *We know we are useless, but don't take it out on our staff.*
> > *Sure, your train is running late for the third day in a row, but don't take it out on our staff.*

So often it has little or nothing to do with the employees themselves. The problems are caused by system failures, by management decisions, insufficient staff and resources and so on - but it is the employees who feel the brunt of the public's ire. Engaged staff? Difficult to feel happy with employment that causes customers to insult and abuse you. The natural reaction is for staff to circle the wagons and see both customers and management as the enemy.

O'Rourke says that when all is said and done, more is SAID than DONE and customers and staff know it. They have heard many promises of value added solutions, superior customer service and proactive advice. The truth is that if actions speak louder than words, they have to experience the difference.

> Fair enough, sometimes changing the system is impossible. Sometimes it is totally out of your control. So do you do nothing or do you do what the cruise terminal in Vancouver does?
>
> Almost all the cruises leaving Vancouver enter US territorial waters and visit US ports. As such, anyone who goes aboard the cruise ship has to go through US Customs & Border Protection. This is a decidedly unpleasant experience and could easily lead to those of less than average patience saying something they (and the cruise line) will subsequently regret. So the terminal authorities have used some imagination and have employed a number of retired ladies, dressed in what is very obviously a Canadian uniform, to act as buffers.

> The unspoken message is, '*We know getting through US immigration can be a very off-putting experience and we don't want your holiday to start on a sour note. So here is your own personal assistant to smooth the way.*'
>
> The ladies take you aside; give you the forms; explain how to complete them; tell you that '*Yes, you do have to put your name and address in three time but just bear up and it will be over soon.*' They smile constantly; escort you to the US officials and get you though. Afterwards they meet you again and say, '*There. That wasn't so bad was it?*' In fact it was awful but the ladies are so nice, you don't want to upset them.

That is doing something.

YOUR CALL IS IMPORTANT TO US

It used to be possible to telephone a company. It is becoming increasingly difficult with the advent of what are known as interactive voice response systems (IVRs). What is the impact on employees? They have to talk to customers who are already annoyed by the telephone answering maze. They have to face emotions which are not of their making but which are upsetting and challenging. They have to attempt to justify a system which they themselves abhor. Do they feel engaged? No, they feel put upon.[181]

As John Seddon says[182], the problem with many call centres has been that they not only annoy customers and make employees' lives miserable, they are also frequently a herd response with little value. Take a typical example of one call centre design, one concerning computers.

> The customer calls the centre, is put into an IVR and asked to choose whether the problem is hardware, software, printer, monitor etc. The choice having been made, the customer is routed to a diagnostic group who decides what action is to be taken and then routes the action to a controller who decides what parts are required and which engineer is available to handle the matter. The engineer collects the parts, visits the customer and fixes the problem.

Simple. The IVR gets the customer to the right place, the diagnosticians, being experts in their area, diagnose the problem and the controller gets the right parts and the engineer together to fix things. Costs are controlled because only the right parts are released, only the right engineer is despatched and only those problems which the diagnosticians are experts in reach them. Great. Costs are further controlled by the diagnosticians being given set target times for a diagnosis; monitors taking no more than 8 minutes, servers allowed up to 20 minutes.

Did it work?

Work? Of course it didn't. Fifteen percent of calls were repeated calls, indicating the original solution had not provided the right fix. If customers routed themselves to the wrong diagnostic group, they were put to the back of the queue in the right group. (Otherwise their figures would have looked bad.) Over half the calls were re-worked by the controllers, who were more experienced than diagnosticians. Engineers were able to resolve customers' problems only 40% of the time. Engineers would often swap a part as directed by the diagnosticians even when they could see this would not fix the problem. It would look to the customer as though something was being done. In short, only 30% of the work flowed cleanly from start to finish with no re-work or other forms of waste. Rational? No. Controlling costs and activity? No. Measuring the right things? Absolutely not.

The thing to measure is whether the customer gets his or her machine fixed and the overall costs of achieving that end. Using this apparently rational system meant that only 30% of the time the system worked well and that only 60% of customers' problems were ever fixed.

> In a UK bank, the organisation and methods personnel had measured the volumes and durations of telephone calls into the bank's branches. This sized the work. They moved this work to three new call centres, routing all the phone calls to the new centres and making the surplus branch staff redundant, replacing high cost with low cost staff.

> However, because of higher than anticipated demand, managers added another call centre and then another. When they got to five call centres the chief executive started to express concern about costs. Managers rationalised the reason for the unanticipated volume of calls.
>
> They claimed customers must be enjoying the service and were making more use of it. They compared their experience to that of the advent of the M25. Just as this motorway had experienced unexpected volumes of traffic when it opened, their call centres were attracting unanticipated demand. [183]

There are two broad types of demand on any service centre. Value demand is what the service centre exists to serve. It represents the demands customers make for things they want, things that are of value to them. Failure demand is created by the organisation not working properly. Seddon defines it as *demand caused by a failure to do something or do something right for the customer.*

Such failures to do something – turn up, call back, send something that is anticipated and so on – causes the customer to make a further demand on the system. A failure to do something right – not solve a problem, send out forms that customers have difficulties with and so on - similarly creates demand that represents extra work.

> Failure demand is a major form of sub-optimisation. In the case of the bank, failure demand was 46% of the total volume of demand. That's how the bank got to five call centres. Nearly half the calls were failures - not great for customers or staff.

How do staff feel?

Do the call centre people feel engaged? Do the engineers, swapping a part as directed by the diagnosticians even when they know this will not fix the problem, feel engaged? The system is so often the emperor's clothes. The fact that it seems logical does not mean that it is – and the criterion of an effective system is not its apparent logic but its impact on customers and staff.

> I have spoken of Jan Carlzon who became head of the Scandinavian Air System (SAS), an airline which in common with most others, was losing money. However, while other airlines went on to lose even more, SAS returned to profitability and became airline of the year. Carlzon's approach was customer service which he achieved by empowering the front line staff. Carlzon reversed the normal pyramid view of organisations that shows the boss at the top and the people who actually meet customers at the bottom. In Carlzon's view, the only justification for management is that it should enable and facilitate the people in customer contact to do their jobs well. He drew the chart with himself at the bottom, the customer at the top and the customer contact people just below them - a reverse pyramid.

B: THE APPRAISAL PROCESS

Think about your appraisal system. Does it add value to the company or does it get in the way? Is it just another example of an emperor with no clothes? In his iconic article for Fast Company, *'Why We Hate HR'*, Keith H. Hammonds asks: [184]

> *Why are annual performance appraisals so time-consuming - and so routinely useless?*

He reports a 2005 survey by consultancy Hay Group which concluded that:

> *... just 40% of employees commended their companies for retaining high-quality workers. Just 41% agreed that performance evaluations were fair. Only 58% rated their job training as favorable. Most said they had few opportunities for advancement - and that they didn't know, in any case, what was required to move up. Most telling, only about half of workers below the manager level believed their companies took a genuine interest in their well-being.*

Michael Landa, writing in the *Canadian Manager* in 1999, said:

> *... it has been an article of faith that investment in employee performance appraisal has contributed significantly to increased worker productivity.*

However, he goes on:

> *For most employees, appraisal is at best a highly stressful process with little or no perceived connection to their compensation. At worst, employees see it as a figurative whip in the hands of management. The appraisal process has become little more than a pro forma. Employees and their supervisors often find appraisal both painful and demotivating.*

As Keith H Hammond famously says:

> *Companies are doing it to protect themselves against their own employees. They put a piece of paper between you and employees, so if you ever have a confrontation, you can go to the file and say, 'Here, I've documented this problem.'*

No connection to compensation, highly stressful, a management whip, painful and demotivating? And this is not just a recent view. In the *Harvard Business Review* as long ago as July 1959, Rensis Likert wrote:

> *The aim of reviewing the subordinate's performance is to increase his effectiveness, not to punish him. But apart from those few employees who receive the highest possible ratings, performance review interviews, as a rule, are seriously deflating to the employee's sense of worth. Not only is the conventional performance review failing to make a positive contribution but ... it can do irreparable harm.*

Appraisals simply do not work. It is not just that they add no value to a company, they actively damage it. The seminal article is from the 1965 *Harvard Business Review* by Herbert Meyer, Emanuel Kay, and John French Jr, a study on the effectiveness of performance appraisal systems at General Electric.

They found that performance appraisals more often than not eroded rather than improved performance. They added that employees tend to ignore positive comments in appraisal interviews, viewing them largely as a cushion for negative points. Such negative comments make employees defensive and the more criticism they hear, the more their performance declines after the appraisal. Most importantly they found that employees believed that negative points are not made with any interest in helping them improve their performance but only to justify a low raise in pay.

More recent research conclusions bear this out:

- 50% of respondents claim that appraisals have no positive effect on the workforce. (Industrial Society)

- 43% of employees say performance appraisals do not serve any purpose. Despite 71% of all workers in the survey receiving a regular performance appraisal, 50% of all employees said that they had no real feedback on how they were doing. 77% said that appraisals are tangential to performance. (Bayt.com)

- 87.6% of employees have various kinds of complaints about their internal performance management system while 83.2% of the managers confessed that their performance would not be affected at all if their performance management system was abandoned. (Price Waterhouse Coopers Consulting)

- Appraisals fail to motivate employees. 90% of respondents to a survey cite employee motivation as one of the main objectives of appraisal. Not a single survey respondent stated that appraisal was a very good way of doing this. (Consultants Saville & Holdsworth)

- Performance appraisal decreases motivation in public sector workforces. Appraisal is particularly ineffective for those whose motivation is intrinsic. (Professors Seong Soo Oh and Gregory B Lewis, Georgia State University)

The Watson Wyatt Worldwide study[185] of 2,004 Canadian workers found that:

- 43% said their performance was rated unfairly

- 40% of employees said they did not understand the measures used to evaluate their performance

- Only 19% reported a clear, direct, and compelling linkage between their performance and their pay

- Only 42% reported regular, timely performance reviews

- Only 47% said that their managers clearly expressed goals and assignments

- Only 37% said that their manager talks with them regularly about performance related issues

Appraisal expert Bill Robb says that many people have terrible experiences when being appraised, that they generally think appraisals are a stick for management to beat them with and see appraisals as threatening events. Employees feel their pay-rises and continued employment depend on performing well in a short interview and worry about appraisers who may not like them.

He argues that most appraisers know that appraisal interviews are just bureaucracy and that the company doesn't intend doing anything with the information gleaned from them. Many appraisers treat appraisals as a time-waster - to be completed and forgotten as quickly as possible.

There is a view that it takes an organisation six months to recover from an appraisal round and that individual performance decreases after an appraisal. Far from increasing motivation, appraisal lowers it.

Inaccurate and costly

Appraisal judgements appear to have little accuracy. Studies carried out by Gary P. Latham, Marie-Helene Budworth, Basak Yanar and Glen Whyte suggest[186] that the best predictor of a performance rating is the past performance of the evaluator rather than the effectiveness of the person being assessed. Smart employees would be wise to find a boss who is seen as stellar within the organization. They found that:

> *A manager who receives a favorable performance appraisal subsequently evaluates the performance of another significantly more positively than a manager who receives an unfavorable performance appraisal.*

(You want to improve matters by using a 360 degree feedback system? Watson Wyatt's 2002 *Human Capital Index®* lists 360 as one of the three HR practices most associated with a decrease in financial performance.)

Writing for *The Working Manager*, Fred Nikols says of appraisals:

> *The costs are extraordinary and many of the supposed benefits cited do not withstand serious scrutiny. If you do scrap your company's performance*

appraisal system you will do more than realize a sizable cost saving, you will also, in one bold move:

- *unfreeze your organization's culture*
- *eliminate one of the chief structural obstacles to any changes you and your management team might be contemplating.*

He warns:

The one thing you should not do is listen to those who will implore you to let them redesign the performance appraisal system to make it more supportive of the changes you have in mind. As Craig Brooks, the director of a Winona, Minnesota human services organization and a 26-year veteran of performance appraisal redesign sessions claimed, 'I could retire on the salary I earned during those meetings.'[187]

What are appraisals for?

Here are some claimed uses of appraisals together with what is said about them.

A formal, recorded and regular review of performance

77% of responders say that appraisals are tangential to performance. 46% do not believe that appraisals in their company lead to improved performance while 31% say that appraisals only occasionally do. Only 40% of employees say they understand the measures used to evaluate their performance despite appraisals. 83.2% of the managers confess that their performance would not be affected at all if their performance management system were abandoned.

Annual pay and grading review

Only 19% report a clear, direct, and compelling linkage between their performance and their pay while 43% say their performance was rated unfairly. Employees see negative feedback as only a way to justify low pay rises.

To set objectives (delegation of tasks)

Only 47% say that their managers clearly expressed goals and assignments.

To provide constructive feedback

Only 37% say their manager regularly discusses performance related issues. Despite 71% of all workers in the survey receiving a regular performance appraisal, 50% of all employees said that they had no real feedback on how they were doing. Employees tended to ignore the positive comments and viewed them largely as a cushion for the negative points. Negative comments tended to make employees defensive. The more criticism they heard, the more their actual performance declined after the appraisal.

To motivate staff

Research has found that performance appraisals are of questionable value and, more often than not, erode rather than improve performance. In particular it has been found that performance appraisal decreases motivation in public sector workforces. Appraisal is particularly ineffective for those whose motivation is intrinsic. 90% of respondents to survey cite employee motivation as one of the main objectives of appraisal. Not a single survey respondent stated that appraisal was a very good way of doing this. There is a strong view that it takes an organisation six months to recover from an appraisal round. Far from increasing motivation, performance appraisal lowers it for half the year.

For attitude and behaviour development

Many people being appraised have had terrible experiences when being appraised and think appraisals are a stick for management to beat them with. For most employees, appraisal is at best a highly stressful process.

For training needs analysis, career and succession planning

Most appraisers know that the company doesn't intend doing anything with the information gleaned from them. Many appraisers and appraisees treat appraisals as a time-waster to be completed as quickly as possible and think they are introduced by the Personnel Department to justify its own existence - merely form-filling to keep senior management happy.

So, given that the Emperor has no clothes, let's cease to pay the charlatans who are pretending to make the cloth. Let's avoid de-motivating and de-engaging people through the appraisal process. That's what Apple did. They stopped all appraisals in 2000.

C: COMPETENCIES

It is difficult to avoid the feeling that the wheels are disengaged when people talk about competencies. What are they? Let us start with the definition given by the Office of Human Resources in the US Government.

> *Competencies are a set of behaviors that encompass skills, knowledge, abilities, and personal attributes that, taken together, are critical to successful work accomplishment.*

The consulting firm, Opinion Research, in the UK says:

> *Competencies describe the knowledge, skills and attitudes necessary to achieve job objectives.*

while the Cultural Human Resources Council of Canada says:

> *The Competency Profile enumerates the full range of necessary skills as identified by a group of practitioners on the basis of their combined experience and expertise.*

What are competencies used for? The US Office of Human Resources, again, says:

> *Individual competencies are those that each employee brings to his or her function. Individual competencies are critical components of organizational competencies. If the individual competencies in the workforce are not in accord with those needed by the organization, workforce planning will point out these gaps.*

A more detailed view of the use of competencies is given by Future Learning Inc. of Canada who say that competencies are used to:

- provide a systematic approach to planning training
- customize training delivery to the individual or organization
- evaluate suitability of training programs to promote job competence

- provide employees with a detailed job description
- develop job advertisements
- interview and select personnel
- conduct performance appraisals
- target training to skills that require development
- give credit for prior knowledge and experience
- focus on performance improvement
- promote ongoing employee performance development
- identify employee readiness for promotion
- guide career development of employees
- develop modular training curricula that can be clustered as needed
- develop learning programs

One or two of these sound a bit circular – using competencies to *'evaluate suitability of training programs to promote job competence'* - and there is a bit of an oddity in the objective *'provide employees with a detailed job description,'* but there you go. Jargon is often an end in itself.

The general trend is clear. Competencies are 'what you have to be able to do' and 'what you have to know' in order to do a job. So the idea of competencies is to ensure that an organisation recruits, trains, promotes and manages its people towards the goals of the organisation – the competencies being, in theory at least, derived from these goals.

Is it new?

Is this really new? Well, very few things in management are really new. The golden age of the development of management theory – from perhaps the early 1940's to the mid 1960's – probably said it all and companies have long spoken of job descriptions and person specifications.

> Traditionally, a job description lists what the job is for, what duties it contains, the limits of its authority and so on. A job description exists to show an employee what he or she will be expected to do in a job and to enable a company to see that each job has a purpose
>
> Traditionally also, a person specification is a list of the experience, skills and knowledge which a job holder needs to be able to do the job well. It would not seem that there is much of a difference between the job description/person specification analysis and that of competencies.
>
> I am not saying that the creation of job descriptions and person specifications was or is consistently carried out. Indeed, it has always seemed to me that the main impetus for writing a job description has always been to get the job graded, after which the need to update it is conveniently forgotten until the job holder seeks an another upgrade.

RESEARCH OR WHAT?

How are competencies established? Bernadette Allen, President of Future Learning Inc. in Canada, says that:

> *Competencies are developed based on information collected by studying what top performers do in the defined job context. Competencies focus on the attributes that separate the high performers from the rest of the workforce.*

She says:

> *Information can be gathered in a variety of ways, including employee questionnaires, focus groups, and interviews with managers and employees.*

Cultural Human Resources Council of Canada says that it

> *... has chosen the DACUM (Developing A CurriculUM) model to conduct competency analysis. One of the key features of DACUM is to rely on a group of practitioners to review all the competencies required to function effectively in a given occupation.*

So there are at least two ways to decide what competencies are required in a job. You can:

- research what people who are good at the job know and are able to do
- ask people who know about the job to tell you what is needed to do it well.

The first method is what researchers of selection tests ought to do. They should select a group of high performers and get them to complete a battery of tests to see how high performers score on them. They should also select a group of low performers and contrast their scores with those of the high performers. (They ought really to select a group of average performers as well.) If the tests differentiate, the difference between the high and low performers is reflected in the difference in the scores on the tests.

It is the same with competencies. To isolate the skills and knowledge that are necessary to be a top performer in a job, it will be necessary to measure both high and low performers and identify and isolate the knowledge and skill differences.

Does it work?

Well, it certainly could but it is not as easy as all that. When you are trying to find out whether a battery of tests will work in recruitment, you are trying to discover whether an independent variable (the test) will co-vary with the dependent variable (performance.) That is to say, you are seeking to discover whether a high score on the test battery is correlated with high performance and low score on the test battery with low performance. (I simplify.)

It is not always easy to measure performance, even sales performance which is usually shown in numerical terms. You have to allow for experience in the job, recency of training, the nature of the sales territory, the market position of the product and so on. You can indeed often allow for all these, but it tends to mean that you need a very big sample.

In a job which, unlike most sales jobs, does not have numerical measures, you have to set up some independent criterion of 'doing a good job.' Not only is this more difficult than it sounds, it often comes down to subjective considerations of managers' opinions or performance appraisal records.

And jobs change, perhaps today faster than ever before. With selection testing and competencies, the dependent variable can, and often will, change on you and when it does, the skills and knowledge required for the job change as well.

> I remember well a study that we did in Xerox many years ago on sales people recruitment. It was a very detailed study that took a long (a very long) time and the results of it were a set of tests which did indeed seem to indicate which candidates were most likely to make a success in the Xerox sales force (at that time.)
>
>> A couple of years later, when I had left HR and was in line management, my successor came to me and said, almost accusingly, *'Those tests you developed. They don't work!'* Actually, I was not surprised and had in fact already dropped a note to my erstwhile boss, indicating that I thought HR should stop using the test battery. Why? Because the dependent variable had changed.
>
> Instead of selling copying machines (then called 'box selling'), the sales force had now been asked to build copy volume on already installed machines. It was a different job and I could see from the results in my own sales teams that different people were succeeding. To use the test battery in the new circumstances, the company ought to have re-validated the study, choosing a new cohort of sales people successful in the new selling situation and contrasting them with people less successful, looking again at the test results. To do this would have meant starting the whole research process over again – another long, very long period of time. It was simpler to drop the idea and the tests, which is what they did.

THE WALLY WALLINGTON EFFECT

Competencies are rarely set by genuine research. At best they are set by a panel of experts.

I very much hope that no one would use a panel of experts to research and develop a test battery for recruitment! However, it is clear that organisations do use panels of experts to develop competencies (lists of skills and knowledge required.) Again going back to Xerox days, I remember my time in Marketing. We were about to launch a new machine, very different from anything we had marketed before; much bigger, much faster and much more complex. A group of us, experts all, were asked to come up with the profile of the sales people who should be selected and trained to sell this new machine. We worked very hard on this.

It was a good team and we worked well together. In not too much time, we prepared a list of the education, experience, knowledge and skills required of people who should be selected (the competencies if you like.) We thought that they ought to have good education in mathematics and finance, systems experience, wide product and customer knowledge, ability to work with IT departments and print rooms and so on.

The most successful sales person with the new machine was dear Wally Wallington. Now I fear gathered to the great sales *No. 1 Club* in the sky, Wally was the antithesis of our list of competencies. To give you the idea, when on the beach during his numerous, and even constant, attendances at sales award conventions, he was usually to be seen dressed in trousers (pants) rolled up to his knees, normal dress shirt with braces (suspenders) over the top and a handkerchief, knotted at the corners, on his head. (Actually, he was the most lovely man but he had no obvious mathematical skills or systems experience, nor was there any evidence of his working with IT departments or print rooms.)

Experts can be wrong – and they can certainly overdo things.

RESULTS?

What are the results of competency studies? Well, a large scale study on teachers is reported by Dr Anne M. Jasman of the Australian Institute of Education at Murdoch University in Western Australia[188]. With due respect to Dr Jasman, the list that the study came up with is not enlightening. For example, the list for Level 3 Classroom teachers was:

- Utilise innovative and/or exemplary teaching strategies and techniques in order to more effectively meet the learning needs of individual students, groups and/or classes of students.

- Employ consistent exemplary practice in developing and implementing student assessment and reporting processes.

- Engage in a variety of self-development activities, including a consistent high level of critical reflection on one's own teaching practice and teacher leadership, to sustain a high level of ongoing professional growth.

- Enhance other teachers' professional knowledge and skills through employing effective development strategies.

- Provide high level leadership in the school community through assuming a key role in school development processes including curriculum planning and management and school policy formulation

I mean there is nothing wrong with this list – apart from its use of words such as 'exemplary' and 'high level' which do not describe but evaluate - but did it need a study to formulate? If it is not a dazzling glimpse of the obvious, it comes close.

The Cultural Human Resources Council of Canada carried out a study of competencies for Cultural Export Professionals. The study came up with a set of 'professional' competencies:

- assess export readiness
- research export markets and issues
- develop a strategic export plan
- finance export projects
- develop a marketing strategy
- negotiate contracts and agreements
- manage projects
- cultivate relationships

... all of which sound a lot more like components of a job description. The general competencies they arrived at were (wait for it!): *'Communicate and demonstrate personal skills.'* Not exactly earth-shatteringly original is it? Did we need a research study to come up with this either?

One cannot escape the view that the wheel is spinning freely here. The overwhelming sense is one of bathos. The study is described in scientific-sounding terms, even written largely in that specific style that academics choose, expectations are raised and then the result is disappointing: obvious, uninspiring or even wrong: not justifying the effort put into it. As Drucker says, someone has been *'polishing stones or collecting footnotes.'*

> The Council members break down what they mean by communication. They say, perhaps not with the greatest originality, that communication is composed of oral and written communication. Oral communication, according to this study, implies the ability to:
>
> - Give clear directions/instructions
> - Explain complex issues/material in plain language
> - Make one-on-one presentations
> - Make presentations to small groups
> - Make presentations to a large audience
>
> None of which is very interesting and, if you read most of the guidance on communication and selling, all almost entirely wrong. For example, listening is usually taken to be the major skill in communicating and indeed selling.

Genuine research?

Of course, the number of competency sets in management which are genuinely researched or even the result of a panel of experts can be numbered on the metaphorical fingers of no hands. Most competency sets are created not by research and certainly not by research of the form that we have described. Most competencies are merely the opinion of their authors, following on from statements in other organisations and heavily edited by political concerns. The most important criterion in setting out competencies is what the senior management will accept or what makes them feel good.

Consequently, there is no evidence that the *knowledge, skills and attitudes* contained in the competency sets, have any relevance to the job or job level under consideration.

> The chairman of one major organisation completed an appraisal form for one of his direct reports by ticking the '*Fully*' box against all the attributes listed on the appraisal form – such as '*Does this person consult with members of his team?*' and '*Does this person seek the creative ideas of everyone involved?*' Then, at the foot of the form, under the heading '*weaknesses*', he wrote '*Getting results.*'

Remember that the herd will emphasise doing the right things (defined as what everyone else in the herd says is right) more than doing things right. With unconscious humour, the then head of Learning and Development at John Lewis said of her work to create an appraisal system for the company based upon 'behavioural indicators' – competencies under another name:

> *We needed to emphasise the importance of behaviour rather than outcomes. But there became an increasingly popular view that someone can be a great manager (in terms of the behaviours) and still not achieve adequate results … so at more senior management levels there's been a move toward changing the balance, giving more weight to performance measures to get a better balance with behaviours.*

In other words, the correlation between the competencies that her system called for and getting results was imperfect to say the least. It seems that it was largely inversely proportional. There was no evidential basis to the behavioural indicators.

Such unscientific thought frequently leads to management competencies being expressed in a way that only a superhero (and a self-contradictory one at that) could fulfil them all. For example, and this is a genuine example, consider the situation of a manager expected to:

- give clear direction
- set clear priorities
- set day to day targets
- act with a sense of urgency
- work with speed and accuracy
- always meet deadlines
- communicate with passion

and at the same time:
- consider all the facts before making a decision
- be open to different ways of doing things
- encourage open communication
- always listen carefully to the views of others
- be tolerant of all views
- seek opinions of other people

Managers who operate with the first set of skills rarely if ever operate with the second. The skills sets are, if not incompatible, the next best thing to it. What would a manager or employee think when faced with such a contradiction?

So what is the reality of management competencies?

They would be of some use if there were a real correlation between the competencies and effective management performance. That would let managers know what to do and let employees know what they could expect of their managers and indeed what to learn themselves to get promotion. However, since any correlation is accidental at best, they do not serve such purposes.

This Emperor has no clothes. Except for some very specific jobs, competencies have no use whatsoever. The few jobs they are useful for are typically those which have clearly observable behaviours or skills[189] which can be directly tested for. Management is not one of these.

Are they of any use to line managers? No. Are they of any use to employees? No. And when unresearched competencies (and worse) are used to create systems in which employees have to jump through irrelevant hoops to be thought ready for promotion, another source of disengagement occurs.

What is the impact of competencies on employees? It is negative. It is another layer of nonsense which impedes performance, takes up time that no one has and reinforces the view that they are just another stick to beat people with.

D: THE PLANNING PROCESS

The massive effort put into the annual planning round, the massaging of figures just to arrive at the answer that management wanted in the first place and the dishonesty that it creates are all part of disengagement. Remember what Kenichi Ohmae says in *The Mind of the Strategist*[190]:

- *Corporate strategy has as its aim to alter the company's strength relative to that of its competitors in the most efficient way.*

- *Such a process is as much about insight and intuition as it is rational, to combine, synthesise or reshuffle previously unrelated phenomena in such a way that you get more out of the emergent whole than you have put in.*

- *Most people in big companies have forgotten how to invent. Invention is crucial because success lies in creating sustaining values for the customer far better than those of competitors. It therefore means first of all invention and the commercialisation of invention.*

As Professor Robin Stuart-Kotze has said, writing for *The Working Manager*:

> *The economic environment in the western world has remained relatively stable, certainly since the second world war, and arguably since the mid-nineteenth century - stable in the sense of steady growth (barring periodic depressions and recessions, all of which have been of a temporary nature and have not significantly affected the basic structures of economies and organisations), of steady progression of technology, and of steady progression of knowledge.*
>
> *A relatively stable environment is compatible with the role of 'stewardship' - to keep things on course; to maintain consistency; to protect the investment in procedures and systems that forms the backbone of any organisation; and to make sure that things run as they were designed to run. Stewardship believes in, and relies on, planning. The Steward is uncomfortable without a clear plan; without a clear view of the future and the role of the organisation in that future. After World War II, the view of the future had a marvellous predictability to it, and so began the Great Age of the Planner. Certainty was the goal; qualifying uncertainty and removing all possible risk was the task.*
>
> *However, as the pace of change has quickened, it has become clear, at least to some, that different behaviours are necessary to make organisations run effectively - effectively, as opposed simply to efficiently. Managing the changing, the unknown, and the unpredictable requires vision and leadership. Leadership behaviour is about changing things, about doing things differently. Ordinary management (stewardship) behaviour is about taking the given and making it work optimally. One tends to lead people and manage things.*

The idea that the manager's role is to work out a plan of action and to assign people to implement that plan, implies predictability; something which has certainly disappeared today. Plans laid in 2007 would have been meaningless by 2008. Plans laid in 2009, outlooking some form of recovery, would have been meaningless by the end of 2010. I doubt whether any planning has even been started in 2012. It is obvious that no one knows what is going to happen next.

> *The Governor of the Bank of England, Sir Mervyn King, said November 2011,[191] that economic activity is likely to be 'broadly flat' until the middle of next year. But the MPC report also admitted that it has 'no meaningful way to quantify the most extreme outcomes associated with developments in the euro area.' The report forecasts that CPI inflation will fall to 1.3 per cent by late 2013 ... but Sir Mervyn was keen to stress the uncertainty of the inflation picture. He said: 'We do believe that inflation is likely to come down sharply next year but who knows what's going to happen tomorrow, let alone in the next 12 months.'*

Planning as setting out the sequence

Joe Kelly wrote in *How Managers Manage*[192]:

> *Planning means working out where you want to go and developing a possible sequence of events that will get you there.*

An unexceptional remark, is it not? Well, I find myself taking exception to it! I do so both because it is not specific enough and at the same time is too specific.

When my crew and I planned our annual trip with the boat to the National Championships, either of us would have been somewhat disconcerted to find the other was developing *'a possible sequence of events that will get (us) there.'* No, what we needed was a definite sequence: route, ferry booking, hotel, sails, tool kit and so on. You cannot make a possible booking on a ferry, take a possible turning in the road nor stay in a possible hotel!

Now it is true that when journeying to the Nationals, my crew and I knew where we wanted to go. That is because the class association had planned for the Nationals to be at a specific location. However, in business life, *'knowing where you want to go'* is not necessarily as easy as that and this is where I find Kelly's definition too specific. How definite can anyone be about the corporate goals in times of constant change? Robert F Waterman, in his book *The Renewal Factor*[193], says:

> *It's common for the big decisions made by companies or divisions to come as a surprise - not just to the company's competitors or the business press, but to the company itself.*

He gives examples of Wells Fargo who, he says, do plenty of planning but whose acquisition of Crocker was unplanned; of 3M's invention of the Post-it Note[194] and so on. Waterman goes on to say:

> *The big opportunities that lead to renewal, and the strategic decisions that capture them, seem more like the whimsical flight of a butterfly than the path of a carefully directed arrow.*

If the corporate goals can shift like a butterfly's flight; if where we want to go changes almost without notice, then planning as a means of working out where you want to go and developing a possible sequence of events to get you there, does not make a lot of sense.

LOGIC FAILS

In fact, there is a big difference between ordinary planning and Corporate Planning. The small scale plans that we make - to go on holiday, decorate the dining room, organise a conference or produce the corporate report - are easy to understand and cope with. They are short term, have concrete objectives, are uncontroversial, involve sequential steps and generally speaking have been done before.

Joe Kelly, writing in the 1970's, talked about strategic and tactical planning. At that time, he was able, in all seriousness, to talk about 5-10 year corporate strategies, 5-15 year R&D goals and 3-5 year market plans. In a world in which a whole industry - the internet for example - can rise, become the most important business area of all, decline and virtually die within five years only to rise again, such planning horizons are meaningless. In this sense Planning, as I have used the word with a capital 'P', is at best obsolescent. Business and organisations have to be opportunistic and seize the moment.

Planning works under the assumption that there is a logical sequence of activities that can be put in place to produce a desired end. However, the logic fails if the end is uncertain - as it is increasingly with modern corporate life.

Linear thinking, such as in the great age of the planner, inhibits opportunism just as strict roles and territories inhibit creativity (and success on the football pitch.) Organisations have to create a culture of flexibility, of readiness to change and concepts, for example, like job descriptions, largely get in the way. Controlling matters less than empowerment.

So, the trouble with formal, old-style Planning is that it assumes certainty and predictability where none now really exists. It causes punishment of people who do not achieve plan, even when circumstances have made the plan obsolete and, worst of all, it encourages people to think that their roles are stable and thus inhibits change and opportunism.

> Robert Waterman writes[195]:
>
> *Planning includes communication, elements of control, ways to keep organizations and the people in them from doing dumb things, ways of embracing opportunity on the fly, techniques for generating data, schemes for asking 'What if?' and getting sensible answers, means for reinforcing cultural values, and a whole lot more. The last thing that planning seems to do is to cough out a plan that anyone takes seriously.*
>
> Note the last sentence. This makes it messy and complex, as Waterman says, but that is reality. For me, the most important aspect of planning is communication. A plan says, in effect, not *'this is what you must do and in this order'* but more *'this is the direction that we are taking at the moment so keep this to the forefront of your mind - but stand by for change almost at any moment.'* To quote Waterman again:
>
> *Planning as communication is a powerful force for integration. People can use plans to let one another know what they intend to do. Thus Mr Right Hand knows what Mr Left Hand has in mind. If potential problems exist, they can get to them sooner. Planning as communication enables large organizations to deal with complicated issues of integration.*

A WASTE OF TIME AND WORSE

Possibly the most hard core of all planning gurus was H Igor Ansoff[196] who created what he saw as a rational planning model which required a daunting set of steps. Like many of his time and upbringing, Ansoff believed that a plan could arise complete unto itself for as long as there was total information and rigorous logical analysis. The fact that there never is total data and that complete analysis would take an inordinate amount of time did not, in the end, escape him. He came to regard strategic planning as an 'incomplete invention' - and indeed Ansoff himself coined the phrase 'paralysis by analysis.'

In other words, the planning process as we have come to know it is a chimera: *an impossible or foolish fantasy, hard to believe,* as Wikipedia glosses the term. As such, it causes an enormous amount of effort for little or no return and, even more dangerously, causes that effort on the part of those who know that the effort is wasted: the managers and employees. But it is even worse than this.

We hear almost a chorus that planning must be bottom up. The sales teams, manufacturing units, departments and so on say what they think they can achieve and the planning department pulls everything together in a coherent plan. Right?

This never happens. The top knows what results it will accept. The lower units can wriggle, under-call so as to be over plan in eventual performance and so on but if the top does not like the result, they will say, in that glorious phrase I once heard in a boardroom, *'Make those numbers go away.'* The planning process operates on assumptions which everyone knows to be false and does so in a way that everyone knows to be a lie.

Dr. Alper Alsan, Strategy Director for Siemens Turkey, has created an unusual planning approach. Quite opposed to the traditional linear process, Alsan's view is that planning is best operated by people who:

> *... know how to create alternative ways to implement his/her passionate targets and able to select one way without being afraid of change and being right or wrong.*

> The planner, he says[197]:
>
> *... looks for patterns in trends in order to spot opportunities (and) develops scenarios with teams via continuous communication and chooses among them.*
>
> He says that:
>
> *The mind of the strategic thinker is always hungry for new input. It works not only by analysis and synthesis but also listens to intuition or better put 'gut feeling' because without it no insights can be formulated. The Strategic Thinker learns from experience and strives to increase his or her understanding of the world around, always desiring to become better through intellectual growth and behavioural improvement.*
>
> This does not sound much like the usual planning process.

So what to do?

- Set your values - your strategy in Porter's[198] sense of the word.
- Communicate them and ensure that everyone understands the full implications of them.
- Estimate what you can do and achieve in the short to medium term in your current and desired markets.
- Do some planning with a short term focus to achieve this.
- Get as much knowledge as you can about what else you might do and sort out where you will best invest your energies.
- Have an outline plan for what you might do next but make sure everyone knows that this is up for discussion - that it might (will) change and indeed that the discussion might well be the agent of change.
- Keep everyone looking around for opportunities and keep everyone on their toes to seize opportunities as and when they arise.
- Keep everyone looking for possibilities, seeking to do things differently, researching ideas and talking about them.

- Remember that planning is communication - and communication is two way.

- Remember also that the whole thing is iterative and involves feedback.

- Oh, and never, ever, have copies of your plans bound!

However, don't believe that any answers you get can be expressed to any places of decimals or that they will withstand two or three months of reality.

THE MORAL?

The traditional planning process is just another mythical suit of clothes, one that rarely does much good but always wastes people's time and disengages them.

And remember what we found about performance against plan for senior executives: that a Hay Group study of executive pay in 2010 found that annual bonuses had jumped back up but they were not related to companies' profits; that bonus payouts had been helped by companies revising the bar for performance-based bonuses. If you read the footnote to this, you will have seen that Ira Ozer's research[199] shows that companies did not reduce sales targets during the recession and as Ozer says:

> *Without attainable goals, very few salespeople will achieve their numbers... when few salespeople earn bonus compensation or incentives, an attitude of cynicism can take hold and become a negative influence on everybody.*

This dissonance will add to the disengagement.

ARE YOU SHORT OF CLOTHES?

So, don't march through the streets of the town, dressed in the processes of the herd. In a traditional control orientated company, all who see you may well exclaim, *'The emperor's new suit of clothes is wonderful! How well they fit him!'* You may be unlucky and find that there is no child, with no important job to lose, to cry out, *'But he has nothing on at all. The Emperor is naked.'* You may have frightened people enough that if they tell the truth, someone will hiss, *'Fool! Do you want your head chopped off?'*[200] You will have wasted an awful lot of money, time and effort and reinforced the disengagement of your people.

* * *

9

TOWARDS A SOLUTION III:
THE ONLY WAY IS ETHICS

Employee engagement is about loyalty. It is in this sense a question of morality. If the company has no moral sense, if its actions repudiate the moral dimension, then it is hard to see how its management can call for loyalty, engagement - and that extra mile.

The (UK) Financial Services Authority reported that nearly 2500 people were mis-sold investments by advisers from a company owned by the high street bank HSBC, between 2005 and 2010. Vulnerable elderly people were mis-sold unsuitable investment policies - unsuitable in that they were sold to people with an average age of 83 and who had a life expectancy less than the recommended length of the investment. The FSA imposed a record fine of £10.5m and ordered the bank to provide £29m in compensation.[201]

In 1873, Friedrich Nietzsche wrote, *'The liar is a person who uses the valid designations, the words, in order to make something which is unreal appear to be real.'* Does this not strike you as a wonderful description of PR and spin?

Nietzsche's comment pre-dates the beginnings of public relations. Ivy Lee (1877-1934) is often considered to be the first practitioner of PR, establishing a firm in 1905. He later worked for Standard Oil after the coal mining rebellion in Colorado known as the Ludlow Massacre. Upton Sinclair, the Pulitzer Prize-winning American author[202], called him 'Poison Ivy', referring to the occasion when Ivy Lee issued press bulletins claiming that several miners, who were shot by the Colorado militia, were killed by an overturned stove.

> The Ludlow massacre is the stuff of legend. Miners were being paid extraordinarily low rates and worked in extremely dangerous conditions, none more so than the Colorado miners who had twice the chance of any other miner of being killed. Miners were frequently not paid in cash but in vouchers – known as scrip - which they could spend only in the company store, which then overcharged them. The miners formed a union and went on strike.
>
> The Rockefeller family evicted striking workers and their families out of their homes in the Colorado winter and brought in an armoured car with a machine gun that was called the 'Death Special'. This weapon was used to fire on the tent cities that the miners put up and what was virtually open warfare broke out. In 1918 a monument was erected to commemorate those who died during the strike. You may recall the song, *Sixteen Tons*, made famous by Tennessee Ernie Ford and recorded by many artists including Johnny Cash. The chorus runs:
>
>> *You load sixteen tons, what do you get?*
>> *Another day older and deeper in debt.*
>> *Saint Peter, don't you call me, 'cause I can't go;*
>> *I owe my soul to the company store.*

Your employees know when you are lying. They know when the company is lying. They know when top management is on the fiddle and they know when the company is. How can one feel loyal and committed to a liar or a cheat? Nietzsche also said:

> *I'm not upset that you lied to me. I'm upset that from now on I can't believe you.*

Lying disengages. It also legitimises copycat behaviour by employees. Laura Bramble, writing for eMoney, speaks of a vicious cycle:

> *Low morale and unethical behavior develop into a vicious cycle. Bad behavior and the mistrust it fosters create low morale and a feeling of isolation. Isolation breeds a feeling of 'everyone's only out for themselves,' leading to a 'what's in it for me?' attitude. Once that attitude develops, minor ethical lapses occur, such as abusing sick time, taking small company property, fudging figures and cutting corners.*

At one level, corporate lying simply annoys employees and makes them feel unclean. At a higher level it damages the company and puts people – often not enough of them – in jail. If the company has no moral sense, if its actions repudiate the moral dimension, then it is hard to see how its management can call for and expect loyalty, engagement - and that extra mile.

In *The Working Manager*, we created as one of the 'quizzes', the *Practical Ethics Exercise* which asked users to read descriptions of situations in ordinary management life and select from five options each time. These options loaded on to five factors described as follows:

Look after number one

Perhaps ethics begins by looking after yourself and your family. We live in an imperfect world, which is often 'dog eat dog.' If you are the only one who is acting ethically, you are going to miss out. There are times when it makes sense to take advantage of a situation for your own benefit.

Be practical

Ethical concerns are all very well but you have to live in the real world. Businesses have to survive and make money and people have to work together. Insisting on ethical concerns too strictly can make companies unprofitable and make working with people impossible.

No fuss

Recognise the importance that some people place on ethics. However, there is rarely a need to make a fuss about it. Most events can be handled quietly. Noise just calls people's attention to the event.

Find a compromise

Do what you can to do the right thing but recognise that no one gave you permission to make your company or your team a martyr by damaging results and relationships. Often talking to people will get the result.

Ethics first

Ethical action is not optional. If a business suffers financially or if people get upset because of an ethical decision, then so be it. The company or the people should not have got themselves into the position in the first place.

Employee engagement requires that our answers load on the 'Ethics first' factor. By insisting that 'Ethical action is not optional', we make it plain that the company will always be straight in its dealings and can always be trusted. It will always say what it means and will always mean what it says.

WORDS

> *'When I use a word,' Humpty Dumpty said in rather a scornful tone, 'it means just what I choose it to mean - neither more nor less.'*
>
> *'The question is,' said Alice, 'whether you can make words mean so many different things.'*[203]

Words do matter and the way a company expresses itself describes the company. Take what seems a very minor issue, the concern over 'difficult conversations'. I have never seen a definition of 'difficult' as used here but the conversations under this heading seem to be those where a manager is worried about upsetting an employee. Thus, we get advice to introduce difficult topics in a very odd way:

- *Tell the employee that you need to provide feedback that is difficult to share.*

- *If you're uncomfortable with your role in the conversation, you might say that, too.*
- *Seek permission to provide the feedback.*

We get advice to use some pretty weird forms of words:

- *I'd like to talk about x with you, but first I'd like to get your point of view.*
- *I have something I'd like to discuss with you that I think will help us work together more effectively.*
- *I need your help with something. Can we talk about it?*
- *I think we have different perceptions about y. I'd like to hear your thinking on this.*
- *I'd like to see if we might reach a better understanding about z. I really want to hear your feelings about this and share my perspective as well.*

This form of words verges on a con trick. The words are dishonest and dishonesty is never the foundation of good management. More, such weird uses of language lead employees to be suspicious of anything you say.

> *I'd like to talk about x with you, but first I'd like to get your point of view.*

… doesn't really mean what it seems. What it actually means is:

> *I am going to tell you how to behave but I want you first to think that I am a nice person who is open to your ideas. I am not. I just want you to do what I say and be nice to me about it.*

The statement:

> *I need your help with something. Can we talk about it?*

… really means:

> *I need you to help me by making me feel good about myself, by accepting what I am about to say and by not bursting into tears which will make me feel bad.*

Oh – and:

> *I'd like to see if we might reach a better understanding about z. I really want to hear your feelings about this and share my perspective as well.*

... doesn't seem to mean much at all in the context. In all cases, the only proper and human response is *'Get lost.'* As Sheila Heen[204] says:

> *Anxious about a confrontation, we instead come at the topic sideways, and this is bound to leave (the other person) feeling ambushed. You're implicitly communicating, 'What I want to say to you is so bad, I can't even say it directly.'*

The late, great Bill Reddin was fond of the reply 'Whose needs are being met here?'[205] when asked for advice about various courses of action. He meant, of course, that management is about the needs of the organisation. The problem with these approaches is that they are all about the needs of the manager.

There is nothing wrong with a desire to be loved, in and of itself, but everything wrong with it when it interferes with your duties as a manager. People who wrap things up like to think they are doing it to protect the feelings of the other person. They are not. They are protecting their own feelings.

Worrying about what people may think of us, how they will feel about us, how we will be perceived, we freeze, unable to act. The remedy for this is found in Paul Simon's song *'Fifty ways to leave your lover.'* You will remember the chorus:

> *There must be fifty ways to leave your lover.*
> *You just slip out the back, Jack.*
> *Make a new plan, Stan.*
> *You don't need to be coy, Roy.*
> *Just get yourself free.*
>
> *Hop on the bus, Gus.*
> *You don't need to discuss much.*
> *Just drop off the key, Lee*
> *And get yourself free.*

It is like taking off the Elastoplast. If you pull it off slowly, it hurts like hell. If you rip it off, there is a short burst of pain and then it is over and done with. So get on with it. Yes there are procedures that need to be followed in certain situations – but once you are sitting face to face with the employee don't dress it up. Straight talking connotes a straight organisation.

- *Jean. Your performance has not improved. In the downturn, we cannot carry passengers. Do what we have agreed or your employment may be terminated.*

- *Harry. Putting no finer point on it, you have a body odour problem. Is there a medical issue? If not, you need to get your personal hygiene sorted out.*

- *Amanda. Your gossiping about people's private lives is upsetting the team and really annoying me. It's disruptive and inappropriate in the work place. Stop it.*

If you feel you need to seek permission to give feedback, if you're uncomfortable giving it or if you find feedback difficult to share (and feel you have to use the word 'share' in this context[206]), then don't be a manager. Simple. Feedback is the major part of management and if you have to wrap it up, it doesn't work. Leave management to someone who doesn't need permission from employees to manage.

OK, so this sort of thing is fairly minor, if annoying. However, it is an instance of how words are used to set a culture and cultures can be very dangerous.

Abu Ghraib

Philip Zimbardo is Professor Emeritus of Psychology at Stanford University. In 2004 he acted as an expert witness in the court martial of Sergeant Ivan Frederick who was accused, with others, of abuse and torture of detainees in Abu Ghraib prison in Iraq during 2003. The crimes of which Sergeant Frederick was accused, and subsequently found guilty, were made infamous by the publication in the international press of disgusting photographs of prisoners being physically and sexually abused.

At his trial, he pleaded guilty. Sentenced to 8 years in jail, he was released in October 2007. Sergeant Frederick was not alone in his acts. He was merely the highest in rank of those charged. What he did was widespread. The fact that these acts appear to have been committed by women soldiers as well as men seems to make the whole thing even more horrifying and even more difficult to comprehend.

Professor Zimbardo supported the accused, not because he believed Fredericks and others innocent but because of his research that shows that much of the evil in the world is the result of the actions of very ordinary people.

Stanford Prison Experiments

Philip Zimbardo is most famous for his 1971 experiments, not repeatable today, in which a group of volunteers were divided into guards and inmates and the conditions of a prison simulated. A large part of his book is devoted to a detailed account of these experiments. The behaviour of the guards was so shocking that the experiments were terminated early.

The parallels between the Stanford Prison Experiments and the events at Abu Ghraib are there. Not that there was actual physical abuse or sexual deviation in the experiments, but the de-humanising treatment of 'inmates' was all too similar. Zimbardo says:

> *The Stanford Prison Experiment began as a simple demonstration of the effects that a composite of situational variables has on the behaviour of individuals role-playing prisoners and guards ... However, over time, this experiment has emerged as a powerful illustration of the potentially toxic impact of bad systems and bad situations in making good people behave in pathological ways that are alien to their nature.*

He argues that the most important lesson to be learned from the Stanford Prison Experiments is the power of systems. The rules, the way we do things around here, what is deemed acceptable, what we get used to, what is normal; all these things appear to be controlled and even defined by the system, or the organisational culture as Ed Schein would say.

The people in the Stanford Prison Experiments were normal people. Zimbardo and his colleagues applied selection procedures to ensure this. Thus:

> *One of the most dramatic outcomes of the Stanford Prison Experiments was the way in which many healthy, normal young men began to behave pathologically in a short time.*

The banality of evil

The Stanford Prison Experiments were in effect research on how normal people *'begin to go mad.'* In his book, *The Lucifer Effect*[207], Philip Zimbardo speaks of the banality of evil. We all wish to believe that evil can be contained, that in general it is the result of a bad apple, that those who do wrong are in some way different from us, that we would never act in any such way ourselves. Zimbardo shows that much of the evil in the world is the result of the actions of very ordinary people.

Zimbardo talks about the horrors of Abu Ghraib and few of us will ever be exposed to them. However, there is a myriad of lesser evils. The 'little evils' we might call them that happen in business and management almost every day. They are perpetrated by those we might call ordinary folk.

Are they evil? Are they even bad people? We can be relatively sure that few of them are into torture. We may be relatively sure that few of them have a prison record, beat their wives, poison their husbands or sell drugs outside school gates. Indeed, we can be relatively sure that most of them are ordinary decent folk living ordinary decent lives.

There grows up in the organisation a culture of dishonesty which, after a while, people come to accept and even cease to notice. The results are behaviours which range from the deceitful to the criminal.

The deceitful

> *The ASA, the Advertising Standards Authority, held that InBev, the brewer of Stella Artois, can no longer boast that its lager is produced by a family that has been dedicated to brewing for six centuries. The authority said the Artois brand was no longer family-owned and it was untrue to claim that one family of common ancestry had been involved in the brewing of Stella Artois for six centuries.*[208]

> *The advertising watchdog criticised L'Oreal for a mascara commercial featuring actress Penelope Cruz that exaggerated the product's effects. The Advertising Standards Authority said the company broke its rules and misled consumers by failing to make it clear that Cruz was wearing some fake lashes. It ordered L'Oreal to make it clear in future adverts if models are wearing fake lashes.*[209]

The dangerous

> *An Italian truck was travelling from Fort William to Dover when it was pulled over at a check point near Stirling. The number of defects, which included faulty brakes, a shock absorber and a damaged tyre, has been described as 'staggering' by police.*[210]

> *An undercover survey into car servicing revealed that none of the six garages targeted spotted all the faults they should have done. The survey was carried*

out by Swindon Council's trading standards department, which planted 18 deliberate faults on cars. Phil Thomas, of the department, said: 'The real shock was that none of them fixed the faulty light bulbs and most missed the tyre pressure, both of which are safety items.' The best garage failed to find five of 18 faults and the worst missed 12.[211]

And some that appear to be simply criminal:

Network Rail, the successor organisation to Railtrack, which was responsible for Britain's railway infrastructure at the time the King's Cross-Leeds train was derailed at 115mph, was convicted of safety breaches. Balfour Beatty, which was responsible for track maintenance, had already pleaded guilty to breaking safety regulations.[212]

Rail infrastructure company Network Rail and rail maintenance company Jarvis today announced they had accepted liability on behalf of the rail industry for claims brought over the Potters Bar crash. The admission of responsibility has long been called for by those injured in the crash and the families of the seven people who died at Potters Bar station in Hertfordshire in May 2002. The train derailed because of faulty points and hurtled into a bridge at 100mph.[213]

What is the impact on anything that might be termed employee engagement from such actions? Since the company is acting irresponsibly or illegally, it surely has no moral right to ask its employees to go that extra mile. Indeed, since the employees usually know that the company is acting in this way, they become totally cynical about its statements.

Trust is difficult to rebuild once it is lost. Inconsistencies in behaviour which appear to be in the interest of the company may also appear hypocritical, which further damages trust.

There is a true story of a branch of a global accounting firm which contacted a client to chase payment of a long outstanding bill, only to be told that the accounting firm itself had advised the client to pay its bills as late as possible to improve cash flow.

Professor Robert Cochrane writing for *The Working Manager*

Corporate lying

Cheating and lying can take many forms. Some are even amusing. The *Independent* carried[214] a story of a young man, an airline employee seeking asylum from Afghanistan, who pleaded guilty to diverting air (reward) miles from genuine passengers to fictitious accounts he had set up. As a result of his legerdemain, he was able to fly first class around the world and enable his family and friends to do so as well.

Dishonest behaviour? Yes, of course, but not a corporate crime. It is a simple example of dishonesty which admittedly has a touch of amusement to it — the poor refugee living the high life until he gets caught.

Another story with its amusing side, said to be true, was that of the bank employee who diverted amounts of money, in 'unreal' decimal places beyond two, to his own account. One supposes that an interest calculation resulted in a credit to someone's account of, say, $40.3521. There being no coins which add up to $0.0021, the bank employee simply set up a computer programme to credit his account with the odd $0.0021. It does not sound much - but do it enough times and it adds up to a fortune.

The only thing corporate about these crimes is that they occurred in a corporate environment. Both people used their knowledge of the corporate system to steal but the only thing that the respective corporations were guilty of was designing a system with holes in it and few system designs can outlook every clever but dishonest act.

Positions of trust

How much do these cases differ from that of the Adelphia Communications Corporation? According to the *Washington Post*:

> Adelphia Communications Corp. founder John J. Rigas and two of his sons siphoned off millions of dollars in corporate funds for personal extravagances, including using Adelphia funds to pay for 100 pairs of bedroom slippers and for corporate jets to deliver Christmas trees to another family member, a federal prosecutor told jurors.

Well, I do not know if the bank employee was also a slipper fetishist, and enabling one's family to fly around the world seems a lot more imaginative than having corporate jets deliver Christmas trees, but otherwise the cases seem to be identical - fiddling the system for personal benefit.

However, there is a difference, isn't there? The Adelphia case is a bit more than a case of simple dishonesty. There is little amusement value in a founder using millions of dollars for personal extravagances, if indeed it is proved that he did. It just sounds extravagantly greedy and an extreme abuse of a company position. Worse than this is the Rite Aid case. Again, the *Washington Post* reports:

> *The son of Rite Aid's founder, Grass pleaded guilty to one count of conspiracy to defraud the company and its shareholders, and one count of conspiracy to obstruct justice. Grass ... has admitted to a series of illegal activities, ranging from backdating contracts and severance letters to hiding a $2.6 million real estate deal from the company and federal regulators.*

Abuse of significant trust is one thing but there is another factor to these high level cases. I doubt very much that the airline employee or the bank clerk told anyone what they were doing, so no one else would know of their crimes until they were discovered. However, the founder and the son of the founder were involved in actions which, of necessity, involved others. After all, someone had to fly the corporate jets to deliver the Christmas trees. Their actions must have been well known.

MORAL CORROSION

So what does it do to a company when its leaders are known to be on the fiddle? What example does it set to the rest of the organisation? How much did senior management actions legitimise other actions, perhaps in aggregate just as damaging to the company's cost base and shareholder returns? How, for example, can a leader call for extra effort from employees in difficult times if he, or she, is acting like the Adelphia/Rite Aid crew allegedly were?

> *Harry Stonecipher, the former CEO of Boeing made the restoration of corporate ethics in the organization a top priority but was soon after embarrassed by the disclosure of an extramarital affair with a female employee. The board asked him to resign.*[215]

Dishonesty at the top can very easily cause dishonesty lower down, on the basis of what is good for the goose is good for the gander. It damages the basis of high rewards for hard work, the contract between employer and employed, the very norms of behaviour that the company lives by. Such behaviour at the top has a corrosive effect on the company. It corrodes trust, the social contract and morale. It not only is, but also causes dishonesty. It is a disgusting (as opposed to slightly amusing) betrayal of trust.

If you think these examples are not representative and that dishonesty at the top of organisations is rare, I fear the accounting firm KPMG will disabuse you. In a report issued in June 2011, they revealed that fully half of all UK corporate fraud is perpetrated by senior managers and board members. Not surprisingly corporate crimes are only infrequently brought to light by management. The most common way that such frauds are discovered is through whistleblowers and anonymous tip-offs.

I once invited quotations for the replacement of windows in my house. In the event, I selected an excellent firm who did a professional job for the right amount of money. However, one company, for essentially identical windows, quoted more than twice the amount I eventually paid. They offered to drop their price by 10% if I would sign the contract then and there. Following my (natural) refusal, they went away and later telephoned me with a quote half their original one. On being told they were still more expensive than the company I would be buying from, they offered to beat any price I had received. This meant that they were prepared to do the job at 42% of the price they first quoted.

Now, I am not as likely to be conned into paying a vastly inflated price as the proverbial little old lady but it upset me to think that perhaps some little old ladies (or indeed gentlemen) had ended up paying perhaps 200% of a fair price, due to the sales techniques of this company. How can anyone think of themselves as a professional sales person while adopting, no doubt on orders from the boss, such dishonest techniques?

> *It is no surprise that the quality of this company's installations is very poor and keeps the local law firms busy. After all, if the bosses do not care about the customer, why should the sales force or anyone else in the company? Who will work for this company? Well, those who cannot get a job elsewhere (and who will leave as soon as they can) and those whose ethical stance, or absence of one, matches the company's. And is someone with an ethical stance of this nature likely to be someone loyal, engaged and ready to go the extra mile?*

THE SHELL CASE

The Shell Oil Company[216] was found to be vastly over-stating its oil and gas reserves. It cost Shell a sizeable amount of money. They had to pay out:

- $340.1m to investors who bought shares between April 1999 and March 2004
- $12.5m divided equally among those investors who submitted a claim for relief
- $6.5m to organisations representing individual shareholders
- $120m to investors in the US
- $120m in fines

Perhaps in response to the Brent Spar case (when Shell were wrongly accused of putting profits before environmental concerns), Shell had launched a major ethics initiative. You can read their publicly stated ethics policy on their website. Part of it reads:

> *The corporate scandals of the last year have underlined the importance of not just having core values, but living up to them consistently in practice ... (We) have global standards for critical areas of our business, covering, for example, governance, financial control and accounting, security, diversity and inclusiveness, environmental management and emissions from our sites, biodiversity, health management and animal testing.*

It went on:

> *The executives responsible for each Shell business and country operation must inform our Committee of Managing Directors every year, in writing, whether his or her organisation has acted in line with Group policies and standards and, where not, to describe actions being taken to achieve compliance.*

How can anyone read this statement, made very publicly and as a corporate strategy, without feeling nauseated knowing that the top people were well aware, at the time of approving it, that they were being dishonest about their reporting of their oil reserves? The *'global standards for critical areas of our business, covering, for example, governance, financial control and accounting'* (and oil reserves can only be a critical area) were being ignored and indeed flouted by the very people who initiated and approved this ethics policy.

It turned out that they were doing no more than mouthing words. They should not have been just words. If actions had followed these words, they would have been fine words indeed. What must it have felt like to work for Shell at that time? The employees must have been feeling rather soiled, a bit dirty.

And yet more

> *In 2005, the US Securities and Exchange Commission charged Time Warner Inc. with materially overstating online advertising revenue and the number of its Internet subscribers, and with aiding and abetting three other securities frauds. Time Warner agreed to a $300 million penalty. Time Warner agreed to restate its historical financial results to reduce its reported online advertising revenues by approximately $500 million.*[217]

> *In 2002, the Senate's Permanent Subcommittee on Investigations*[218] *concluded that Riggs executives and bank regulators failed to monitor suspicious financial transactions involving hundreds of millions of dollars. The scrutiny of the bank involves accounts it held for General Augusto Pinochet, the former Chilean dictator, and for the Saudi Arabian Embassy. When regulators asked Riggs in 2000 for a list of its accounts controlled by political figures, the roster provided by the bank did not include General Pinochet's name. The bank – in a move that it acknowledged was improper – changed the name on accounts of the general and his wife from 'Augusto Pinochet Ugarte & Lucia Hiriart de Pinochet' to 'L. Hiriart &/or A. Ugarte,' ensuring that searches*

for Riggs accounts named 'Pinochet' would draw a blank. In 2002, Riggs sent $500,000 in cashiers' checks to the general. Later analyses by Senate investigators indicated he cashed them to pay personal expenses. Sometime between the spring and summer of 2002, according to the Senate report and testimony last week, Riggs tried to withhold information about the Pinochet accounts from regulators and then, rather than freeze the accounts as is customary, closed them and returned the money to General Pinochet.

In 2005, Ernst & Young was barred from accepting new public-company audit clients for six months after an SEC judge ruled the firm violated conflict-of-interest rules. E&Y then found itself negotiating with the Justice Department to avoid criminal prosecution for the sale of improper tax shelters.[219]

These are not the actions of one or two dishonest people. They sound more like systemic failures of ethics.

- To book $500 million of questionable advertising revenue is not the action of one or two dubious sales directors. It implies that the practice of cheating in reporting sales performance is widespread throughout the company – involving not just the sales force itself but also those responsible for both management and financial reporting.

- To permit millions of dollars in suspicious transactions implies not just a bad decision by one bank manager but widespread acceptance of rules disobedience.

- For a major firm of chartered accountants to be barred from accepting new public audit clients for six months is not an insignificant matter. The Washington Post calls it *'one of the most serious sanctions the government has attempted to impose on the accounting industry,'* and Allan D. Koltin, a management consultant to the accounting sector, describes it as *'almost as close to the death penalty as one could get.'*

For a major firm to be barred like this, implies more than an isolated case of over-enthusiasm by an accounting manager or partner. The judge wrote:

The overwhelming evidence is that during the relevant period, EY's day-to-day operations were profit-driven and ignored considerations of auditor independence in relationships with PeopleSoft.

Such examples tend to show that the organisations concerned lost sight of their ethical duties or indeed deliberately flouted them. They disobeyed the rules of business, the rules of competition. As cultures, they accepted, and obviously in some cases encouraged, behaviour which was simply immoral. The norms of behaviour, the 'way we do things around here', had become immoral.

Punishment of the innocent

There is indeed a penalty for illegal behaviour. In the accounting world, Arthur Andersen paid the ultimate penalty: death. However, the penalties often fall upon the innocent. Take the WorldCom case. Here is an abstract taken once more from the *Washington Post*:

> *In February 2002, the stock took another big tumble after the company sharply lowered its revenue and earnings projections ... Investors got another dose of bad news the next month when the SEC announced it was investigating WorldCom's accounting practices as well as some loans it made to executives. Another worry was the company's high debt, which had reached $30 billion by April 2002. By this point, WorldCom Group's stock was trading below $7 ... The following month, the company announced it would end its separate tracking stocks for WorldCom and MCI in July 2002, which will save $284 million by doing away with the MCI Group dividend.*

The first people to suffer were the shareholders. Not only did the share price tumble but a reporting decision cost them $284 million in dividends.

> *In April 2002, the company said it would lay off 3,700 employees - about four percent of employees. The company said the layoffs were part of a cost cutting measure that also included the freezing of salaries, stock options and the elimination of free coffee for some employees. Then in June 2002, the company started laying off another 17,000 employees - more than 20% of its remaining workforce.*

After the shareholders, the next people to suffer were the employees. Twenty thousand or so lost their jobs as the board took exceptional cost saving action, including the dramatic decision to eliminate free coffee! Eliminating free coffee is supposed to compensate somehow for all the money lost through fraud at the top?

One hopes that those responsible for these forms of dishonesty get punished, and severely. No doubt our refugee airline employee and the bank clerk were punished immediately. However, the famous saying about the stages of project management - *enthusiasm, disillusion, panic, search for who to blame, punishment of the innocent, promotion of the guilty* – encapsulates the view that while the employee is punished, senior management gets away scot free. Employee engagement? Why?

IDEALS

Barak Obama said, 20 January 2009

> *We reject as false the choice between our safety and our ideals. Our Founding Fathers, faced with perils we can scarcely imagine, drafted a charter to assure the rule of law and the rights of man, a charter expanded by the blood of generations. Those ideals still light the world, and we will not give them up for expediency's sake.*

Jharna Sengupta Biswas wrote for *The Working Manager*:

> *In virtually all areas of human endeavour, both 'how' and 'what' matter. No company, organisation or even state can really afford to ignore either of these aspects. The need is always to balance the task compulsions with the task constraints - the 'what' and 'how'.*
>
> *In quoting for the building of a bridge, an engineering firm must take account of professional engineering standards when setting its price. A drug company bringing a new molecule to the market must have tested it for side effects according to accepted scientific methods. A motorcar manufacturer must have tested all the components of a new vehicle such that it lives up to its expected, safe working life.*

The high ground in business ethics is where legal requirements are considered as purely the minimum requirement for business action. The ethical company will rarely be bothered by legal requirements because its natural ethical stance is far in excess of the minimum. The company is seen as an ethical agent, capable not only of obedience but also of positive ethical leadership. This is the stance taken to a large extent by Johnson & Johnson and particularly by Body Shop. As Anita Roddick said:

> *I also learned that we have to enshrine our shared values of honesty, respect and care for people, animals and the environment, and that, if we didn't they would become no more than a hollow add-on and we would be no different from any dime-a-dozen cosmetics company. If you mess around with the values, you mess around with the company's reason for existing.*

GREED IS GOOD?

Sir Adrian Cadbury, a business leader well-known in Europe for his concern for business ethics and corporate governance, wrote an introduction to the book *Case Histories in Business Ethics*[220] in which he argued that business ethics have become more visible:

> *First of all, business has become more international ... (and) it is seen, I suspect, to be less accountable. Since it is spread across the world ... it is held to be responsible to no single jurisdiction. A second reason why governance has risen up the corporate agenda has been the occurrence of disasters. The Exxon Valdez tragedy, Bophal, Maxwell, corporate collapses - all of these highlight this question of accountability. Third, there is the interest shown by shareholder groups, and by governments themselves, in ethical and environmental issues.*

He goes on to talk about greed.

> *Consider the well-known quote from Ivan Boesky*[221]: *'Greed is alright. I want you to know that. I think greed is healthy. You can be greedy and feel good about yourself.' The interesting thing about that quote is perhaps not just that he said it, but that he said it at the commencement address for UCLA, to all those bright new students coming up to the University, prior to making their own way in life. The message they got was that. That does make one think.*

One can feel the distaste coming through in his account of this speech. Sir Adrian Cadbury goes on to argue that a business's ethics matter because reputation is an asset and distrust is a barrier to trade. He goes on to say that condoning unethical practices leads to a slide in standards and, importantly, that a business cannot engage people of integrity and ability unless it has high ethical standards.

LEGISLATION AND MORALITY

In 2003, *StepStone*, the European Career Portal, reported that more than half of the European employees feel embarrassed when asked for the name of their employers. Italian employees top the list with 64% who said they felt uncomfortable when asked while only 14% of Italian employees took a pride in their companies. In Germany, Holland and Sweden, 50% of all staff are ashamed of their employers and only one third of the German, Belgian, Dutch and Swedish employees and 40% of all Danish employees feel pride in their companies. Employee engagement surely requires that the employees are not ashamed of their employer.

A fairly common view is that there is nothing unethical in a company taking the law as the only limit on its behaviour. Thus, it is held that the only ethical duty for the managers of a company is profit maximisation on behalf of the shareholders.[222] Such a view holds that it would even be wrong to do more than obey legislation, if doing so would increase costs and reduce profits.

A more extreme view holds that a company should seek to avoid being caught by legislation, and indeed its duty to its shareholders requires this. Thus, a company may use PR, lobbying, legal argument and special pleading to avoid legislative constraints and the costs implied. It is possible that Union Carbide's actions, post Bophal, are a case in point.

> *In 1984, an explosion at the Union Carbide plant in India released poison gases including hydrogen cyanide and carbon monoxide, allegedly causing some 16,000 deaths. The company paid US$470 million as part of an out-of-court settlement that granted company officials immunity from prosecution. Groups representing the victims claim that much of the compensation has never been paid and over 120,000 survivors are still in need of medical attention. Legal argument has continued and as late as 1999 lawyers filed a class action lawsuit in New York charging the corporation with violating the human rights of the victims and survivors and with fraud and civil contempt for their perceived failure to comply with orders of the courts of the United States and India.*

If this is true, it may be an example of a company minimising its losses by the use of legal argument. The story has continued.

> *On April 19, 2004, Agence France Presse reported that two Bhopal women, Rashida Bee and Champa Devi Shukla, who have defied social norms, poverty and sickness in a quest to hold Dow Chemical Company accountable for the 1984 Union Carbide disaster, were among seven grassroots activists from around the globe being awarded this year's Goldman Environmental Prize in San Francisco.'*

Union Carbide was taken over by The Dow Chemical Company in 2001.

> *It was reported April 21, 2004[223] that about 8,000 tonnes of toxic waste is still lying scattered and exposed in the Union Carbide factory premises, nearly two decades later and that an appellate court in the US held Union Carbide responsible for contamination of the groundwater.*

If you take the view that a company should argue with the law, seek to minimise its impact and avoid its effect on the company if this can be (legally) done, Union Carbide did nothing wrong in attempting to minimise their losses. The only question that should arise is whether 'doing the right thing' would have been less expensive in the longer run. On this view, Union Carbide's decision is seen to have been wrong mathematically, rather than morally.

The story came back to bite Dow Chemicals in 2011, when their sponsorship of the London Olympics was criticised. Associated Press reported that UK Member of Parliament Keith Vaz tabled a motion expressing reservations over Dow's ties to the Olympics, which were expected to stir concern among Britain's Indian community. *'This is not the right kind of sponsorship for the world's greenest Olympics,'* Vaz is reported to have said.

> *CNN-IBN December 15 2011*
>
> *The Indian Olympic Association (IOA) will not boycott the 2012 London Olympics, but will lodge a strong protest over the 1984 Bhopal gas tragedy which tainted Dow Chemicals sponsoring the sporting event. The victims of the Bhopal gas tragedy have been demanding that India boycott the Games if Dow stays on as a sponsor.*

It is difficult to see Dow as a company one would proudly announce as one's employer, is it not? Dow may be legally correct but their reputation is damaged anyway. Employees might find it difficult to be engaged with a company with that reputation. Engagement requires a company to be more than legally correct.

Morality and brand image

It pays to be very careful about what one's company is doing. Nike was accused of employing child labour. The *Independent* newspaper reported in 2001:

> *Philip Knight, the company chairman, clearly stung by reports of children as young as 10 making shoes, clothing and footballs in Pakistan and Cambodia, attempted to convince Nike's critics that it had only ever employed children accidentally. 'Of all the issues facing Nike in workplace standards, child labour is the most vexing,' he said in the report. 'Our age standards are the highest in the world: 18 for footwear manufacturing, 16 for apparel and equipment, or local standards whenever they are higher.' But in some countries (Bangladesh and Pakistan, for example) those standards are next to impossible to verify, when records of birth do not exist or can be easily forged.*

The *Independent* report went on:

> *Mistakes, however, continue to happen. In recent years, Nike has been criticised for its employment of child labour in Cambodia, but the company defended itself by saying fake evidence of age could be bought in Cambodia for as little as $5. When it was exposed by the BBC as having employed children there, the company claimed it then re-examined the records of all 3,800 employees.*

In 2010, Nike issued a code of conduct which included the rule that its sub-contractors should not employ workers under the age of 16. It also invited the Fair Labour Association to conduct an independent assessment of the football production in the Shanghai Wande Sporting Goods Company.

The *Independent* was not accusing Nike of illegal behaviour. I am just pointing out that the brand was damaged by such reports – and may still be being damaged.

The book *Brand Manners*, by Hamish Pringle and William Gordon,[224] argues that every organisation has a brand whether or not it indulges in brand management. Such a brand is no more and no less than the customer's perception of the quality of goods or services that the organisation delivers.

It applies as much to hospitals, government agencies, law firms, sports teams, churches and schools as it does to brand management companies like Coca-Cola or Unilever. *Brand Manners*, the authors argue, are the amalgam of all the behaviours which enable the board, the management, and the staff to align the internal values of the organisation to the external values of the brand.

Organisations make contact with the external world through their brands. In anything other than a pure monopoly we make decisions about which brand of goods or service we wish to purchase. Advertising may get our attention, but what decides the issue is how the brand is delivered - and that comes down, in most cases, to the people behind the brand. The challenge for management, as Pringle and Gordon put it:

> ... is to ensure that the whole company, and in particular its customer-facing employees, actually live their brand and convey its essence in everything they do.

Management's behaviour, the ethical stance of the company, its ethical record and the match or mismatch between its words and its actions are all part of this. Anita Roddick wrote[225]:

> I sometimes wonder why we're not more outraged by the fact that three billion people live on less than $2 a day while the wealthy have stashed away $8 trillion in tax havens. What is needed in business is a return to kindness and a rejection of obscenities like huge compensation packages for CEOs. I think that it is a sin to sack thousands of people and then accept a million-dollar bonus, a sin of the human spirit.

Engagement and Morality

Drucker, in *Management Challenges for the 21st Century*, says:

> *Knowledge worker productivity is the biggest of the 21st century management challenges. In developed countries it is their first survival requirement. In no other way can the developed countries hope to maintain themselves, let alone maintain their leadership and their standards of living.*

You will remember the book *Funky Business*. In it, Ridderstrale and Nordstrom say:

> *The most critical resource wears shoes and walks out of the door around 5 o'clock every day.*

The BBC News reported, December 2011, that five orthopaedic surgeons had resigned from an East London hospital in protest at the fact that patients had allegedly been left with life-changing injuries because of a dangerous shortage of surgical facilities.

> *'I can no longer stand idly by when patients are physically harmed by the care they receive,' said Dr David Goodier. He claimed that patients were left with open wounds for six days while waiting for a slot. When they were finally operated on, bones often healed badly or infection set in leading to long-term complications. 'We have become so used to this situation it is no longer seen as a crisis, it is the norm.'*

The surgeons resigned over what they clearly regarded as an ethical failure. Some staff are extremely difficult to recruit and orthopaedic surgeons are among them.

The 'brains', the knowledge workers, those who are most in demand by companies are also those who march to their own drummer and have strong values. They can afford to have them. They can be choosy and they will fairly clearly choose not to work for companies whose leaders' ethics resemble those of the average alley cat. Yes, ethical behaviour by the bosses does matter if a company wants to survive and prosper.

In talking about employee engagement, do remember we are not talking about something very ordinary like turning up on time or wearing a tie at work. We are talking about hearts and minds. Employee engagement:

> *... describes employees' emotional and intellectual commitment to their organisation and its success. Engaged employees experience a compelling purpose and meaning in their work and give of their discrete effort to advance the organisation's objectives.*

as the Work Foundation put it and which I quoted at the beginning of this book. If employees are to feel engaged with a company, they need to feel proud of the organisation they are supposed to commit to. Only a company with a good reputation, one that goes beyond the law and takes a positive view of its ethical position, can expect employees to experience that *'compelling purpose and meaning in their work.'*

Much more than a programme

The message of this book has been that employee engagement can only result from really effective leadership in an organisation which has:

- leadership committed to the long term development of the organisation
- rewards which are transparently equitable, themselves leading to the long term health of the organisation
- systems and processes which enable and reinforce engagement rather than destroy it
- loyalty to its employees in return for loyalty to the organisation and a respect for the psychological contract
- honesty in all its dealings with its customers and staff and a sense of pride emanating from that.

It also demands from the company's leadership an understanding of the how and why of engagement and a genuine interest in leadership and management.

I summarise what has been said in a bullet point summary following this page. If you sincerely wish to gain the engagement of your employees and stand ready to make the changes required, then I wish you every success and an enjoyment of the (immense) efforts required. If you don't, then I sincerely hope that you will not use the words 'employee engagement' again.

* * *

10

SUMMARY: THE MESSAGE OF EMPLOYEE ENGAGEMENT AND WHAT HAS TO BE DONE

If people are committed to making decisions work, if they support the boss, understand and appreciate what is going on, believe that the company is doing its best, believe that their owns efforts are respected and rewarded and that they are valued, then they are all the more likely to get behind decisions and work to make them come right.

The Working Manager

Forget socialism, capitalism, just in time deliveries, salary surveys and concentrate upon building organisations that achieve that most difficult of all challenges: making people look forward to coming to work.

Ricardo Semler

SUMMARY

This whole leadership thing, it's like losing weight. We know it will happen if we do the right things but this takes commitment, sacrifice and concentration. Instead, the natural human condition is to say, 'Is there a pill I can take?'

Robin Stuart-Kotze

LET PEOPLE BELIEVE

- If the pay is poor, the conditions of employment unfriendly, the supervision untrained, the management uncaring, job security unlikely and status low then it is obvious you have a prescription for staff turnover and absenteeism. No such jobs? Don't be so sure!

- In 2010, the CIPD reported that employee satisfaction was at an all time low.

- Intrinsic motivation is so much more important than extrinsic.

- There is a world of difference between doing a job and doing a good job.

- There is a world of difference between doing a good job and putting your heart and soul into it.

- People do want to feel engaged.

- The great majority of employees are anxious to believe in what they spend a rather large slice of their lives doing.

- The trouble is that management just makes it so difficult.

- Ensure that people in the organisation are doing things that enhance their lives.

- If you are a manager, ask yourself why you stay in your job. If you love your job, ask yourself how you can engender the same feelings in the people who work for you.

Not a programme

- Employee engagement is not a programme that someone (HR?) can take care of while line management get on with the job (which would be what exactly?)
- Unless you are prepared to change the way you lead, you will end up with just another programme.
- Such programmes, with the exception of TQM, have no effect whatsoever on engagement.
- People are now immune to programmes.
- The attempt to engage employees in their work is not a process isolated from management and leadership. It is management and leadership.
- It is primarily what managers are for.
- The only correlation with employee engagement is with a company culture which genuinely prizes people and their involvement.
- Engagement depends upon organisational values, culture and management style.
- If you are convinced that top down management is right, then keep clear of employee engagement.
- Please don't pretend. You don't really want employee engagement, so don't make things worse by saying you do.
- The idea of employee engagement does not live in a vacuum. If you want to treat the subject seriously then you must know its background.
- If you don't, then you have no right to be monkeying around it. That is as dangerous as driving a car before you've had a lesson or passed a test.
- Engagement is correlated with complexity.
- If you wish to keep things simple and avoid giving employees discretion over decisions, then you will get very low involvement.

All in this together?

- Employees, bargaining for perhaps a tiny increase in pay, find it difficult to express loyalty to an organisation paying a CEO tens or even hundreds of millions a year.

- Until such time as senior executive pay is tied properly to performance and is calculated using methods which are both transparent and similar to those used to calculate employee pay, the CEO and his or her immediate staff will still be seen as aliens. [226]

- To that extent, nothing that they say about extra miles, or being all in this together, will connect in any way with those who are being asked to put in extra effort.

- People are most upset by finding out that someone who does the same work is paid a lot more. They expect some people to be paid more than them but they also expect a rationale to this and for the discrepancy to be within bounds.

- Principles of fair pay are urgently needed both to guide those who determine pay and to reassure the wider public that such principles exist and are being followed.

- Fairness in pay is defined as the due desert for discretionary effort which delivers desired results; reward should match the employee's actions and contribution.

- The relationship between CEO pay and performance is astonishingly small. One meta-analysis found that company performance accounted for less than 5% of the variation in CEO pay.

- The compensation and the failure experience of CEOs, alienates employees when it ought to be clear that leadership of a company is an honour, a recognition of skill, knowledge and performance, which also brings duties towards the organisation.

Leadership

- An organisation is not for making CEOs feel good and rich.
- It is the way that we bring together people, investment and raw materials to create economic growth, products, jobs and, equally important, human well-being and satisfaction.
- Leadership implies not demanding extravagantly better terms and conditions than anyone else. Indeed it can demand the acceptance of worse.
- It certainly implies making sure that everything that is done is in the interests of the organisation: its shareholders, employees and other stakeholders – not just the fat cats.
- Senior management should be asking serious questions:
  - How can we create a company where the spirit of community binds people together?
  - How can we create a sense of mission throughout our organization to justify extraordinary contribution?
  - What are the biggest gaps between the rhetoric and reality in our company?
  - What are the values we have the hardest time living up to?
  - What's the espoused ideal we'd like to turn into reality of action?
- Loyalty is a two way street and so is engagement.
- While employees have little trust in senior management, they still have some in their immediate managers.

The psychological contract

- Such a contract covers informal and imprecise mutual expectations – from working late when something needs to be completed, covering for several colleagues off sick, digging the boss out of trouble when he or she has made a mistake, making allowances when a loyal employee has a bad day, ante-ing up some expenses when overtime cannot be paid or doing one's damndest to avoid a redundancy.

- Loyalty cuts both ways.

- Lay-offs and redundancies damage the psychological contract. They are also dangerous to your long term health.

- Downsizing brings decreased loyalty and morale, lower trust levels, break-up of high performing groups, cultural damage, self-protection strategies among employees, decreased risk-taking, lower levels of employee involvement, increased top-down management and stress.

- Companies which engage in downsizing experience declines in customer satisfaction.

- Downsizing does not reduce costs.

- There is little doubt that in most companies today, the contract between managers and people has broken down and with it has gone employee loyalty.

- The interests of the employee and the interests of the senior executives seem diametrically opposed.

- If senior management is successful in reducing headcount, resisting pay increases and minimising costs of employment, they are seen to be successful, and can pay themselves more. (42% more as it turns out.)

- Senior managers are seen not just as aliens but as enemy aliens.

It's a paradigm shift – believe it

- A paradigm shift occurs when the facts start to rebel. We have reached such a point in management.

- Laughter may be a sure sign that a paradigm shift has occurred.

- We need to change many of the assumptions we have lived with over the last 50 years.

- The new world is one in which the ideas of control, job descriptions and skill sets are about as useful as an investment in sub-prime mortgages.
- Some people appear to want it both ways: to maintain control, to be in charge but at the same time to have empowerment, creativity and initiative in others. They can't.
- Responsibility now has to be a shared matter. Decisions are not made by one person but by a consensus of many people, experts in one or more fields of knowledge and endeavour.
- The aim is management by vision.
- There are times when less management is more.
- There are no doubt times when management style has to emphasise control but there are more times when it should emphasise delegation and inspiration.
- One of the most important phrases is loose-tight, as used by Peters and Waterman in their first book, *In Search of Excellence.*
- Delegation is controlled by the value system inherent in the culture.
- Maintaining control is not an objective in itself nor is protecting your ego.
- The simple and simplistic idea of asking people to participate without any change in management style is doomed to failure.

Lack of creativity kills

- It's all down to evolution; the survival of the fittest.
- The essential characteristics of creativity are a willingness to embrace problems and a belief that destruction and creation go hand in hand.
- Creativity does not happen to order nor is it the result of piece work.
- Creative people will not respond to command and control.

- Creativity requires a culture where lateral thinking and new ways of looking at processes are normal, accepted, encouraged and supported.
- Creativity is not only about product. It can also create dramatically reduced costs, dramatically improved service and new ways of selling and buying.
- As Tom Peters says: *'The reality is that millions - literally an unlimited number - of innovation/improvement opportunities lie within any factory, distribution center, store, or operations center. And you can multiply that by more millions when you can involve the factory and distribution center and store working together as a team. And multiply that again when you add in involvement in innovation by suppliers and customers.'*
- Station X. Chaotic? Yes. Successful? Yes. In line with views on target setting, activity measurement and competencies? No.
- This is not rocket science.
- Creativity matters but the creation of an organisational culture in which creativity can flourish matters even more.
- Extrinsic rewards, internal competition and performance evaluations are detrimental to creativity and problem solving, which depend upon intrinsic motivation.
- Monetary rewards decrease cognitive flexibility in problem solving.
- Such rewards also decrease performance on complex tasks.
- Anita Roddick said: *'There aren't many motivating forces more potent than giving your staff an opportunity to exercise and express their idealism.'*

THE EMPEROR'S NEW CLOTHES

- So much of what happens in organisations is a matter of clothes that people are too scared to tell the Emperor do not exist.
- Much of what goes on in the typical organisation disengages people.

- At the very least, avoid disengaging people through processes that do not work.

- It is not just that appraisals add no value to a company, they actively damage it.

- Competency sets for management have no basis in research.

- Planning processes work under the assumption that there is a logical sequence of activities that can be put in place to produce a desired end. That is rare today.

- Many processes seem to go on for years with no one ever believing they are adding anything to the organisation. Get rid of them.

- Be very chary of best practice.

- Harvard Business School Professor Clayton Christensen: *'Good management was the most powerful reason (leading firms) failed to stay atop their industries.'*

- The reason, says Peters, *'Because, all too often, good management means big, bureaucratic blobs ... peopled by big, bureaucratic, blobby employees ... paying attention to big, bureaucratic, blobby customers ... supplied by big, bureaucratic, blobby suppliers.'*

- For an example, take customer service.
    o People in the company have to talk to customers and clients who are already annoyed by the company's systems.
    o They have to face challenging customer emotions which are not of their making.
    o They have to attempt to justify a system which they themselves abhor. Do they feel engaged? No.
    o If customers' demands put strain upon the way they work, successful organisations change the way they work.

Leave the Herd

- Don't hang on to the old ways of doing things. Now is the time for radical change.
- The rules say that we should do things certain ways and we follow the rules.
- Ask how correct the rules are first.
- Management is full of preconceived notions that control the way we manage.
- Our preconceptions are inadequate in the face of changed circumstances.
- Challenge the preconceptions.
- Many managers reject learning and even avoid the need to think differently.
- The theories that are implicit in what we do are theories-in-use. What we like to think we do is espoused theory.
- Most company reports say somewhere that people are their greatest asset. This is not cynicism but espoused theory. Actions that cut training spend are part of the theory-in-use.
- The 2008/11 recession was caused by the inane activities of major banks, not one or two but a whole chorus line of them, all doing the same thing, making the same mistakes, ignoring the same warnings and using the same amateurish bonus systems.

It is a Matter of Morality

- How can one feel loyal and committed to a liar or a cheat?
- Your employees know when you are lying and when top management is on the fiddle.

THE MESSAGE OF EMPLOYEE ENGAGEMENT AND WHAT HAS TO BE DONE

- If the company has no moral sense, it is hard to see how its management can call for and expect loyalty and engagement both of which are about morality.
- Organisational leadership in today's organisations is not easy.
- If people slip from the highest standards that such leadership demands, then they are not worthy.
- In such cases, society has to take the most severe action, to protect its very way of being.

A NEW APPROACH TO STRATEGY

- CK Prahalad argues that growth depends not on analysis but on imagination.
- Competing for the future is about competing for opportunity share rather than market share.
- How can we talk about market share in markets that do not exist, markets that have yet to be created?
- The role of senior management is to generate a deep commitment to change, imagination and the future.
- The past is not a good guide to the future.
- Gary Hamel has said that if a company is interested in finding the future, most of what it needs to learn it must learn outside its own industry.
- Peter Senge wrote that companies that succeed will harness the imagination, spirit and intelligence of people in ways that no authoritarian organisation ever can.
- Strategic planning is not a financial exercise, not a numbers ritual, but a matter of strategic intent, having an aspiration which is widely shared and an obsession with winning.
- Thus, companies need to engage everyone in thinking about strategy.

- The organisation must challenge its own orthodoxies and re-think its most fundamental assumptions.

Employee engagement is the result of great management

- Employee engagement has a strong moral dimension.
- Leadership is many things and directing is not often one of them.
- In the sophisticated organisation, the person with the title of manager will almost never attempt to give commands. He or she will almost never expect obedience.
- A manager's job is to get things done (willingly) through people.
- The essence of the managerial job is therefore to inspire, teach, develop and ultimately to delegate to people of ever-increasing knowledge, skill and confidence.
- This is not about being soft.
- 'Niceness' is not the end point.
- People can be challenged, exhorted, tested, extended and pushed a bit harder.
- Accepting low standards, for fear of upsetting someone, is not acceptable.
- Engagement demands consistency up and down the hierarchy.
- Failure must be treated the same everywhere.
- There are good examples of senior management: Dan DeMicco, James Lincoln, Wim Roelandts, Ricardo Semler, Roger Milliken, Julian Richer and Anita Roddick.
- These leaders have been successful beyond the wildest dreams of the herd.

Culture

- Organisational culture is a vital part of organisational life.
- Corporate culture is 'the way we do things around here.'
- It controls more of what is done than managers do.
- No set of rules, no procedure manual, can cover every eventuality. It is the culture that fills in the gaps.
- The creation of an effective culture is the most important job a leader has.
- Culture is the single most important driver of employee engagement.
- Tom Burns offered a key distinction:
  - *The mechanistic organisation* is one in which the parts (departments, units and so on) are connected by the 'proper' channels. Commands and decisions flow from the top while information is passed up from the bottom. Such an organisational structure is suited to stable, well-defined tasks where change is gradual and predictable.
  - *The organic organisation* is open to the environment so that each of its parts can react to local and current conditions as appropriate. Such an organisation is not efficient, if only because the attempt to create efficiency would make it rigid and controlled and this is exactly what it seeks not to be. Such an organisation is suited to an ambiguous, changing environment and is constantly seeking to capitalise speedily on new opportunities.
- We are in transition and a number of different types of organisational cultures, systems, and structures are in operation.
- Many companies are groping for ways that will enable them to compete more effectively in the high-tech global economy.
- A low-level employee today can access information in seconds that 20 years ago was available only to top managers. Similarly, computer technology increasingly allows employees anywhere in

an organization to communicate with anyone else without going through formal channels.

- The concept of authority and maintaining the chain of command are increasingly less relevant as operating employees are being empowered to make decisions that previously were reserved for management.

- The employer who works at creating a culture of trust will occasionally get cheated.

- But the culture will be more productive and so the occasional cheating will not matter.

- When you find the cheat, don't appraise them, fire them!

THE KEY TO CULTURE IS RECRUITMENT

- Getting the right people is ever more vital.

- You can only truly delegate to people who share your values and beliefs.

- To the degree that the right people are on board, to the extent that people share a common vision and hold values in common, to that degree decisions will be more easily taken and the degree of hostility to any outcome or change will be less.

- Those who do not share the values, understand the nature of the organisation, work well with others nor respect the culture, will be dangerous and destructive.

- According to HR managers themselves, the accepted ways of recruiting don't work.

- 87% of managers believe hiring the best people should be No. 1 to a company.

- 79% of managers said their companies did little to make sure hiring was a priority.

- 87% of hiring professionals did not think they were interviewing the best candidates available.
- 81% of hiring professionals said only one-third of the people they hired performed as well as expected. Another third fell short, and the final third should never have been hired.
- Successful recruitment is about getting to know people, not about systems, processes and banks of pre-prepared questions.
- It is not an impersonal matter. Recruitment is carried out by people.
- Getting the right people on board depends almost always, in the end, on a human, subjective judgement.
- The skills needed are not specific to any job.
- You need people who are flexible and able to learn new skills.
- Nucor's criteria are personal skills.
- Robert Pearse spoke of the need for:
    o Strategic adaptation skills
    o Individual skills
    o Interpersonal skills
    o Team skills
    o Organizational skills
- Daniel Goleman groups personal skills into:
    o self-awareness
    o self-regulation
    o self-motivation
- If you want to keep the highly skilled staff that you have fought hard to recruit and train, you had better go for enrichment and advancement.

Responsibility

- A sophisticated organisation today has
    - complex products
    - major investment in R&D
    - a global marketplace
    - a need to recruit and retain people with brainpower
    - a desperate need for creativity and innovation
    - a pressing need for speed in bringing new products to the market.
- It exists in highly competitive markets, not only for its products but also for its staff.
- It has to take account of a large number of pressure groups and legislations.
- Price competition is fierce.
- Responsibility has to be a shared matter, an organisational one.
- Decisions are not made by one person but by a consensus of many people, experts in one or more fields of knowledge and endeavour.
- Staff, who hitherto may have been said to report to a boss may well be more skilled and have more knowledge through the recency of their education.
- The view that a boss makes the decision alone, that he or she can impose this on the rest of the organisation and that everyone who reports to him or her can be expected to obey is a plain nonsense.
- Communication is management, not an add-on to it.
- The history of bad decisions at senior level is long and colourful.
- Studies show that fewer than 20% of mergers and acquisitions achieved any business success.

- A study by Ohio State University's Paul Nutt suggests that one-third of all business decisions are never implemented by the organisations involved.

- It is luck to make the right decision. It is commitment that makes the decision come right.

- If people are committed to making decisions work, if they support the boss, understand and appreciate what is going on, believe that they are doing their best, believe that their owns efforts are respected and rewarded and that they are valued, then they are all the more likely to get behind decisions and work to make them come right.

- Applaud great failures. If there is no failure, there is no creativity.

CREATE GREAT MANAGERS

- Great managers are interested in and fascinated by management.

- Will Rogers said, *'If you want to be successful, it's just this simple. Know what you are doing. Love what you are doing. And believe in what you are doing.'*

- Invest in management education.

- The function of management education is to
    o   broaden the minds of managers
    o   equip them to think about and debate management
    o   help the company create the culture that will lead to success.

- Management must aim for total trust, minimal controls, maximum delegation and a focus on creativity in the workplace.

- This can only be achieved by exemplary values, a really strong culture of honesty, achievement and openness and a strong sense of belonging.

- We need management by communication and vision and not management by objectives.

Genuine leadership

- People show more loyalty to leaders from the inside than to leaders recruited from outside.
- People are more loyal to leaders seen to be prepared to sacrifice for the group.
- A strong commitment from the leader is more effective in eliciting sacrifice from members than the possession of traditional management skills.
- Individuals cooperated more with committed leaders than with those who scored well on a standard management skills test.
- Group members are more willing to sacrifice for their leader if they had a say over who it should be even if their favourite person was not elected.
- Autocratically led groups have far higher attrition than democratically led groups.
- When group members feel that they are treated disrespectfully, and subsequently experience a decline in their status, they no longer feel obliged to cooperate with the leader's objectives.
- Leaders who make a promise and then break it quickly lose employee confidence.
- Perceived procedural unfairness from management is a key reason for employee turnover.
- When group members as a whole received praise from the leader, this positively influenced their self-esteem and their willingness to sacrifice for the group.
- As Tom Peters says: *'Today's successful business leaders will be those who are most flexible of mind. An ability to embrace new ideas, routinely challenge old ones, and live with paradox will be the effective leader's premier trait.'*

Individual performance pay schemes are just wrong

- The fact that they are common does not make them right.
- Individually based incentive schemes motivate dishonesty.
- Managers are not just measurers. They exist to bring out the best in people; to develop, to coach, to facilitate, and to communicate.
- Motivation derives from having a sense of achievement, recognition, responsibility and opportunities for personal growth. The nature of the job may itself be motivational.
- Herzberg rightly criticises management for ignoring the motivational factors and trying to motivate through hygiene factors like money and benefits - expensive and not successful.

The real team

- A very good group of individuals will beat a group of less good individuals.
- A genuine team of good players will beat a group of better players.
- A team is different from a group.
- What makes a team is emotional inter-dependency with common purpose and goals.
- Teams are rare in business life.
- People do not often engage their emotions, their values or their life journey with the managers they work for or with the colleagues whose work place they share.
- Managers can create teams.
- This involves processes very different from those normally listed under the title of team-building.

- A team is a group of people who share among themselves and the leader:
  - Trust
  - Mutual commitment
  - Shared values
  - Common opinions
  - Loyalty
  - Common goals
  - a shared will to win.
- Leaders of such teams are:
  - Always investing in the people
  - Not autocratic
  - Ready to make sacrifices for the team
  - Concerned about team status
  - Consistently fair
  - Ready to listen

It will take time

- Taking on a new paradigm, a new culture and a whole new set of values will take time.
- But that is what employee engagement requires.
- It is not only managers that have to cope with the change.
- Just like their managers, employees have to understand what shared leadership entails.
- Charles Handy cautions that we live in an organisational world that has many paradoxes and ambiguities.

- Executives who are looking for a quick fix solution to their organisation's change problems are doomed to disappointment.
- Lofty corporate mission statements that are full of glittering generalities won't get the implementation job done.
- Senior management must demonstrate every day that it is committed to the task.
- Never promote anyone who does not display the ethics necessary for employee engagement and the skills to facilitate its occurrence.
- Every wrong promotion is a slap in the face.

A REMINDER

Employee engagement is the single most serious issue in management today. Its apparently inexorable decline will soon spell the end of Western economies. If you cannot compete on price (and the West cannot) you must compete on creativity and quality. Without employee engagement, neither of these is possible.

Employee engagement is not the result of some initiative quite detached from leadership. It is not something that someone (HR?) can take care of while line management get on with the job (which would be what exactly?)

The commercial organisation is the primary way that we bring together people, investment and raw materials to create economic growth, products, jobs and, equally importantly, human well-being and satisfaction. Profitability enables this social purpose. Such organisations are not for short term gains or making CEOs rich, attitudes which have brought capitalism to a crisis point.

Most employees in most organisations seek to do their best, often in spite of management, much of which disengages people, adds useless cost and serves as grist to the cynics' mill. This applies equally to not-for-profit and public sector organisations.

The only way is ethics. If employees are to feel engaged with a company, they need to feel proud of it. Only a company that takes a positive view of ethics can expect employees to find compelling purpose in their work.

* * *

FOOTNOTES

[1] *In the Heart of the Heart of the Country* in *Root and Branch: The Rise of the Workers' Movements*, edited by Jeremy Brecher, Rick Burns, Elizabeth Long, Paul Mattick Jr, and Peter Rachleff

[2] Thesis presented at Ohio State University in 2009, *The Little Car that Did Nothing Right: the 1972 Lordstown Assembly Strike, the Chevrolet Vega, and the Unraveling of Growth Economics*

[3] *How managers manage*, Prentice Hall, 1980

[4] http://www.glassdoor.com/Reviews/Employee-Review-Southwest-Airlines-RVW539145.htm

[5] *Working life: employee attitudes and engagement*, Truss, K., Soane, E. C. and Edwards, C. 2006. London: CIPD.

[6] *Creating an engaged workforce; findings from the Kingston employee engagement consortium project*, Kerstin Alfes, Kingston Business School, Catherine Truss, Kingston Business School, Emma C. Soane, London School of Economics and Political Science, Chris Rees, Royal Holloway, University of London, Mark Gatenby, University of Surrey, CIPD 2010

[7] *Understanding the Deal*, Wilson Wong, Laura Blazey, Jane Sullivan, Ksenia Zheltoukhova, Alexandra Albert and Ben Reid, The Work Foundation, 2010

[8] *Good Jobs*, Susannah Constable, David Coats, Stephen Bevan and Michelle Mahdon, The Work Foundation, 2009

[9] Gallup, *Employee engagement index*, 2008. Gallup's employee engagement work is based on 30 years of research involving more than 17 million employees.

[10] *Why Managers Should Care About Employee Loyalty*, IPSOS loyalty study, 2009, Paris.

[11] Article contributed to *The Working Manager* core site.

[12] CIPD 2010 *op. cit.*

[13] http://www.glassdoor.com/index.htm

[14] Southwest Airlines, General Mills, Slalom Consulting, Bain & Company, McKinsey & Company, MITRE, Boston Consulting Group, Continental Airlines, Procter & Gamble

[15] All references to *The Working Manager* are to the core site of this organisation. The opinions expressed in the core site do not necessarily express the opinions of the clients of The Working Manager Ltd. www.theworkingmanager.com

[16] *The Living Dead Switched Off, Zoned Out: The Shocking Truth about Office Life*, David Bolchover, Capstone, 2005

[17] For *The Working Manager*.

[18] http://edelman.co.uk/

[19] *Top Talent: Keeping Performance Up When Business Is Down*, Sylvia Ann Hewlett, HBS Press, Harvard 2009.

[20] *Workers Need a Morale Boost*, Gregg Lederman, Brand Integrity, quoted by Bain & Co at http://

www.bain.com/bainweb/publications/

[21] In a public speech widely reported. See http://www.guardian.co.uk/business/2010/mar/31/myners-urges-fsa-to-investigate-shareholders-role

[22] *Relative Deprivation and Social Justice: a Study of Attitudes to Social Inequality in Twentieth-Century Britain*, Routledge, London 1966

[23] *Fair pay*, Will Hutton, December 2010

[24] The High Pay Commission is an independent inquiry into high pay and boardroom pay across the public and private sectors in the UK. The Commission was established by Compass with the support of the Joseph Rowntree Charitable Trust. http://highpaycommission.co.uk/

[25] 5 July 2010

[26] March 2010 http://www.bnet.com

[27] Professor Rick Roskin says that most studies show no correlation but that the Forbes data appears to show a negative correlation. If it is genuinely performance pay, the correlation ought, of course, to be strongly positive.

[28] http://www.forbes.com/lists/2011/12/ceo-compensation-11_land.html

[29] June 2010

[30] As reported in the *Independent*, 21 November, 2011. On the same page, no doubt with deliberate irony, the newspaper reports, *Government plans to curtail workers' rights*; that the intention is to make it easier to fire people.

[31] Work Foundation, *op. cit.*

[32] Hutton, *op. cit.*

[33] *Op. cit.*

[34] Edelman *op. cit.*

[35] 10 September 2010

[36] 20 January 2010

[37] *The Truth Behind Executive Severance Packages*, April 2003, MSN Money Insight

[38] Business Insider, November 16, 2009

[39] *The 5 richest payoffs for fired CEOs* Michael Brush, MSN Money 28 November 2007

[40] *As long as oil flows, BP chief Hayward's job is safe*, Slate, Wednesday, June 9, 2010

[41] Ulanoff is arguing for Hurd's return at http://mashable.com/2011/09/22/hp-bring-back-mark-hurd-opinion/

[42] http://www.charlesrussell.co.uk/

[43] Hewlett-Packard's directors faced a class action lawsuit from shareholders claiming they violated their fiduciary duties in connection with Mr H's resignation and seeking to recover the $12m paid as severance to him.

[44] *Executive Excess 2010: CEO Pay and the Great Recession*, Sarah Anderson, Chuck Collins, Sam Pizzigati, Kevin Shih, September 1, 2010

[45] *Investors want greater transparency on boardroom pensions*, 15 June 2010, NAPF press release

[46] *Delta CEO Mullin stepping down*, Marilyn Adams, USA Today, 24 November 2003.

[47] Bob Diamond Barclays, 2010 Reward: £6.75m, Share Price Performance 2005-2010: Negative 46.8%; Eric Daniels Lloyds 2010 Reward: £2.5m, Shares 2005-2010: Negative 66.3%; Stephen Hester RBS, 2010 Reward: £3.5m: negative 90.7%; Stuart Gulliver HSBC: £6.2m +0.8 per cent. Figures exclude the long-term share deals of up to £4.5m in Mr Hester's case. (Source *Independent*) Barclays own pay report shows that if people had invested £100 in the bank in 2005 they would have lost £47 by 2010 compared with a £26 gain in a FTSE 100 tracker fund. Thomson Reuters Datastream research shows that over the same period shareholders in Lloyds would have lost two-

thirds of their money and RBS investors would have been left with just £9.

[48] *Employee survey highlights fundamental lack of trust in UK plc senior management, as redundancy takes toll on the survivors*, Press release, CIPD, 7 August 2009

[49] September 2010

[50] *Many companies are still measuring their performance based on the results of years just prior to the start of the recession, but this is erroneous and creates objectives for salespeople and the company as a whole that are unattainable in this economy. Without attainable goals, very few salespeople will achieve their numbers... when few salespeople earn bonus compensation or incentives, an attitude of cynicism can take hold and become a negative influence on everybody.* Ira Ozer, pipmag.com, *Improve Sales Performance During a Recession,*

[51] The study examined the link between executive pay and company performance and said '*Surprisingly some execs at high performing companies see pay decreases, while their poor performing counterparts receive increases,* Press release August 3, 2010, BDO

[52] From *The Working Manager* core site

[53] Harvard Business School Press, October 2007

[54] High Pay Commission, op.cit.

[55] From the John Lewis Partnership website

[56] Hutton, *op. cit.*

[57] *Anger as pay for top FTSE bosses soars by a third*, Richard Hall, *Independent*, Tuesday, 31 May 2011

[58] *Ibid.*

[59] HarperBusiness, 2001

[60] *Unshrink*, Pearson Education, 2002

[61] The Code is addressed in the first instance to firms who manage assets on behalf of institutional shareholders such as pension funds, insurance companies, investment trusts and other collective investment vehicles. It requires them to actively monitor the firms they invest in and not as a matter of course support the board.

[62] *Independent*, November 5, 2011

[63] As reported by Oliver Wright in the *Independent*, 21 November, 2011.

[64] http://www.i-l-m.com/research-and-comment/8787.aspx

[65] *What makes a true football fan?* Simon Kuper and Stefan Szymanski, *Financial Times*, August 7 2009

[66] ibid

[67] Dorsey Press 1960

[68] *The Employment Relationship: Examining Psychological and Contextual Perspectives*, Oxford University Press, Oxford, 2004

[69] *Human factors in organisational resilience: Implications of breaking the psychological contract* in Journal of Business Continuity & Emergency Planning, August, 2009

[70] *The psychological contract*, Fact sheet, May 2010

[71] *Op. cit.*

[72] *Be honest fellow football fans, have you have ever considered quitting your club?* Mark Apostolou, Sportingo, 19 September 2007

[73] Quoted in Hickok, T.A. *Downsizing and Organizational Culture*. Journal of Public Administration and Management 1998.

[74] The Chartered Management Institute wrote, regarding the 2007-2010 recession, '*In the current difficult economic climate, redundancy is a reality that many managers, their colleagues and family will have to come to terms with.*

[75] Frequently published internet article, *Why Managers Should Care about Employee Loyalty*

by Timothy Keiningham and Lerzan Aksoy of IPSOS.
[76] *Charging Back Up the Hill: Workplace Recovery After Mergers, Acquisitions and Downsizings*, Mitchell Lee Marks, Jossey-Bass, January 2003
[77] *Employee Anxiety Levels on the Rise*, January 2009, Towers Perrin
[78] *Creating a Sustainable Rewards and Talent Management Model: Results of the 2010 Global Talent Management and Rewards Study*
[79] *Executive Excess 2010: CEO Pay and the Great Recession*, Sarah Anderson, Chuck Collins, Sam Pizzigati, Kevin Shih, September 2010
[80] *Loc. cit.*
[81] Ivey Business Journal, May 2009
[82] In *Re-Thinking the Future*, ed. Rowan Gibson and Nicholas Brealy, Penguin, 1998
[83] *Op. cit.*
[84] Washington Post, February 9, 2009
[85] W.W. Norton, 2009
[86] *Op. cit.*
[87] *Op. cit.*
[88] *Downsizing isn't what it's cracked up to be*, Ivey Business Journal, May 2009
[89] As reported in the *Daily Telegraph*, 3 September 2010
[90] Published by Public Affairs, a member of Perseus Books Group, 2010
[91] *In the Black, But No Pink Slips: One company's experience with a no-layoffs policy*, March 1, 2010
[92] In 1879, when the original city premises of the Cadbury company became too small, George Cadbury and his brother Richard bought a green fields site with canal and railway access to build a new factory which became known as Bournville. As a Quaker, George set out to build not just a factory but to provide also good housing that could be afforded by working people. In January 2010, Cadbury was acquired by Kraft who said it planned to invest in Bournville and maintain production at Somerdale in Somerset. By March, it had closed the Somerdale factory.
[93] Silicon Valley Women in Human Resources, http://www.ourhrsite.com/
[94] *Happy Hour is 9 to 5 - How to Love Your Job, Love Your Life and Kick Butt at Work*, Alexander, 2007
[95] *The seeeeeeriously cool way out of a downturn*, positivesharing.com, March 6, 2009
[96] He repeated this in October 2011. Let's hope he was just flying a kite.
[97] *Employee engagement: Enough!*, Paul Hebert, Business Week 29 May 2009
[98] Wooda, S. & de Menezes, L. M. *Comparing perspectives on high involvement management and organizational performance across the British economy*. The International Journal of Human Resource Management, 2008
[99] *Administration industrielle et générale; prévoyance, organisation, commandement, coordination, contrôle*, 1916, H. Dunod et E. Pinat, Translated into English in 1949.
[100] Harvard Business School Press, 2004
[101] BookHouse Publishing, 1999
[102] *Principles of Scientific Management*, 1911, Harper & brothers
[103] Free Press, 1990
[104] *What Business Leaders Can Learn From Moments of Truth*: An Interview With Former SAS CEO Jan Carlzon, at http://www.customerthink.com/interview/jan_carlzon_moments_of_truth, January 2006

[105] W. Edwards Deming, *Out of the Crisis*, MIT Press, 1986
[106] Joseph Juran, *Quality Control Handbook*, McGraw-Hill, many editions from 1951

FOOTNOTES

[107] Philip Crosby, *Quality is Free*, McGraw-Hill, 1979

[108] Six Sigma was developed by the Motorola Corporation in 1986

[109] *Kaizen: The art of continuous improvement*, http://www.thinkingmanagers.com/management/kaizen.php

[110] McGraw-Hill/Irwin, 1986

[111] Gitlow, Levine, and Popovich, *Design for Six Sigma for Green Belts and Champions*, Prentice-Hall 2006

[112] Dr Adrian Banks, University of Surrey, contribution to a meeting of the British Psychological Society, June 26, 2007 as a contribution to a series of discussions entitled *Exploring Mental Capacity*.

[113] *Descartes' Error: Emotion, Reason, and the Human Brain*, Antonio R. Damasio, Harper Perennial, 1995

[114] Back Bay Books, Little, Brown, 2005

[115] Prentice Hall, 1980

[116] *Winning*, HarperBusiness 2005

[117] iUniverse Inc 2004

[118] Mary Parker Follett (1868-1933) was described by Peter Drucker as the 'prophet of management.' Her principal writing on management was accomplished during the 1920s when hard-nosed executives crowded into her famous lectures that were clearly cutting edge for the time and which remain incompletely understood today. She pioneered the multi-disciplinary approach to the study of management, herself drawing from fields as diverse as law and even chemistry; she was possibly the very first to make extensive use of the emerging fields of psychology in understanding collaborative groups and how to manage them. She anticipated the application of general systems theory to the study of management by 50 years. She foresaw and explained in detail the principles of leadership, loyalty, group cohesion, organizational design, power, authority, and self-management that are still only being rediscovered today, and that were almost uniformly better understood and explained by her than by her successors.

[119] University of Oklahoma Press, 2000

[120] November 2005

[121] *Human Motivation*, Cambridge University Press, 1987

[122] *Motivation and Personality*, Harper & Row, 1954

[123] John Wiley, 1959

[124] Plenum Press 1975

[125] Journal of Organizational Behaviour, 2005

[126] *The Human Side of Enterprise*, McGraw-Hill 1960

[127] Journal of Management, 2004

[128] *The Essential Drucker*, HarperCollins, 2001

[129] WW Norton & Company, 2009

[130] Bookhouse Publishing AB, 2002

[131] Harvard, 1985

[132] HarperCollins, 2001

[133] Taken from Project Gutenberg under the terms of the Project Gutenberg License

[134] *Engaging a Changing Workforce, Study of Four Generations*, 2011

[135] The Urban Dictionary explains this as the act of willingly making a sacrifice for the benefit of others. In sport it is to allow yourself to get hit by a pitch in order help your team win a baseball game.

FOOTNOTES

[136] *Heroes or villains? Corruption and the charismatic leader*, Journal of Leadership & Organizational Studies, Summer 2004
[137] *Bandit Capitalism*, The Washington Times, September 18, 2008
[138] http://www.wealthflow.org
[139] Harvard Business School Press, 2007
[140] The University of Chicago Press, 1962
[141] Century, 1993
[142] It is still going strong today. See http://www.semco.com.br/pt/
[143] Harvard Business Press, 2008
[144] http://www.accel-team.com/
[145] *The 7 habits of highly effective people*, Simon & Schuster, 1989
[146] William Collins, 1988
[147] *Independent*, 15 November 2011
[148] McGraw-Hill, 1970
[149] HarperBusiness, 1982
[150] *The Leadership Triad*, Oxford University Press, 1966
[151] *Organizational Culture and Leadership*, Jossey-Bass, 3rd edition 2004
[152] Simon & Schuster, 2002
[153] Macmillan, 1998
[154] In his article, *Autopoiesis of the Enterprise,* Bastias draws upon the work of Chilean Professor Aquiles Limone, international expert in knowledge management and second order cybernetics, the founder of the Valparaiso Autopoiesis Theory.
[155] Pearson Education, 2002
[156] Wang Laboratories became bankrupt in 1992. It was eventually acquired by Getronics of The Netherlands, now itself part of the Dutch IT & Telecommunications company KPN.
[157] *Freakonomics: A Rogue Economist Explores the Hidden Side of Everything*, Steven D. Levitt and Stephen J. Dubner, Penguin, 2007
[158] *Teachers cheating to raise grades*, report for BBC's Five Live
[159] To survive the recession.
What counts as survival?
To increase the revenue of the Brazilian operation from $200,000 to $400,000 by 2018.
Inflation in Brazil in 2008 was about 5%. In 10 years this would account for 63% of the target. If the Brazilian real continues to strengthen against the dollar, then the rest of the target is automatic as well.
Ensure full compliance with Equality & Diversity policy at all times.
What counts as compliance? What work is the word 'full' doing? Why use the phrase 'at all times'? Something smells fishy.
Reduce water use in 2009.
What methods are allowable? Don't wash? Stop lavatories from flushing?
Ensure all staff are trained to required standards by end March 2009.
'Required standards'? What is the test for being trained? If you test for knowledge might this not prove that training was not the answer? If so is training still required? Do line managers support training and will they allow staff time off to attend? If so how long? Is this enough?
Ensure all core Health and Safety requirements are met on an ongoing basis.
What is the meaning of 'on an ongoing basis'? What counts as 'core'?

Run 3 skills workshops each for 30 members of staff by 1 March 2009.
Why? What subjects? What types of staff? How long should the workshops last?
Hold one team meeting a month for all team members.
Why? What are the criteria for success? Attendance rate? Relevance? Performance improvement? Will a social gathering suffice? Are there cost implications?

[160] Channel 4 Books, 1998

[161] I think this is 159 million trillion. It would take about 2 weeks to count to a million. To count to 10 million is almost half a year's work. To count to 100 million is 5 year's work. To count to 1 billion would take your whole working life. This may give you some idea of the numbers involved.

[162] We now know that *Colossus* was primarily designed to attack the German High Command cipher known at Bletchley as *Tunny*. *Colossus* was designed by engineer Tommy Flowers. The breaking of *Tunny*, 'one of the greatest intellectual feats of World War II,' was led by Bill Tutte. Flowers died in 1998 and Tutte, Distinguished Professor Emeritus at the University of Waterloo, Canada, in 2002.

[163] Wikipedia is very good on banburismus

[164] While I have not seen it myself, I am led to believe that the TV series of *The Office* provides further examples.

[165] *The Goal: A Process of Ongoing Improvement* (actually a business novel) North River Press, 1984

[166] Allen & Unwin, 2005

[167] The Intergovernmental Panel on Climate Change projects sea level will rise between 18cm and 59cm by the end of this century. However, the IPCC refrains from assessing the impact of a change in ice sheet flow from Antarctica and Greenland. Even partial melting of the Greenland ice sheet, and possibly the West Antarctic ice sheet, would contribute around 6 metres to sea level rise. An increase of 3 degrees C is enough to trigger this.

[168] *Beyond the Stable State*, Penguin, 1973; with C. Argyris, *Theory in practice: Increasing professional effectiveness*, Jossey-Bass, 1974; with C. Argyris, *Organizational learning: A theory of action perspective*, Addison-Wesley, 1978

[169] Peter Senge, *The Fifth Discipline: The art and practice of the learning organization*, Doubleday, 1990

[170] Addison-Wesley, 1969

[171] 4 March 2009

[172] *Consensus decision making in human crowds*, Journal of Animal Behavior, February 2008

[173] *Strangers to ourselves*, The Psychologist, 2006

[174] Texere Publishing 2001

[175] In a series of interviews carried out by Helen Kelly for *The Working Manager*

[176] *Op. cit.*

[177] *Provided you don't kiss me*, Duncan Hamilton, Fourth Estate 2007

[178] *Trends in Change Management*, Professor Veronica Hope Hailey, Director – Change Management Consortium, University of Bath

[179] *Management: tasks, responsibilities, practices*, Butterworth-Heinemann, 1974

[180] http://usablewords.com/blog/how-not-to-talk-to-the-public/

[181] Some IVRs now offer no possibility at all of talking to a person. Many of them are closed loops. Companies simply do not wish to have a conversation with customers. (It many cases, pressing the # key still works but not in all.)

[182] John Seddon, *Freedom from Command and Control*, Vanguard Education 2003

[183] Seddon, op.cit.

[184] He also asks, '*Why is HR so often a henchman for the chief financial officer, finding ever-more ingenious*

ways to cut benefits and hack at payroll? Why do its communications - when we can understand them at all - so often flout reality? Why are so many people processes duplicative and wasteful, creating a forest of paperwork for every minor transaction? And why does HR insist on sameness as a proxy for equity?'

[185] Work Canada 1997

[186] *The influence of a manager's own performance appraisal on the evaluation of others*, International Journal of Selection and Assessment, September 2008

[187] If appraisal design could be improved, you'd have thought that it would have been done in the period since the 1960s. As we have seen, the research results indicate no improvement.

[188] http://www.ecawa.asn.au/home/jfuller/level3/annejasman.htm

[189] They have been very successful in the Royal National Lifeboat Institution for crew members.

[190] McGraw-Hill, 1991

[191] Sourced from the *Independent* 21 November 2011

[192] Prentice Hall, 1980

[193] Bantam Press, 1987

[194] Spence Silver was seeking to produce, says Waterman, *'a supersticky bonding agent. What he actually produced was some goo that was sticky but didn't stick all that well.'*

[195] *Op. cit.*

[196] *Corporate Strategy*, McGraw-Hill, 1965

[197] In an interview with Helen Kelly for *The Working Manager*

[198] *Competitive Strategy*, Michael E Porter, William Collins, 1980

[199] Ira Ozer, pipmag.com, *Improve Sales Performance During a Recession*

[200] CBS reported that about half the whistleblowers who responded to a survey by the National Whistleblower Center in Washington said they were fired after reporting unlawful conduct. Most of the others said they faced on-the-job harassment or unfair discipline.

[201] Reported in many places including the Financial Times www.ft.com

[202] Upton Sinclair wrote about the strike in his novel *King Coal* (1917)

[203] Lewis Carroll, *Alice through the looking glass*

[204] Co-author with Douglas Stone and Bruce Patton of *Difficult Conversations*, Penguin, 2000

[205] Actually Bill Reddin would simply say, *'Whose needs?'*

[206] Such words are part and parcel of the pseudo-caring language of so much meaningless jargon in management. The *Independent* carried another example in its report on sponsorship of the FIFA World Cup following yet another example of Sepp Blatter, FIFA's President, putting his foot in his mouth rather than near a football. The reporter writes, *'When I rang X (a corporate sponsor) 'the woman in the press office thanked me for "reaching out" and then, when I suggested we had a chat about Blatter, kept repeating that if I provided my email address she would send a statement. After two failed attempts to strike up a conversation, I remarked that she was behaving like a robot. Without a hint of irony she just said the same thing again.'* What on earth is the meaning of 'reaching out' in this context?

[207] Rider, 2007

[208] Source: realbeer.com

[209] Source: Reuters

[210] BBC News, August 2007

[211] Press release www.swindon.gov.uk/

[212] Source: The *Guardian* newspaper

[213] *Ibid.*

[214] 20 April, 2004

[215] Source: Iveybusinessjournal.com

FOOTNOTES

[216] More formally The Royal Dutch/Shell Group

[217] U.S. Securities and Exchange Commission, Litigation Release No. 19147 / March 21, 2005

[218] Variously reported emanating from *Money laundering and foreign corruption: enforcement and effectiveness of the patriot act; Case study involving Riggs Bank*. Report released in conjunction with the Permanent Subcommittee on Investigations' hearing on July 15, 2004. http://hsgac.senate.gov/

[219] Variously reported. For example see www.bloomberg.com and www.orlandosentinel.com

[220] Edited by Chris Megone and Simon J Robinson, Routledge, 2002

[221] The quote is from 1986. Ivan Frederick Boesky was an American stock trader convicted, fined $100m and imprisoned for his role in a Wall Street insider trading scandal that occurred in the United States in the mid-1980s.

[222] The Association of British Insurers, which represents some of Britain's biggest institutional investors, has written to the chairmen of the UK's five publicly traded banks (HSBC, Barclays, Royal Bank of Scotland, Lloyds and Standard Chartered) demanding fundamental reform on pay. *'The move demonstrates that shareholders have finally lost patience with the huge rewards earned by top bankers at the expense of investors,'* says the Independent. *'The letter explicitly rejects the argument put forward by banks for years that if they cut bonuses their best employees will leave.'*

[223] Website www.newkerala.com

[224] Wiley, 2001

[225] *Business as unusual*, Thorsons, 2000

[226] In early December 2011, the UK Deputy Prime Minister, Nick Clegg, said that the government intended to act to stop the excessive and irresponsible behaviour demonstrated in the levels and nature of boardroom pay. He said, 'I believe that people should be well paid if they succeed. What I abhor is people who get paid bucket loads of cash in difficult times for failure.' He promised to prevent the old boys network by which executives sat on each other's remuneration committees, and said that employee representatives should be represented on such committees. He promised that shareholders would be given more power concerning executive pay decisions and that companies would be made to publish figures on the relationship between top and median salary levels. By the time you read this book, we will know if anything happened.

Printed in Great Britain
by Amazon.co.uk, Ltd.,
Marston Gate.